Learning and Teaching in
Higher Education

Greg Light is Associate Director of the Searle Center for Teaching Excellence at Northwestern University in Chicago. He is also an associate of the Institute of Education, University of London where he is a member of the Centre for Higher Education Studies (CHES). In 1998 he established the Professional Accreditation of Teaching in Higher Education programme at the Institute of Education, of which he was the Director. Recent publications have focused on student learning and the professionalization of teaching in higher education.

With a background in psychology and philosophy **Roy Cox** has a wide experience of research and practice in learning and teaching in higher education. He helped to establish one of the first centres for learning and teaching in higher education in the world at London University, where he is currently a visiting academic. His many publications draw on his educational research in a range of disciplines and his teaching in higher education in over 30 countries.

Learning and Teaching in Higher Education

The Reflective Professional

Greg Light and Roy Cox

SAGE Publications
London ● Thousand Oaks ● New Delhi

ISBN 0-7619-6552-1 (hbk)
ISBN 0-7619-6553-X (pbk)
© Greg Light and Roy Cox 2001
First published 2001
Reprinted 2003, 2004, 2005

Paul Chapman Publishing Ltd
A SAGE Publications Company
1 Oliver's Yard, 55 City Road
London EC1Y 1SP

SAGE Publications Inc
2455 Teller Road
Thousand Oaks, California 91320

SAGE Publications India Pvt Ltd
B–42 Panchsheel Enclave
PO Box 4109
New Delhi 110 017

British Library Cataloguing in Publication data
A catalogue record for this book is available from the British Library

Typeset by Anneset Ltd., Weston-super-Mare, Somerset
Printed and bound in Great Britain by
Athenæum Press Limited, Gateshead, Tyne & Wear

Contents

Preface

This book is, above all, a book about learning. It is primarily for 'faculty' engaged in learning and in facilitating student learning in higher education, including professors, lecturers, teachers, researchers, teaching assistants and all those who are in one way or another supporting learning. It draws upon over three decades of research, scholarship and teaching experience – at the Institute of Education (University of London) – providing programmes for enhancing learning through improving the quality of teaching. Indeed, the joint authorship of this book reflects a fifteen year collaboration of research, scholarship and teaching about learning and teaching in higher education which has immeasurably enriched our own learning.

The authors do not for a moment pretend there is a 'solution' to the many challenges confronting learning and teaching in higher education. If anything, the book extends the range and scope of the challenge. It does, however, propose a comprehensive way of approaching this challenge, a way embodied in the book's subtitle: *The Reflective Professional*.

Learning and Teaching in Higher Education: The Reflective Professional addresses the practice of learning and teaching within a rapidly changing higher education sector challenged by escalations in the number and diversity of students, tougher demands for professional accountability, increasing calls for educational relevance, thinning resources and the exacting demands of a global education market. In this respect, the book brings together key issues of theory and practice to develop an overall professional 'language' of teaching situated within communities of academic practice. This 'language' provides teachers with a conceptual 'vocabulary' and 'grammar' for understanding and improving practice, enables them to critically reflect upon their teaching in a range of key 'genres' of practice, and proposes a strategy for conducting and producing evidence for continuous professional development in learning and teaching. It is not intended to be prescriptive but, rather, to provide a structure for developing teaching and learning strategies appropriate to the distinctive subjects and conditions of the individual university teacher and his or her academic community.

The book is divided into four sections: an introduction and three parts. Chapter 1 introduces the context of the book and the challenges which teaching in higher education faces. It is concerned with the theoretical issues surrounding the changing nature of higher education, the changing role of the teacher within higher education, and the development of the teacher as both professional and reflective practitioner. In response to the challenge, we propose the concept of the 'reflective professional' and sketch a model for a professional 'language' of practice with three interrelated components: a critical conceptual framework, relevant and appropriate genres, and a general strategy for professional realization.

In Part 1 of the book, we examine the themes of the first component of this language. It is chiefly concerned with situating this 'language' within three conceptual locations. Chapter 2 addresses the first of these – a general theoretical framework of human communication and knowledge. The second location is taken up in Chapter 3 and explores a model of the reflective professional within academic practice, suggesting that the three roles of student, teacher and researcher converge in one model centred on learning. Chapter 4 focuses on the character of learning in higher education. It develops a critical matrix of learning, providing teachers with a conceptual tool for designing, developing and implementing their teaching across the various 'genres' of their teaching practice.

Part 2 of the book is concerned with different 'genres' of teaching practice. While it recognizes that teaching is a holistic practice not comfortably divided into different sections, it nevertheless accepts that teaching in higher education has come to recognise certain distinctive core 'genres' of teaching, which may be usefully addressed separately. Chapters 5–11 focus on these 'genres'. They are, respectively, designing, lecturing, facilitating, supervising, innovating, assessing and evaluating. Each of these chapters addresses key practical teaching issues and activities of the 'genre', relating them to relevant theory and recent research. Part 3 is concerned with the professional development of the 'language' in practice. In this respect, Chapter 12 draws upon the discussion to propose and describe a general strategy of 'professional realization': a strategy for engaging with and mastering the critical 'language' of the reflective professional.

Greg Light
Roy Cox

Acknowledgements

The authors of this book gratefully acknowledge the widespread encouragement and important contributions of many, many colleagues, friends and family members. We would like to record our appreciation to all the members and graduate students of the Centre for Higher Education Studies and the Lifelong Learning Group at the Institute of Education, University of London. They provided an ongoing, stimulating and critically acute intellectual climate for debating and developing the essential ideas and issues presented in the book. Particular thanks, in this respect, go to Ronald Barnett, Gareth Williams and Michael Young for their conversation, insights and continuing support. A very special thanks must go to David Guile and Angela Hobsbaum who read the whole of the manuscript and offered insightful and practical comments throughout its development, bringing their experience and expertise as researchers and teachers to bear on our project.

We would also like to acknowledge an immense debt of thanks to the faculty and teachers from over 20 universities who have participated in the Institute's Professional Accreditation of Teaching in Higher Education (PATHE) programme over the past 3 years. Their generous reflections, comments and willingness to engage openly with the ideas of this book have made it immeasurably richer.

Finally, Caroline Steenman-Clark and Janet Harding deserve special thanks for their patience in managing the diverse programs from which this book derived and for their help in preparing the manuscript.

All of the above have been for the authors, teachers from whom we have learned immensely.

1

The Challenge of Professionalism

The millennium 'storm'

Written at the end of one millennium and published at the beginning of the next, this book is situated on the edge of a transition apparently massive in its power to focus minds and cultures and, yet, chronologically rather trivial: another year has simply passed. Nevertheless, in the longer term this transition may very well be assigned rather more substance. It may well be regarded as a transition defined by transition, a shift revealing a future increasingly characterized by the condition of uncertainty and ambiguity which announced it: the defining date of the postmodern condition (Lyotard, 1984). It is a condition which higher education – through its vast contributions to the technological, social and cultural insurrection that lies behind it – has played a central role in creating. Ironically, it is condition, as we shall see, which has also come back to haunt the university.

As for many other professionals, for academics working in higher education today, this condition often feels more like a 'storm'. The demands on their time and the complexity of those demands are changing and escalating almost exponentially. They have been overwhelmed with a rapid expansion in both the number and diversity of students, without a corresponding increase in staff or resources. The burden in terms of staff–student ratios, teaching time, tutorial provision, assessment responsibilities, evaluation and feedback has swelled enormously. Pressures to increase research and scholarship activities have mushroomed as they have taken unprecedented priority in university preoccupations while research funds have remained relatively static, become more fiercely contested, more complex to win and increasingly the realm of fewer and larger departments. New academic practices and 'consultancy' activities have grown and/or demanded more time and attention in the competition for new income streams. At the same time, the relationship of these activities in terms of academic career progress and status has become murkier, many of the practices (although expected and encouraged) not counting at all. At the same time, mounting criticism of the quality and

1

efficiency of the twin pillars of academic practice – research and teaching – has increased the proportion of time spent on what has now become the third pillar of practice, administration.

Like most storms, it is the result of changes in powerful and prevailing systems. The academic 'storm' is the result of changing relationships between higher education, knowledge (its primary material) and society. Historically, as Barnett (1994) has noted, higher education has been an institution 'in society', privileged and governed by an almost linear relationship through which academics defined and produced knowledge which was then imparted and infused within society through its graduates and the dissemination of its research. This relationship characterized the university's separation and freedom, gave rise to its description as an 'ivory tower' in a 'real world'. The one-way nature of this relationship may be exemplified by the phrase 'academic freedom', a concept central to the fabric of academic life, but rarely accompanied by its customary social counterpart, responsibility. 'Academic freedom', as Donald Kennedy, the past president of Stanford University, notes 'is a widely shared value; academic duty, which ought to count for as much, is mysterious' (1997: 2). This, he suggests, is due to a dissonance in the way in which society and higher education see their relationship. It is a dissonance, moreover, which has recently seen an escalation of public criticism and policy concern with respect to the accountability of higher education (Robertson, 1997: 86-8).

This concern for accountability is representative of the wider change in the complex relationship between higher education and society. Higher education no longer simply resides 'in society', it is 'of society', and being of society it has increasingly become subject to its prevailing ideologies, ways of viewing the world, its transitions and upheavals. Higher education no longer simply shapes society through its 'knowledge' contributions, it is rather shaped by society through the 'knowledge specification' (Light, 2000) – both in terms of students and research – which the latter contracts with higher education to deliver. This 'specification' is characterized by the current social and economic transitions; particularly those associated with the concepts of 'globalization', the widely discussed shift to a 'knowledge-based economy' and 'lifelong learning'. Given the nature of these social changes – converging on knowledge and the lifelong education of the workforce – higher education has become a key recipient of society's focus and demands. It is firmly within the social gaze and that gaze is not about to let up. Neither is it content to be more explicit and hard-nosed in the detail and content of its 'knowledge specification'. It has also concluded that the traditional structures of higher education are not adequate to effectively deliver the requirements of the specification. Consequently, it has insisted that higher education transforms itself, remakes itself in the new social mould.

The new social mould, into which higher education is being levered, is characterized by what may be described as the 'discourse of excellence'

(Readings, 1996). This discourse, focused on delivery and performance, heralds a new way of thinking and talking about higher education. It is not an accident that in a relatively short space of time, the idea of 'excellence' has come to dominate higher education. Very few university mission statements risk omitting the term. Its very universality makes its absence more telling than its presence. Not pursuing excellence is tantamount to an admission of failure. In respect of the values and ideals of higher education, excellence has been criticized as having 'no content' and as marking 'the fact that there is no longer any idea of the University' (Readings, 1996: 39) – and mission statements as being 'ubiquitous, vacuous and inter-changeable' (Coffield and Williamson, 1997: 1).

On the other hand, the idea of excellence (imported from industry) does function extremely well as the torch-bearer of the structural revolution that has embraced higher education as a whole. Because excellence is not so much concerned with 'what' but rather 'how', it brings a whole new way of conceiving higher education. It is a way less encumbered by issues of cultural significance or educational value, as by issues of social and economic effectiveness and efficiency. Excellence is a measure of the way in which the university performs its social role, not a measure of the role itself. It is measured in terms of inputs and outputs. It is therefore accountable: accountable to externally agreed marks of itself within 'the knowledge specification' that society 'contracts' with higher education to provide: the 'new bargain' (Robertson, 1997: 77). This specification defines excellence in terms of performance indicators of both the efficiency with which higher education delivers the product and the quality of product. Drawn up under a social and economic agenda characterized by such issues as globalization, a knowledge-based economy and lifelong learning, the 'specification' is replete with notions of competitiveness in terms of number: expansion of student numbers, expansion of knowledge base, competitive advantage, efficiency gains, employee productivity, and so on. It is a conception of accountability in which 'the quite proper demand that universities be *accountable* gets translated into the reductionist idea that everything is simply a matter of *accounting*' (Harvey, 1998: 115). This is clearly light years from how the university understands academic duty, however mysterious it might be.

The discourse of excellence

This 'storm' of excellence is not simply an abstract way of conceptualizing large changes in the higher education system; it has serious repercussions on the day-to-day affairs of academic practice. Indeed, the features characterizing academics' life and work epitomize the challenges of professionalism facing the academy today. A word of caution: living in the eye of a storm is often accompanied by an impression of calm and security, an impression which remnants of the university's 'ivory tower' legacy still robustly strive to sustain. Given the diverse range of institutions, disciplines, practices and roles that differentiate the affairs of higher education, perceptions of this social tempest and its impact on academic practice will vary widely between individuals and institutions, some feeling more sheltered and less buffeted than others. Nevertheless, such perceptions neither do much to halt or reverse its impact nor to reduce the challenge it poses to academics.

The most exceptional characteristic of this 'storm' is the profound change in the language in which higher education is increasingly discussed. The successful colonization by terms such as excellence, competition, and efficiency has been accompanied by an attendant 'industrialization of the language' (Coffield and Williamson, 1997: 1). Higher education is business. It is big business, international business, part of the burgeoning global service sector. This language has infiltrated most if not all of the features of higher education, sitting uncomfortably alongside older terms it augments or even replaces. It 'sells' 'products', jostling with banks and travel agents, films and restaurants, hairdressers and accountants to retail its wares, ever more conscious that it is competing for a limited sum of expendable income with a wide range of other services and products. The essence of that product is knowledge which its 'customers' 'buy' or 'consume' as they deem it relevant, regard it as serving their needs and/or believe it provides value for the money and time they are investing in it. In making its 'pitch', higher education focuses on the specialized skills it possesses in the generation and dissemination of that knowledge: research and teaching. And in this language, research and teaching are not distinguished so much by their activity as by the nature of their customer and the description of the financial relationship which holds between them: be that through block grants, research contracts, student fees, etc. (The allocation of university funding based on research assessment exercise – RAE – scores, for example, says as much about how the UK government perceives the status of the constituencies it is serving as it does about productivity and performance within the university sector.) This product is increasingly 'marketed' and 'delivered' in accordance with the perceived needs and trends of the market. The whole 'operation' is managed by 'line managers' (course leaders, heads of departments, deans, etc.) who are responsible to 'senior management teams' and 'chief executives' for meeting 'targets' all of whom are looking for both increases in 'efficiency gains' and in 'product quality'.

Within the discourse of excellence, efficiency gains and, to a large degree, product quality are accompanied and driven by a culture of competition. Higher education institutions not only compete generally for expendable income within the national economy; within their own knowledge sphere they are competing ever more aggressively with other national and regional universities and colleges for research and students, for consultancy and status. With the globalization of the economy, competition has extended into a race to develop foreign markets, while simultaneously defending home markets. If this competition was not enough, universities have seen escalating direct competition for their 'products' from non-academic sources, including 'commercial laboratories, government research centres, think tanks and consultancies' (Robertson, 1997: 91). In addition, higher education is measured, scored and rewarded for their competitive success. League tables provide measurements of 'quality' and 'excellence' in both research (RAE) and in teaching and learning (subject review or teaching quality assessment – TQA).

The impact on individual academics of 'excellence' in the guise of both increasing efficiency/competition and ever more intrusive measurements of quality is extensive and pervades all aspects of their academic practices. Efficiency and competition have meant that the activities of academic staff have been scrutinized more minutely for efficiency gains and tied more directly to their personal role in income generation. Concerns about having fixed staff in areas of declining customer base, whether this be due to changing market trends or the result of poor competitive operations, has led to management looking to use more flexible arrangements and patterns of staff deployment. This has resulted in a vast increase in part-time and short-term contracts, and includes the 'outsourcing' of academic staff to agencies with all the insecurities such policies engender. Pressures have subsequently increased on staff to become flexible, both in terms of the kinds of duties and the range of subject areas in which they are engaged. Ability to teach, for example, in subject areas progressively more distant to one's areas of subject expertise and to engage in work developing new income streams – such as consultancy – for which one has little or no training, are quickly becoming the rule rather than the exception. An indication of the triumph of a culture of efficiency and productivity gains has been the dramatic fall in the relative strength of academic salaries in the UK, simultaneously improving productivity and reducing academic status in the market economy.

There is also a growing focus on the development of abilities that are more akin to the modern entrepreneur than the traditional academic. These include the talent for marketing oneself, one's teaching, one's research and one's institution. They encompass a diverse range of skills from media presentation to brochure and leaflet design, from product development (research, scholarship, courses) to product design (more accessible and customer-friendly modular programmes) and product packaging (online courses delivered to the home). In more extreme cases it may even require academics to become direct sales people: universities have sometimes acted like call centres, providing lecturers with lists of potential students whom they were required to 'cold call' to inform them of the advantages of their various courses ('products').

Where the impact of competition and efficiency on individual academics leads, the impact of intrusive systems of quality assessment and assurance follows. The recent intense focus on academic accountability in terms of quality has had significant repercussions on the nature of the academic's changing role. For many academics, research and scholarship activity is increasingly perceived and conceived within the scaffolding of numbers: numbers of published articles, numbers of citations, quantity of research funding, five-year RAE cycles, publishing lead in times, and so on. There is, moreover, a 'gallows' silhouette to this scaffolding – 'publish or perish' – as academics are reminded that their probation, employment contracts and promotional prospects are directly linked to their ability to scramble and clamber within it, the dark image of a 'noose' ever present and threatening. While productivity may have increased, it has not done so without significant repercussions on the process and nature of research and scholarship. This includes, for example, uncomfortable trends towards more hurried work published before it is ready, towards work which is more practical or applied, less theoretical or pure or 'blue skies', more trivial work and/or work which is increasingly felt to be isolated and irrelevant. It has also be accompanied by an explosion of journals (paper and electronic) but with ever more specialized articles read by fewer and fewer readers. In addition academics are also finding that more of their time is being spent on developing, writing and sending off research proposals which are more likely to be turned down as funds are more hotly contested.

In teaching, similar accountability, 'scaffolding' has added further pressures to academic time. Quality assurance, quality assessment, quality audit, quality enhancement and quality transformation (Middlehurst, 1997) have not only introduced a new, often confusing vocabulary, they have also added a multitude of more formal and systematic administrative practices to the academic workload. These practices have come to characterize more fully the three key relationships academics maintain between their institutions, their students and themselves. New and changing institutional quality assurance systems, for example, require academic staff to spend additional time complying with and contributing to institutional policies, strategies and paperwork, increasing considerably as external audit and assessment exercises approach. In addition, relationships with students have been characterised by increased paperwork, including administering more formal and comprehensive systems of monitoring student assessment, evaluations, support, completions, destinations, etc. coupled with developing strategies to learn and improve from such monitoring. Finally, these strategies have included increasing responsibilities for staff to engage in a wide and diverse set of personal development activities. These may range from relatively undemanding one-off lunchtime discussions with colleagues on issues of mutual relevance and importance to ongoing, long-term programmes of continued professional development. They are increasingly accompanied by formal systems of appraisal, peer observation and, particularly for new staff, mandatory programmes in teacher training. In the UK, the Dearing Committee report recommended that all 'institutions of higher education begin immediately to develop or seek access to programmes for teacher training of their staff, if they do not have them, and that all institutions seek national accreditation of such programmes from the Institute for Learning and Teaching in Higher Education' (NCIHE, 1997: recommendation 13). The higher education sector subsequently established this new institute in 1999 as a professional body for teachers in higher education. While not yet mandatory, such accreditation is regarded as yet another burden by many academics, requiring substantial time commitment without substantial increase in resources.

Living in the eye of the 'storm of excellence' – with its industrial vocabulary manifested in twin guises of competition/efficiency and quality/accountability – has undeniably presented a substantial test for academic life. This test has been exemplified by changes in the nature of academic roles and the pressures associated with these changes. In the next section, we shall briefly look at the specific challenges it presents to the academic in terms of how he or she is being asked to think about their roles in relation to both knowledge and the student. The disposition of these challenges both announces the new call for academic professionalism in teaching and learning and supports the nature of its response.

The challenge of excellence

The challenge of 'excellence' is not entirely a negative phenomenon. The move towards professionalism in teaching and learning is a natural manifestation of the discourse of excellence. In terms of the social and economic accountability of higher education to society, it is long overdue. While the nature of the challenge – immersed as it is in an 'accounting' mode – is deeply suspect, it provides a necessary jolt to critical thought and reflection. This does not mean, however, that it should be passively accepted or, for that matter, that academics should rage blindly like modern 'Lears' within their 'towers', as the 'storm' strips off the last remnants of ivory veneer. It is vitally important that academics take up this challenge to think. This section will briefly look at the nature of the challenge with respect to both the new and developing relationship with the student that it projects, and the edifice of knowledge which surrounds that relationship.

If, as we have seen, *knowledge* characterizes the 'specification' which the *knowledge-based economy* 'contracts' with higher education to provide, *economy* increasingly characterizes the way in which that knowledge is developed, managed and disseminated. Knowledge is the 'product' of modern society and subject to its market structures: it is traded as is any other commodity or service. It is increasingly traded on global communication and information systems that, by virtue of their growing impact, have themselves become a serious component of the knowledge market. In this model, universities no longer sustain the monopoly they once enjoyed. They are simply one of many social and corporate organizations developing, managing, disseminating and competing with knowledge. Indeed, they are often in partnership with corporate organizations that by virtue of financial muscle demand and are given the 'knowledge' control (Chomsky, 1998; Press and Washburn, 2000). The academic relationship with knowledge is increasingly dominated by competitive economic structures which any dominant and powerful product ('knowledge is power') engenders.

Within such a framework, the nature of knowledge and our perception of what it entails inevitably change. Traditional elitist distinctions between 'high' knowledge (culture) and 'mass' or popular knowledge (culture), for example, begin to dissolve (Usher et al., 1997). Produced, moreover, within new sites with different priorities and a wider set of organizational and technical goals, knowledge has 'mutated' and increasingly taken on an 'active voice'. Active forms of knowledge that can be employed to increase economic competitiveness and personal effectiveness are increasingly displacing the passive knowledge of truth, contemplation and personal awareness. Gibbons et al. (1994) have described this change in terms of a move from mode 1 knowledge, primarily 'disciplinary' based and situated in an academic context, towards mode 2 knowledge which is transdisciplinary and located in a context of application. Echoing this distinction, Barnett describes the university as 'a site of rival versions of what it is to know the world', (1997a: 30), embodied in the distinction between 'academic' and 'operational' competence. Academic competence is, for example, described as having a focus on 'knowing that' and stressing 'propositions' evaluated by criteria of 'truth'. Operational competence, in contrast, focus on 'knowing how' and stressing 'outcomes' evaluated by 'economic' criteria. The pressures in the direction of operational competence are, he suggests, changing our very epistemological existence (Barnett, 1997b: 140).

If the challenge of excellence is interrogating our traditional ways of conceiving and using knowledge, it is also contesting the academic relationship to the student. In particular there is pressure to regard students as 'consumers' to whom we are accountable in terms of the product (knowledge) which we are providing. Aside from the changing nature of this product, this has always been a role of the academy. Within the terms of the 'knowledge specification' presented to higher education, however, students have themselves now become more firmly regarded as 'product' for whom the university is accountable to society. In the language of excellence, and the ironic paradoxes that it raises, students have become 'product' through consuming 'product' in order to become 'productive' within our society. As such, it is precisely the nature of student-as-product which has recently become the focus of social and economic concern. The 'knowledge specification', moreover, stipulates in some detail the main collective and individual features of this 'product'. Such terms as 'mass' and 'diverse' describe the collective features and 'transferable' and 'meta-learning' describe the individual features.

Within a generation the student body which higher education serves has radically changed from an 'elite' to a 'mass' system (Trow, 1981), student participation rates more than trebling and the number of institutions called universities more than doubling. Accompanying this enormous rise in student numbers has been an increase in the diversity of students, including growth in the participation of women, mature students, ethnic minority students, students from less privileged classes and overseas students (Watson and Taylor, 1998). Underlying both the increase in numbers and in diversity has been the focus on widening access, again primarily 'to contribute to improved economic competitiveness and to local economic success' (Robertson, 1997: 88).

This economic imperative is also manifested in the individual features specified by society, more recently under the expression 'graduateness' (HEQC, 1996). Higher education should be aiming to 'deliver' to society individuals (students/graduates) who have developed both a range of 'transferable' or key skills and the more general ability and willingness to 'learn to learn' or meta-learning. The former – including communication, teamwork, problem-solving, information technology, etc. – supports the economic requirement of flexibility and adaptability graduates might take into a range of different employment and life practices and activities. The latter – the 'core skill' of transferable skills – characterizes individual 'lifelong learning' or the graduate's ability to continue to learn new knowledge, skills and practices. What this points to for teaching and learning 'is not a core "subject" curriculum so much as core characteristics, qualities and kinds of outcomes for all who enter and re-enter higher education' (Duke, 1997: 67).

In essence, then, these four terms epitomize the nature of the challenge of professionalism to teaching and learning in higher education:

1 the increasing numbers of students in our classrooms;
2 the increasing diversity of background, experience and needs which our students present;
3 a curriculum of transferability;
4 the conceptual shift in our thinking about our practice from teaching to learning, from delivering knowledge to developing and fostering independence of learning in which students develop the ability to discover and reconstruct knowledge (and their lives) for themselves.

This, very roughly, outlines the shape of the professional challenge. Alongside and largely in response to this challenge, has been the development of what might be referred to as a new 'paradigm' in the realization of learning and teaching expertise in higher education. This paradigm – a professional paradigm – is a third paradigm, contesting two earlier paradigms of teaching development. The first *ad hoc* paradigm is located primarily within the individual teacher. Associated with 'elite' systems of student participation and prevalent up until the late 1960s and early 1970s (although still rife in much of higher education), its underlying assumption is that teaching is something you pick up and grasp informally and individually. The teacher is left to their own devices and draws upon past experience of being taught, trial and error, help from sympathetic colleagues when available and 'natural' affinities for teaching. The second paradigm – expanding more or less in tandem with the growth of student numbers from the 1970s onward – is the *skills* paradigm. Its basic assumption is that the development of teaching is an 'add on' process and rests in the accumulation of performance and communication skills, competencies and tips. These skills are 'generic' and provided by trainers and consultants who often have no formal experience of the discipline in which the teachers are working or even of higher education teaching. The provision of training is generally located within the institution's support staff development services, and separated from its core academic activities.

Ironically, the very teaching and learning challenge which 'excellence' has articulated has often failed to address the substance and complexity of the challenge itself. While demanding higher education go beyond the *ad hoc* first paradigm answers to the challenge, it has confined its own general response to the narrowly prescribed *skills*-centred approaches of the second paradigm. 'Excellence' has often elicited approaches for developing expertise in teaching and learning which address the new state of complexity by imposing a reductionist (and 'accounting') framework to simplify it. Curiously, they engage the uncertain by assuming, as Barnett notes, 'a known situation and well understood attributes' (1997a: 41). The result is an approach that specifies increasingly narrow outcomes and competencies of expertise, establishes behavioural standards for them and insists on compliance with these standards irrespective of the professional, disciplinary and institutional context (ILT, 1999a).

The third paradigm – the *professional* – is the focus of this book. It is a relatively recent development and is only beginning to overlap with and compete with the first two paradigms. Like most professions, the location of the *professional* paradigm goes beyond the practitioner's self and institution to embrace wider issues raised by society. Professional status, here, 'rests primarily on three propositions . . . that society attaches value to higher education; that specialized knowledge is involved; and that there are higher order intellectual judgements and skills required in the largely independent acquisition, extension, and application of that knowledge' (Bennett, 1998: 44). It is not detached from the core academic and professional activities of the academy but integrated within it and subject to the same critical requirements and standards with respect to knowledge, theory, values and practice. In the next section we shall begin to examine a third-paradigm approach that we believe more adequately addresses the challenge.

The reflective professional

The different responses elicited by the challenge of professionalism in learning and teaching may be illustrated by an important distinction between the call 'for' professionalism and the call 'to' professionalism. The former is primarily a call from the discourse of excellence for accountability, an external call for standardized professional organization, practice and evaluation procedures. It reflects the overall desire for increased efficiency and competitiveness within an 'accounting' framework of quality. The latter, on the other hand, is a call 'to defend' academic values and practices from the worst excesses of externally imposed frameworks of excellence, but also 'to acknowledge' the challenge, to take possession of and transform it. The 'call to' is a call towards a new way of thinking about learning and teaching which neither falls back on traditional 'laissez faire' academic versions of the benign 'amateur' (Ramsden, 1992: 8) nor succumbs to newer versions of behavioural competence. It is a call to change, but it is also a call to ongoing reflection and change, to an ongoing transformation centred in the learning situation and reflecting the changing nature of that situation as characterized in the four features described above. It is a call to a professionalism that can successfully negotiate and ride the 'storm'.

Riding the 'storm' is an apt metaphor because the storm is not about to disappear or subside. It will change as the forces within society change and impact upon higher education. The very changing social and economic forces will continue to feed it. Vanquishing or weathering the 'storm' are not options. Riding it is the only one. One of the corollaries of 'riding' is that any adequate model of practice must not only account for the events and situations that arise in practice, but also the changing social context of that practice. Here, the model of practice most commonly advocated in opposition to the narrow competence model – the reflective practitioner (Schon, 1983; 1987) – is not sufficient. Both the competence model and the reflective practitioner model describe two very different ways of responding to the multitude of situations and events describing practice, but they both essentially assume a 'storm-less' environment in which these situations and events take place. 'Reflective practice' has been successful in articulating a conception of professional practice that goes beyond the application of previously mastered competencies which are then rather mechanistically applied to events. Stressing the conception of 'reflecting-in-action', this model describes the practitioner's ability to employ professional knowledge during practice in such a manner as to devise, choose and apply appropriate responses to unexpected and complex events and situations. Nevertheless, the model of reflective practice is primarily located in and bounded by those events and situations.

Extending the concept of the reflective practitioner to the reflective professional embraces not only the locus of practice but the sphere of the professional as well. It encompasses what Barnett refers to as 'professing-in-action' (1997b: 135), which includes an understanding of the wider professional and academic context. If the former reflects on practice, the latter critically reflects on multiple and diverse discourses, on practice within the broader contexts and critical frameworks of his or her professional situation, however situated, constituted or clustered: teaching–research–administration; discipline–department–institution; ethical–social–economic–political; local–national–international. These provide a changing set of multiple discourses in which the reflective professional works.

> The key challenge of modern professionalism is just this, of trying to make sense of disparate discourses in one's professional actions. It may be that, on occasions, the discourses collide such that one cannot act under them coherently . . . The challenge, then, that faces the modern professional is the management of incoherence. (Ibid.: 141)

Riding the 'storm' is managing this incoherence. It rests in the ability to critically situate oneself and one's practice within an environment of substantial uncertainty and change – and to manage that change:

- changing academic roles;
- changing knowledge bases;
- changing ways of knowing;
- changing nature of the student body;
- changing student needs;
- changing departmental requirements;
- changing institutional demands;
- changing external agency demands;
- changing professional accreditation demands.

Academic faculty will need to make sense of these changes, understand them, and find ways of working within them as they happen. But, as Barnett (2000) suggests, this is precisely the problem. There are no longer any solid conceptual frameworks for doing so. We are – particularly in higher education – living in an age of 'supercomplexity', that situation when even 'our very frameworks for making the world intelligible are in dispute' (Barnett, 2000: 75). This, of course, does not mean the end of such frameworks – if anything, rather more of them. It does mean managing them, finding ways to be comfortable with them, developing new ones. It will 'depend on having the appropriate language linked to theoretical ideas' (Entwistle, 1998: 1). In this it requires a 'language' which is both critical and open, a language in which concrete 'problem-solutions' (Kuhn, 1970) can be devised, implemented, evaluated, negotiated, modified and/or set aside in an ongoing cycle of critical performance. Such a language must be suitably open and elastic to accommodate a diversity of personal circumstances within rapidly shifting curriculum expansion and development; over a wide range of disciplines (and their escalating disciplinary and interdisciplinary 'contours'); set within a diverse cluster of higher education departments and institutions. The aim of this book is to describe the nature of such a 'language' and how it might be used in practice.

There are three interrelated components to the 'language' developed here: a critical conceptual framework, relevant and appropriate genres, and a general performance strategy (see Figure 1.1). The first component is concerned to situate this 'language' within three conceptual locations: a general theoretical framework of human communication and knowledge, a model of the reflective professional within academic practice, and a critical matrix of learning in higher education. The themes of the first component are considered in Part 1 of the book, and its three locations addressed respectively in the three chapters of that part. The second component is taken up in Part 2 of the book and addresses what we refer here to as 'genres' of the language or 'genres' of 'practice'. It includes that range of activities which teachers in higher education perform in their teaching. While these 'genres' focus on a variety of learning and teaching activities in which academic staff engage, they are not presented as an exhaustive list, nor are they intended as closed systems within themselves. They may be separated and combined in a wide array of 'sub-genres'. The third component proposes an integrated 'strategy of realization' based on an action research model of developing and improving practice. The essence of this component is to (a) locate the development of teaching and learning within the concrete disciplinary and departmental situation, and to (b) link this development with the ongoing improvement of practice. This will be taken up in detail in Part 3.

These three components are not intended to coalesce into a prescriptive generic programme but, rather, to provide a structure for opening

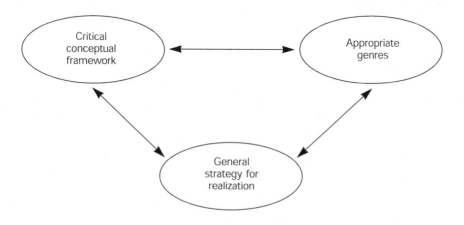

Figure 1.1 The language of learning and teaching

up a wide range of individually located and devised teaching and learning strategies. In this respect, this book is written to provide a way into the language and ideas. It is also intended (as suggested in the Preface) to provide a means of negotiating the professional accreditation programmes and routes established by the Institute for Learning and Teaching, a means which is reflectively and critically professional. Like all languages, it has its own structures and 'genres', which, while not exclusive, provide useful ways of thinking about practice, including their critical rejection and/or reconstitution.

Models of practice, finally, are the construction of teachers and students within situated interactions. They may be, usually are, limited historically, socially, institutionally and by discipline and department. They are rarely, however, completely and utterly restricted and solidified. There are cracks, frequently large gaps, in the dense structures in which researchers, teachers and students engage one another; fractures from which they can pry open those 'engagements' and initiate substantial change. While there may be policy moves to close such 'fractures' with new prescriptions, faculty and students together do have substantial means. Traditionally they have not exercised it as fully as they might. They have rarely had any training in exercising it. The model of practice proposed here is that of mutual empowerment through an engagement with the language(s) of teaching and learning, through a critical understanding of its principles and through enhanced status. It is not asking academics to submit to a barrage of techniques, tips and prescribed practices which they might 'inflict' on themselves and their students but, rather, to engage in a way of thinking about their own practice. At the very least, it is intended to be mildly subversive and liberating, a subversion encompassing academic practice, engagement with students and personal practice. It aims to provide space for the development of critical being in the world (Barnett, 1997b). This is the essence of the reflective professional.

PART 1: THE LECTURER AS REFLECTIVE PROFESSIONAL

2

Language and Knowledge: A General Theoretical Framework

A house of cards

In the last chapter, we raised the issue of developing a professional 'language of practice' for negotiating the changing context of teaching in higher education. Such a 'language' and its mastery, we suggested, are at the heart of the idea of the 'reflective professional'. In the next three chapters, we shall examine the three conceptual frameworks supporting such a language and the practice it professes. They are:

1. a general theoretical framework of human communication and knowledge;
2. a corresponding model of the reflective professional within academic practice;
3. a critical matrix of learning in higher education.

With these three frameworks we shall, so to speak, be putting our own 'theoretical cards' on the table, cards with which we shall attempt to build a framework for developing and understanding the 'language' of teaching and learning. We recognize, of course, the dangers of using this 'card' metaphor, particularly in the context of 'building' a framework. The prevailing image of a 'house of cards' conjures up a multitude of diffident meanings, including instability, precariousness, unpredictability and uncertainty. They do not normally lend themselves to inspiring confidence in a conceptual apparatus underlying practice, particularly one described as existing in a 'storm'. Together the two depict an almost impossible situation. For this very reason, however, the image is, perhaps, both appropriate and relevant.

It is not our intention to construct an immovable and uncompromising framework in granite, but rather to set out a theoretical 'narrative' (Rorty, 1982) which practitioners might profitably engage with and gainfully use within their own unique situations. The image of a 'house of cards' does not offer a foundational framework (power in terms of hardness and solidity) but, rather, a narrative framework (power in terms of

17

description and flexibility). It aims at adaptive and transformative potency as opposed to fixed and enduring strength. A 'house' in which the 'cards' can be critically reshuffled, examined, negotiated, selected and arranged according to the situation 'dealt'. Our objective, here, is to disclose the broad theoretical framework sustaining the idea of the 'reflective professional' and the associated 'language of practice'. This framework is, of course, a particular arrangement of the theoretical 'cards', embedded in other such 'arrangements' and conceptual assumptions, all of which are contestable. They are, however, not available for such 'contests' if not offered.

A secular religion

The theoretical framework developed in this chapter is essentially 'constructivist'. This in itself, however, is not to say very much, for, as Phillips points out, 'across the broad fields of educational theory and research, constructivism has become something akin to a secular religion' (1995: 5). It has become so, he suggests, because despite the wide number of rival sects within this 'religion', there is general agreement with respect to its most basic tenets. These essentially consist of the view that, despite being born with cognitive potential, humans do not arrive with either pre-installed empirical knowledge or methodological rules. Neither do we acquire knowledge ready-formed or pre-packaged by directly perceiving it. On the whole, knowledge, our criteria and methods for knowing it, and the bodies of public knowledge (disciplines) to which it contributes are 'constructed'. There is, however, significant variation between the many theoretical positions described as 'constructivist'.

Phillips maps the variation along three dimensions (see Figure 2.1). While rough and ready, it provides a useful map for locating the frame-

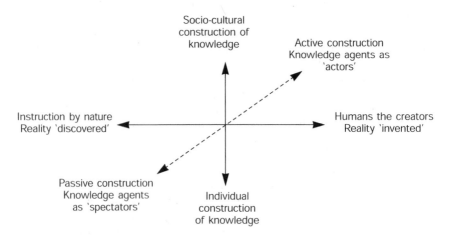

Figure 2.1 Constructivism: three dimensions (adapted from Phillips, 1995; 2000)

work discussed in this chapter. The main horizontal dimension describes the classic dispute 'reality: discovered or invented' (see, for example, Bruner, 1986; Penrose, 1989; Rorty, 1989). At one end, knowledge is independent of human agency: nature serves as a kind of 'instructor', its store of knowledge discovered and absorbed or copied somewhat passively. At the other end of this dimension, knowledge (and reality) is essentially 'made' or 'invented' by creative and active knowers. At some point towards the 'discovered' end of this dimension, a theoretical position is no longer 'constructivist' but takes a strong 'realist' position in which knowledge is in effect 'imposed' from without. There is no effective space for human agency in the formation of knowledge. Theoretical sites towards the other extreme of this dimension take stances describing 'radical relativist' positions. Knowledge is relative to the knower or knowers. It is essentially the result of individual or group 'invention'. Our position will rest between these two extremes, conceiving knowing neither as 'discovery' nor 'invention' but as social 'narrative'.

The 'vertical' dimension of the map in Figure 2.1 describes the tension between theories which contend that the 'construction' of knowledge arises within internal cognitive processes and those which argue that knowledge is socially and culturally 'constructed' and, therefore, largely 'public'. This tension is distinct from the different approaches which theorists take when looking at knowledge and learning. An approach focusing on the individual and the self, for example, does not mean taking a position that regards knowledge as exclusively or even primarily inner or cognitive. Piaget and Vygotsky, for example, are both concerned with how individuals learn and construct knowledge, and approach the subject from an individual psychological perspective, but they differ significantly in their views of what that comprises. Piaget (1950) stresses the biological and cognitive mechanisms, whereas Vygotsky (1986) emphasizes the social factors in learning.

The third dimension focuses on the degree to which human construction of knowledge, whether it is social and public or inner and private, is an active or passive process. Although there are close parallels here with the first dimension, the tensions inherent in this dimension do not map narrowly onto the first. 'Spectator' here is not simply the passive receiver of knowledge from nature and 'actor' is not merely the active constructor of personal knowledge. These terms describe a relationship with knowledge which highlight the active involvement, or lack of it, which human agents have in the process of learning. Again, these 'agents' may be individuals or social communities. The point is the distinction between learning and knowing involving an active playing role in the 'knowledge game' or consisting of merely being a spectator of the 'game'.

This very brief discussion of the broad 'typography' of constructivism cannot, of course, describe in any substantial detail the fine distinctions and nuances which the wide range of different theoretical positions take with respect to knowledge and learning. It provides, rather, a common map for locating and positioning the general theoretical framework that informs this book. Our theoretical framework is broadly located on this map close to the middle of the first dimension but leaning robustly along the other two dimensions towards the 'social' and 'active' poles respectively. Readers will wish to make their own judgements as to where this position might more precisely be located.

Before we embark it is worth reminding ourselves that our theoretical framework is concerned with informing the practice of teaching and learning in the social context of higher education. It has both a personal dimension and a social dimension. The two are inseparable: the personal contains within it the depth and breadth of the social, the exhilaration and the trepidation of the social, the consolations and the threats of the social, the power and the vulnerability of the social. At the heart of this relationship, characterizing and defining its diverse features, is the issue of human communication. The practice of teaching and learning in higher education is the practice of knowledge and communication or the exercise of self and language in specific academic social situations and institutions. In the broad sense, the reflective professional is a critical practitioner of knowledge and language as social being. For the purposes of this discussion, therefore, we shall be probing the issues raised above from a perspective, which focuses on the nature of communication, and on the social nature of the self. It is a perspective that supports our approach of looking at learning and teaching as the practice of a 'language'. It is the theoretical nature of this language as 'intersubjective' or 'dialogical' which we wish to now to explore.

In the stream of life

Language and human existence are inextricably entangled with one another. Life without some sort of human language is almost inconceivable. Pinker (1995) has suggested that language is a human instinct and Wittgenstein has remarked that language 'only has meaning in the stream of life' (Malcolm, 1967). Our understanding of how our minds work and how we communicate has substantial repercussions for how we understand our social relationship and ourselves. In this section we shall briefly explore and unpack the important theoretical issues at the heart of the relationship between language and the self. In so doing, we shall offer a view of both, one that is socially constructed and situated 'in the stream of life'. It will be described in contrast to asocial and/or non-contextual perspectives of language which we suggest tend to characterize (however unconsciously) traditional assumptions of learning and teaching practice in higher education. The latter perspectives are often uncritiqued theories of what Bruner (1996) refers to as 'folk psychology', omnipresent, intuitive theories which are rarely made explicit. In such a context it would be remiss of us to contribute to the development of a new 'folk psychology' by not exploring and making explicit our own theoretical assumptions.

We begin with a distinction that Ong (1982) makes between two models of human communication or language. The first he calls the 'media' model and describes it as 'sending' a message between two separate, independent subjects. Meaning is 'encoded' in a formal 'language' by one subject, sent (by means of speaking, writing, etc.) to a second subject who then 'decodes' the meaning. Knowing and communicating here are separate activities. Such models regard the mind and language in 'computational' terms. The former is a 'computational device' concerned with 'information processing' (Bruner, 1996). They fail, however, as Ong notes, to explain that key aspect of human communication of the sender being, somehow, in the receiver's position before he or she speaks: 'this is the paradox of human communication. Communication is intersubjective'. This second model challenges the linear and reductive nature of the 'encoding-sending-decoding' model, contending that they can only be properly understood within the social or cultural situation in which they occur. Bruner (1996) refers to such a perspective as 'culturalism': meaning is not so much private and exchanged as publicly constructed within exchange; knowing and communicating are 'virtually inseparable'. It is the second model that we shall explore and develop here. In doing so we are not, as has often been assumed, disparaging content in favour of process. Content, knowledge and meaning (be they facts, ideas, concepts, theory, practice, etc.) are central to learning and teaching. It is, in fact, the first model that drains content of the vitality and rigour of social exchange and transformation.

We primarily develop the important issues of this second model through an examination and comparison of the essential conceptual similarities in the work of two writers – Ragnar Rommetveit and Mikhail Bakhtin. Despite their vastly differing approaches and styles, they both describe the main features of what may be called an *intersubjective* or *dialogical* model of communication. The following comparison, at times theoretically technical, nevertheless provides a useful tactic for succinctly disclosing the basic concepts and ideas of the conceptual framework proposed here.

Intersubjectivity

Rommetveit's theoretical stance, set out in what he refers to as 'the architecture of intersubjectivity', takes a social linguistics perspective. In developing it, he begins with a description of the philosophical differences he has with two traditions. The first is the subjective existential approach of writers like Merleau-Ponty who describes the use of a common language as 'a synchronising change of my own existence, a transformation of my being' (1962: 183–4). He assumes an independent, private 'I' which, Rommetveit argues, fails to explain how it is 'possible for any kind of social reality to emerge out of an encounter between two different and entirely private worlds' (1974: 24).

The second and main position with which he is concerned is that of the generative and transformational grammar approach to language of Noam Chomsky and the Harvard–MIT school. In studying language *in vacuo* – independently of their actual use (outside the 'stream of life') – to discover autonomous *deep* or *internal* 'sentence structures' and 'underlying conceptual realities', this school, Rommetveit argues, make 'adventurous' ontological assumptions of an independent reality. Platonic in nature these assumptions concern 'a *finite and already known universe of "conceptual realities"* of some sort, against which the "real" or "underlying" meanings of words . . . can be validated' (Rommetveit, 1974: 19; original emphasis).

Rommetveit's alternative position to the private 'I' of Merleau-Ponty and Chomsky's objective mental structures lies in a refusal to ground meaning in such independent ontological entities: 'the *here-and-now* that constitutes the pre-requisite for any human dialogue appears to be neither entirely public nor purely private, but has to be conceived of as *an intersubjectively established social reality,* (ibid.: 25; original emphasis). Central to this view is the refusal to separate language as system from language as use. Chomsky argues that in order to understand human language and the psychological capacities on which it rests, we must first ask 'what it (language) is and not how or for what purposes it is used' (1968: 62). Rommetveit borrows from the work of the later Wittgenstein who, in contrast to Chomsky, argues that it is not possible to separate language from its actual use: 'To understand a sentence means to understand a language. To understand a language means to be master of a technique' (1968: 81). This is also central, for instance, to Wittgenstein's concept of 'language-game' which he says 'is meant to bring into prominence that the speaking of a language is part of an activity, or a form of life' (ibid.: 11). It is, furthermore, implicit in his arguments against the concept of a 'private language': the other and the social are intrinsic to the very notion of a language.

Utterance

Bakhtin (1986) takes a similar tack with respect to the work of linguists such as Saussure (1966). Saussure accepts that 'taken as a whole speech is many-sided and heterogeneous', belonging 'both to the individual and society', but separates language as 'system' (*langue*) from its use (*parole*) because in the latter 'we cannot discover its unity' (1966: 9). The individual uses of language, as Holquist writes, are 'quickly consigned to an unanalyzable chaos of idiosyncrasy' (1990: 45–6), abandoned as an area of study in favour of the 'system'. Bakhtin claims such abstractions ignore the active process of the speaker (and the role of the 'other') in 'speech communication' in favour of vague terms such as 'speech flow' (Ong's media model) 'interpreted as segments of language' (1986: 70).

Echoing Wittgenstein's famous remark that 'philosophical problems arise when language *goes on holiday'* (1968: 19; original emphasis) – when abstracted from its concrete context – Bakhtin argues that linguistic confusion and imprecision 'result from ignoring the *real unit* of speech communication: the utterance. For speech can exist in reality only in the form of concrete utterances of individual speaking people' (1986: 71; original emphasis). He distinguishes between 'utterance' as a concrete unit of speech communication (inclusive of speaker and situation) and 'sentence' as an abstracted unit in language system.

The essential point on which Bakhtin and Rommetveit agree concerns the central role of the other in 'utterance'. 'Otherness' suffuses the concrete speech situation. In what he refers to as the speaker's 'active responsive understanding', Bakhtin describes utterance as 'determined by a *change of speaking subjects'*. Any utterance, he writes, 'is preceded by the utterances of others and its end is followed by the responsive utterances of others' (Bakhtin, 1986: 71; original emphasis). Speaking (and writing) is by its very nature a response, existing in a 'stream' of related responses and counter-responses distinguished and bounded by a change of speaker not by periods. In his 'architecture of intersubjectivity', Rommetveit describes this definition of utterance – as circumscribed by a change of speaking subject – in terms of the central pairing of 'I' and 'YOU' (self and other) and the 'direction of communication'. The utterance is bounded by the change in control of the intersubjective situation (the here and now) which 'is unequivocally linked to the *direction of communication'* (Rommetveit, 1974: 95; original emphasis). Rommetveit, like Bakhtin, also focuses on the 'real' unit of language defined in terms of the social pairing of 'self' and 'other'. In refusing to separate language from the 'stream of life', Wittgenstein also suggests this idea of utterance serves as a better unit of language than a sentence: 'If I hear someone say "it's raining" but do not know whether I have heard the beginning or the end ... so far this sentence does not serve to tell me anything' (1968: 11).

Three points follow from this discussion:

1 Utterance is a 'real' unit of speech, not 'conventional' (as is a 'sentence').
2 Utterance is defined by dialogue: 'otherness' is presupposed by the speaker as the other to whom the utterance is responding and the other from whom the utterance elicits a response.
3 Dialogue is the fundamental form of communication.

Dialogue

In so far as dialogue characterizes language, language is directed to someone. Bakhtin refers to this aspect of the utterance – whether the recipient is 'an immediate participant-interlocutor in an everyday dialogue [or] ... an indefinite unconcretized *other'* (1986: 95; original emphasis) – as its 'addressivity'. The feature of having 'said or written *everything* (one) wishes to say at a particular moment or under particular circumstances' (ibid.: 76; original emphasis) to say to the particular recipient or addressee he calls the utterance's 'finalisation'. In this view of language and communication, meaning is not a private construction 'transmitted' between people when linguistic conventions ('sentences') are encoded and decoded in such a way as to create a semantic bridge across the 'void' between individuals. Nor is it an act of creative transcendence enabling one 'I' to leap the void to another. Meaning is defined by social 'dialogue' and characterized by being addressed to someone – 'addressivity' – in its very construction. In this respect knowing and communicating are virtually inseparable, and made possible through socially constituted utterances that characterize language in 'the stream of life'.

The 'stream of life', of course, is disclosed in a multiplicity of different social and cultural forms and guises which play a powerful role in the construction and sharing of meaning across a wide range of social and cultural discourses. The central features of 'addressivity' and 'finalisation' that characterize the shared social nature of utterance are themselves embedded in these cultural forms and characterize the construction and communication of meaning within them. Rommetveit and Blakar, for example, note the case of a schizophrenic (suffering from a 'homonym symptom') talking about a grand party, saying: 'I too was invited, I went to the ball . . . and it rolled and rolled away' (1979: 94). The speaker's intention is to make something known about a 'ball' (party) which the listener, in so far as she is listening in accordance with the speaker's intentions and based on his premises, understands. When the speaker pauses and stumbles mid-sentence and follows a different intention regarding 'ball' (as toy), the speaker loses 'control' of the 'temporarily shared social world'. Rommetveit's point is that the speaker's failure to 'make sense' is not merely based on his loss of control over a temporarily shared social world. The prior assumption of such a shared world and a complementarity of intentions within it also determined it. The failure of 'meaning' (or, for that matter, its achievement) is thus founded on a given assumption of 'meaning'. As Rommetveit and Blakar write, 'intersubjectivity has thus in some sense to be taken for granted in order to be achieved' (ibid.: 96).

By changing the context of this sentence, Rommetveit and Blakar argue the shared intentions between speaker and listener is not rigid. It will permit 'variant premises for intersubjectivity' dependent on extra-linguistic features such as the occasion, body gestures, facial expressions, tone of voice and so on. They suggest, for example, the occasion of a poet reciting the following from his work:

I too was invited,
I went to the ball . . .
and it rolled
and rolled away . . . (ibid.: 97)

This second sentence does not evoke the kind of surprise accompanying the occasion of the first. However we may judge the poetry, we share the social intentions of the poet. The often unconscious features accounting for the complementarity of these intentions, Rommetveit (1974) refers to as 'meta-contracts'- as distinct from the contracts of linguistic convention in ordinary language or the sentence aspect of the utterance. Meta-contracts are *'contracts concerning which such potentialities are intended and situationally appropriate'* (ibid.: 61; original emphasis). Thus the picking up of a book of poetry, for example, is an act (meta-contract) in which we decide 'to engage in a different kind of language game' (ibid.: 57). Without this decision, or within a more ordinary 'game', it would not be poetry. This is true of all types of reading. While opening a newspaper may mean shedding a poetic 'game', this is not necessarily the case, other meta-contracts – situation, gesture, voice, etc. – might suggest an extension of the poetic 'game'. As such poetry (as a genre) is not determined by its 'sentence' aspect so much as by the 'game' in which it participates. 'Poetic freedom' is determined, at least in part, by the socio-historical 'legitimation' of certain 'games' which Rommetveit describes as *'institutionalized deviance from other "ordinary" language games'* (ibid.: 58; original emphasis).

Rommetveit's use of 'language game' to describe language forms (utterances) in various 'communication settings' mirrors Bakhtin's notion of speech 'genres' or *'forms of combinations* of these forms (utterances)' (1986: 81). Rommetveit describes them as *'relatively stable types'* of utterances common to and 'determined by the specific nature of the particular sphere of communication' (1974: 60). His further distinction between 'institutionalised' and 'ordinary' language games such as 'poetry' in which there is a 'poetic transcendence of "ordinary" reality' (ibid.: 58) also shadows Bakhtin's distinction between primary and secondary speech genres:

> Secondary (complex) speech genres . . . arise in more complex and comparatively highly developed and organised cultural communication (primarily written) that is artistic, scientific, socio-political and so on. During the process of their formation, they absorb and digest various primary (simple) genres that have taken form in unmediated speech communion. (1986: 62)

The above parallels between 'speech genre' and 'language game' reinforce the similarity between Rommetveit's and Bakhtin's descriptions of human communication. This similarity, as we have seen, centres on the issue of the 'other' (you) with which the self (I) is in 'dialogue' through the exchange of control and direction of the temporarily shared, social here and now. The difference between them rests largely on their differing descriptive perspectives. Thus, stressing the nature of utterance as 'dialogue' – the 'master key to the assumptions that guided Bakhtin's work throughout his whole career' (Holquist, 1990: 15) – triggers a 'dialogic' perspective of language. On the other hand, focusing, as Rommetveit does, on the idea that subjects are intrinsically bound to one another within the concrete utterance, lends itself to an 'intersubjective' description. A third description, 'inner sociality', which Holquist ascribes to Bakhtin, takes a perspective which focuses more clearly on the nature of 'self' as social.

Self

The self is described here as a 'perspective' of human communication in order to stress the social (other-dependent) nature of self. Bruner puts this very strongly: 'It can never be the case that there is a "self" independent of one's cultural-historical existence' (1986: 67). Burgess notes, similarly, that 'personal and human identity does not flower independently of social experience but is, rather, produced by and within it' (1984: 62). Holquist equates Bakhtin's view with that of George Mead who believed, 'the self necessarily carries with it the other-form. Whatever .. . the metaphysical possibilities or impossibilities of solipsism, psychologically it is non-existent' (1964: 103). Rommetveit (1974) also locates the possibility of language in what Mead (1950) called 'taking on the attitude of the other'. This 'attitude', he argues, 'constitutes the most pervasive and most genuinely social aspect of our general *communicative competence* . . . the common denominator of variant architectures of intersubjectivity across different kinds of language games, (ibid.: 63; original emphasis).

Intersubjectivity and 'dialogue', then, are preconditions of consciousness and language, indeed they are preconditions of Being. 'Being' for Bakhtin 'is not just an event, but an event that is shared. Being is a simultaneity; it is always a *co*-being' (Holquist, 1990: 25; original emphasis). Again it 'is an utterance . . . (having) the nature of dialogue' (ibid.:). 'Self' is, finally, neither the *realist* subject bound to an independent objective reality whose *monologue* must be 'discovered', nor the purely free *relativist* subject 'inventing' its own *monologues* (realities). It is *intersubjective*, characterized in its very existence by a social *dialogue* that is lived, shared and wholly subsumed within the torrents and rapids that are increasingly shaping our 'stream(s) of life'.

Revisiting the house of cards

The above conceptual framework stresses the 'situated' nature of language (and of 'being'). In doing so, it provides a means of understanding the vital role that the academic situation plays in the 'practices of knowledge and communication' – researching, teaching and learning – at the heart of higher education. How they are practised reflects, as we shall see in the next chapter, the 'theories' tacitly employed in their practice and understanding, 'theories', themselves, subject to social changes redefining the nature and scope of escalating academic roles and 'audiences'. The reflective professional means having the capacity to deal with this change, to build and rebuild in new, relevant and challenging ways a succession of 'houses of cards'. It includes an ability to integrate different academic 'worlds', to cope with a range of varying and uncertain frameworks and worlds, to construct anew forms of critical being. It is no less a challenge for our students and our ability as teachers to help them accomplish this and their learning will, in no small way, be conditional on our own capacity to do so.

Finally, we must understand the conceptual framework presented in this chapter within the limits of the proviso with which we, ourselves began this chapter. In so far as it is conditioned by its own social and historical situation, we recognize and accept its roots in what Harre (1981) calls source models. Such models are characterized and controlled by 'tacit but pervasive, scientific, metaphysical . . . even social, assumptions of a historical period, since the source-models that seem plausible to a community are those that fit best with the rest of the culture' (ibid.: 7).

That the authors are conditioned by a particular historical and social situation goes without saying. We are, we hope, reasonably aware of the degree to which this approach is characterized and limited by our historical, social and cultural assumptions. Moreover, that we accept this is to take a particular theoretical position which is, again, historically and socially characterized; and this is, again, to take a particular position, again so characterized, and so on. The paradox and incongruities of this infinite regress are symptomatic of the nature of the calls on the reflective professional to rigorously and critically reshuffle, examine, negotiate, select and arrange their cards according to the situation 'dealt'.

3

The Reflective Professional in Academic Practice

Introduction

In stressing the 'situated', social nature of language, the theoretical framework described in the previous chapter provides a way of exploring the vital role that the academic situation and its associated practices play in teaching and learning in higher education. It is a role which not only characterizes the student's first tentative encounters with and deepening experience of that situation, but also shapes the teacher's own professional encounters within it. It is part of what it means to be a reflective professional. The vigour of this theoretical apparatus does not consist solely in its ability to describe the nature of communication and knowledge within a shared situation but also within situations which are less than shared, even at times incommensurate – when the 'stream of life' situations we inhabit are worlds apart. The 'failure' to achieve meaning is often grounded in just such situations, where the underlying 'meta-contracts' or complex 'genres' of organized cultural communication are obscure and unshared. The academic situation – immersed in its disciplinary and institutional histories, discourses and procedures, its ways of thinking and working, of congregating and communicating, of distributing power, authority and status – characterizes the student/teacher encounter before a word is even exchanged. When they are 'exchanged' they carry with them both the wealth and weight of that situation.

In this chapter, then, we examine the second conceptual 'location' through which we are describing the 'reflective professional' in higher education: the key practices of 'knowledge and communication' – research, teaching and learning – which exemplify the academic situation. Drawing upon the theoretical architecture articulated in the previous chapter, we examine the opposing models of teaching and research reflected in the tacit 'theories' employed in their practice and understanding. We contrast traditional assumptions describing 'monologic' models pulling the worlds of practice apart with 'dialogic' models that draw them together under a common point of convergence in learning.

28

Finally, we suggest that academic values and principles rest in dialogic models of practice and, indeed, we cannot genuinely observe them outside such a model.

Worlds apart

For the student the academic situation is typically new and strange, its languages and practices frequently unfamiliar and mysterious, even exotic and bizarre. Their encounter with higher education and their learning is not simply a cognitive or intellectual grappling with new ideas, concepts and frameworks but also a personal and emotional engagement with the situation. If the situation is more familiar for the teacher, its features more explicit and transparent, the teaching encounter with students is immersed in a host of uneven relationships and concerns, including the status of teaching in higher education. Teaching has become the poor relation to research and scholarship. It is a point exacerbated by the financial rewards and status accompanying the latter and, ironically, underlined by desperate concerns on both sides of the Atlantic to improve the status of the former (Boyer, 1990; NCIHE, 1997). It is a difficult task; for at the heart of the struggle is an all too pervasive understanding that teaching is something an academic does, whereas research and scholarship is what makes them special. Where many students approach learning in higher education, hesitant and uncertain, tentatively entering a new language, an increasing number of teachers (including many with a natural love of teaching) approach the encounter with ambivalence and an underlying sense of dissatisfaction.

There is, then, in the general teaching and learning situation an imperfect encounter of three 'worlds' – student, teacher and researcher – which, ironically, are defined by one another in substantial ways and yet have within them underlying tensions separating them. The teacher, for example, is a teacher in so far as he or she has students. They in turn are students because they do not fully share a world with their teacher. There is, by definition, a disparity in the premises they share. The teacher, moreover, has the 'authority' to teach the particular subject of a discipline in 'higher' education by virtue of their work as a researcher or scholar and yet teaching is typically viewed as detached from research and, indeed, as undermining it. Teaching both detracts from the time and effort available to put into research and often contributes to a reduction in the status of the academic, the concern being that 'those who enjoy (teaching) are not good scholars' (Boyer, 1990: 71). Teaching so conceptualized has built into it the seeds of its own undoing: it undermines the research/scholarship that provides the authority to higher-level teaching. Teaching contests and diminishes itself by definition. Evidence of this may, for example, be seen at the doctoral level where the less research/scholarship an academic does undermines their authority to both attract and supervise postgraduates. The 'overlap' or 'correspondence' in the three worlds characterizing teaching in higher education (see Figure 3.1) resides as much in the location of unshared meanings as it does in the potential 'sharing' of a practice. These tensions characterize the ability and ways in which dialogue occurs within these locations.

The achievement of meaning in these locations and practices and the quality of the 'address' are dependent on the extent and quality of the correspondence. How much of the potential correspondence do we permit in practice? How much do we exclude? In a narrowly construed 'correspondence' we construct situations that reduce the potential for the achievement or construction of meaning, irrespective of the quantity of 'meanings' used. In such situations, dialogue can descend into a mechanical and linear process. The listener (or other) is detached from the speaker in the practice not because there is nothing to say but rather because the social situation militates against it. Dialogue becomes 'monologue.' 'Meanings' are merely transmitted across the situation rather than mutually constructed within it. Deeper meaning involving 'self as cobeing' (Bahktin, 1986) and the possibility of 'critical being' (Barnett, 1997b) are not achieved. The potential for dialogue and the realization of genuine engagement ('addressivity') within such 'fragmented' situations and encounters is minimal. The challenge for professionals in higher education (and it is not limited to teaching and learning) is to find ways of critically engaging (reflecting/acting) with the issues of 'intersubjectivity' highlighted by the conceptual framework described in the previous chapter. They are at the heart of the language of reflective professionalism.

In the following discussion we shall look in some detail at these issues with respect to the two key areas of 'overlap' or correspondence characterizing the three 'worlds' highlighted in Figure 3.1: the teacher–student 'encounter' and the teacher–researcher 'encounter'. There is no 'overlap' shown for the third correspondence – the researcher-student 'encounter'. The academic's role as 'teacher' will mediate this relationship for the vast

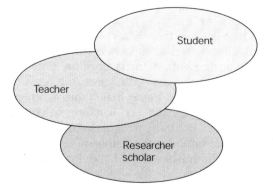

Figure 3.1 The 'worlds' of teaching

majority of students. For a small minority – mainly research students – this encounter may be unmediated in a relationship that we shall suggest transforms the way in which we conceptualize research and teaching.

Teacher–student encounter

Of the two, the nature of the 'overlap' and encounter between teacher and student has been the most extensively examined and researched, although until recently even this has been relatively limited. There are, for example, a wider number of studies looking at how teachers in higher education understand or conceive of their practice vis-à-vis their students. Such conceptions are not the result of innate personal traits or cognitive characteristics but are, rather, 'theories' (often undisclosed or intuitive 'folk' theories) in accordance with which the particular 'world' – the student–teacher encounter – is interpreted and practised. Kember (1997) identified five general conceptions of teaching in higher education that fall under two broad orientations: teacher centred/content oriented and student centred/learning oriented (see Table 3.1). These conceptions of teaching are characterized by five dimensions describing the nature of teacher, teaching, student, content and knowledge.

Teacher-centred/content-oriented conceptions

In the first conception, the teacher/lecturer regards the practice of teaching as one in which he or she imparts or transmits information to the student. The teacher as presenter is a transmitter and the student a passive recipient or receiver. Teaching mainly rests in the content of the curriculum and quality of the knowledge that the teacher has and controls. In this content-oriented conception, good teaching consists of having 'sound academic knowledge'. Teachers holding the second conception still regard teaching as the transmission of information between a presenter possessing knowledge and a recipient, but recognize that the teacher can more effectively order and structure the curriculum and the information transmitted.

Transitory conception

The third conception is a transition conception between substantially different ways of understanding teaching and is often associated with notable development in the understanding of practice. It is characterized by change, particularly with respect to their perceptions of the teacher and student. The teacher regards the student as a participant in a shared situation in which the teacher is presenting but also 'tutoring'. The situation is not now simply a 'void' across which content and knowledge is transmitted but rather they are seen as part of an interactive process. The

Table 3.1 *Conceptions of teaching in higher education*

Dimensions	Teacher-centred content-oriented			Student-centred learning-oriented	
	Imparting information	Transmitting structured knowledge	Teacher student interaction	Facilitating understanding	Conceptual change
Teacher	Presenter	Presenter	Presenter and tutor	Facilitator	Change agent/ developer
Teaching	Transfer of information	Transfer of well structured information	Interactive process	Process of helping students to learn	Development of person and conceptions
Student	Passive recipient	Recipient	Participant	Teacher responsible for student's learning	Teacher responsible for student development
Content	Defined by curriculum	Teacher needs to order and structure material	Defined by teacher	Constructed by students within teacher's framework	Constructed by students but conceptions can be changed
Knowledge	Possessed by teacher	Possessed by teacher	Discovered by students but within teacher's framework	Constructed by students	Socially constructed

Source: Kember, 1997

teacher still defines and frames knowledge but the student is encouraged to 'discover' it within the situation.

Student-centred/learning-oriented conceptions

The fourth and fifth conceptions of teaching describe a qualitatively distinct orientation in which the student becomes the centre of focus. Improving their learning becomes the focus of teaching, but not simply as the accretion of knowledge presented to them. Content and knowledge occur as a result of student learning, of the student constructing it for him or herself. In this situation, the teacher is a facilitator of this learning, having a responsibility to help students in their 'constructions of knowledge'. The fifth conception of teaching extends the role and responsibility of the teacher beyond helping the students' cognitive construction of knowledge towards helping them develop and change their own conceptions of the subject and themselves as a person. It recognizes that knowledge is socially constructed.

The above dimensions not only describe the conception of teaching but also tacit theories of the nature of learning, communication and of self. While these conceptions are a continuum of qualitatively different conceptions, they are not hierarchical. Despite sharing some qualities, the student-centred conceptions do not, as has sometimes been felt (Biggs, 1999), add to or subsume the teacher-centred conceptions. They are distinct: 'when change occurs, lecturers seem to move from one belief to another, and do not retain all elements of previous beliefs' (Kember, 1997: 263). The distinction is theoretically grounded in the conceptual framework comprising the two models of 'language' and 'self' described in the previous chapter.

In this conceptual framework, both the level 1 and level 2 'teacher-centred' conceptions of teaching assume a 'media' or information exchange model of language and self. The first views learning as being located primarily at the student ('other') pole of the communication model: learning consists mainly in the ability of the student to 'decode' well. Level 2 extends good teaching to both poles of the media model, recognizing that difficulties in decoding by the student (self) may also stem from poor 'encoding' by the teacher. Both conceptions, however, dwell in an asocial model of communication in which 'self' and 'other' are fundamentally detached. The teacher fails to recognize the intersubjective nature of both communication and learning. He or she fails to recognize the extent and complexity of the premises shared by teacher and students. Detaching them from the 'stream of life' narrows the available premises and 'genres' upon which meaning might be constructed. In the case of level 1, the premises exclude all but a narrow range of 'encoding/decoding' vocabulary, which it assumes are fully shared. The situation is primarily a monologue. In the second level the teacher does not extend the premises of the situation but rather more clearly signals and uses them. The monologue is streamlined.

Level 3 conceptions are theoretically distinctive conceptions. They retain some features of the media model – that meaning and knowledge are the preserve of the teacher for 'transfer' to student – but they also recognize that transmission is a poor method of 'transfer'. 'Discovery' of knowledge is a more effective method of 'decoding', encouraged through an interactive process between students as participants and teacher as tutor. In viewing the student as more than a passive recipient, the premises defining the overlap between teacher and student begin to permit the personal, social and intellectual experiences of the student within the teaching and learning situation. Teaching begins to resemble the 'dialogue' inherent in 'utterances' rather than the 'monologue' of mere sentences. The 'addressive' quality of teaching encompasses a wider range of shared premises and potential 'genres'.

If level 3 conceptions reflect important aspects of the intersubjective model of communication, this theoretical framework comprehensively supports and sustains level 4 and level 5 conceptions. Meaning and knowledge here are outcomes constructed by students in active dialogue within the social situation. Knowing and communicating are virtually the same and are grounded here within a situation in which the overlap between the premises of the student's 'world' and the teacher's 'world' are extended and as fully shared as possible. Teachers recognize that they are assisting and supporting students; and in doing so they are 'addressing' people in a dialogic relationship the quality of which – in terms of the student constructions of knowledge – they have a shared responsibility. The potential wealth of this relationship is even more acute with level 5 conceptions. At this level, teachers recognize a responsibility which takes them beyond facilitating the 'construction' of knowledge to acknowledging their key role in assisting and supporting the student to develop (or 'reconstruct' themselves) as persons. There is a practical recognition that it is not merely knowledge that is constructed in social dialogue, but also critical 'being'. Moreover, if this dialogic relationship is restricted to limited 'monologue' forms (level 1 and 2) the development of both 'being' and knowledge is limited and undermined.

Teacher–researcher encounter

Since the birth of the idea of the modern university – with Humboldt and the German Idealists (Readings, 1996) – teaching and research have defined the nature of higher education and the university. For the vast majority of academics, the teaching–research/scholarship relationship is the principal feature defining their own academic practice. Even those academics whose practices (and institutions) lie primarily at one or other end of this relational axis will feel the 'pull' of the other end in their academic lives. They will have other roles; an increasing number of roles (as noted in Chapter 1), but for the most part faculty will understand these roles in relationship to this central axis of practice. In this respect, teaching and research are inseparable (Barnett and Hallam, 1999), a unity in which the former (as noted above) derives its authority from the latter. As such this unity is often perceived and conceived by academics as deeply uneven. Research, which confers authority and status, takes precedence. Consequently, it is research, not teaching, which provides the key to their identity as an academic professional. It impels faculty to 'feel primary obligations less towards students . . . and more towards protecting and advancing private interests viewed in terms of discipline' (Bennett, 1998: 47). This situation has been supported by the growth of national and international academic infrastructures almost exclusively focused on research interests. It is research, firmly imbedded in its disciplines, that provides the expertise, the professional qualifications, the membership associations, the scholarly journals, the national meetings, and so on. The very idea of academic professionalism – particularly as it has developed and been understood in this century – has diminished the teacher–researcher 'overlap' and the potential of that encounter.

It is that 'overlap' and the nature of the shared premises and genres that characterize it which our 'intersubjective' theoretical framework impels us to reconsider. It requires a new model or way of thinking about research and teaching. The primary issue here, then, is not so much how do we bring the teaching–research axis into 'balance' but rather how we conceptualize the relationship. Indeed our very use of the words 'axis' and 'balance' can be misleading as it suggests a linear relationship between research and teaching in which positive changes in one bring about negative changes in the other. Figure 3.2 depicts these two ways of conceptualizing the research–teaching relationship.

Diagram A in Figure 3.2 depicts the teaching-research relationship in terms of two detached practices at either end of a scale. One practice is 'achieved' (often in terms of time and status) at the expense of the other practice: the incompatibility thesis (Barnett and Hallam, 1999).

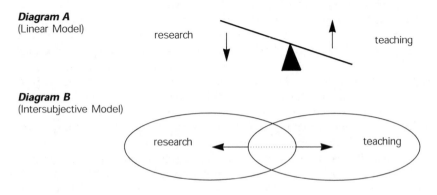

Diagram A
(Linear Model)

research   teaching

Diagram B
(Intersubjective Model)

research   teaching

Figure 3.2   Conceptualizing research and teaching

Professionalism in this model has traditionally tilted towards research, often with negative effects for teaching. Thus, for many academics, one of the essential measures of a more advanced level of professionalism is the distance from teaching responsibilities (particularly at undergraduate level) and from students. Indeed, time spent on teaching – doing it, conceptualizing it, developing it, and so on – has frequently been regarded as distinctly unprofessional. It is a model, moreover, in which the compensations for professionalism – promotion, status, influence and the accompanying financial rewards (facilitated and encouraged by such activities as the research assessment exercise in the UK) – have in recent times increasingly encouraged 'imbalance'.

The development and promotion of teaching and learning in higher education has generally been conceptualized and articulated within the terms of this linear model. It speaks, for example, in terms of achieving a 'balance' between teaching and research (Kennedy, 1997) and of 'raising' the status and importance of teaching separately from the issue of research (NCIHE, 1997). This approach – conceptualizing a new professionalism which, for all intents and purposes, is separate from the existing conceptions of academic professionalism (ILT, 1999b) – may present a challenge to the supremacy of research, but it fails to challenge the existing model. Indeed, the very challenge to research bolsters the model as one in which the two main protagonists are fundamentally detached from one another, competing for time, status and reward. Ironically, success in this new endeavour runs the danger of achieving an alienated academic professionalism encompassing two incompatible components. Signs of this are apparent within the central element of this 'teaching' professionalism: professional programmes for the accreditation of teaching in higher education. Here, for example, the ongoing 'generic versus discipline' teaching skills debate discloses the gap between the discipline location of research and the perceived a-discipline location of generic teaching skills (staff development or educational departments). Similarly, the perceptions of such programmes by many staff who regard them as unrelated to their 'real' academic work as researchers.

This model has also generated a large number of studies, primarily correlation studies, looking at the relationship between teaching and research (Brew and Boud, 1995). Much of this research is predicated on a wide spread view (even 'need') amongst academics that such a link exists (Brew and Boud, 1995; Webster, 1985). The inherent conflict within this model would effectively disappear if it could be established that there was a strong, conclusive correlation between research excellence and effective teaching. Indeed, the few studies that suggest a correlation are used as 'weapons' within the model to suggest that a renewed emphasis on teaching is unnecessary and, thereby, to maintain the dominant position of research. That such a correlation is not, as Brew and Boud point out, interpreted the other way around – 'that being good at teaching makes for better research' (1995: 265) – is telling and symptomatic of a political *need* for a link 'to be sustained until there is convincing recognition and resourcing for good teaching' (ibid.: 264). In the end, the issue is rather artificial. Despite this desire for the inherent conflict within the 'scales' model to be so resolved, these studies are inconclusive overall. They show a negative correlation as often as a positive one. (Feldman, 1987; Ramsden and Moses, 1992; Webster, 1985).

The 'intersubjective' model of understanding research and teaching (depicted in diagram B) describes the relationship in terms of the 'overlap' between teaching and research. Rather than constructing this essential relationship in terms of an inherent conflict, it attempts to reconceptualize it in terms of what the two areas of practice share in common. It looks to further the potential for constructive engagement by developing and extending the 'overlap' or correspondence of shared meanings rather than locking the two practices within a series of incompatible meanings competing across a hostile void. Diagram B suggests two ways for doing so. The first indicates ways in which research practice might share its meanings with teaching (right arrow) and the second suggests ways teaching might share meanings with research (left arrow).

With respect to the first, Boyer (1990) suggests extending the idea of 'scholarship' to teaching. Indeed, he writes of the idea of scholarship – 'engaging in original research . . . but also stepping back from one's investigation, looking for connections, building bridges between theory and practice, and communicating one's knowledge effectively' (ibid.: 16) – as embracing all of academic practice. It is noteworthy that he writes of such a 'scholarship of teaching' that it does not lie simply in transmitting knowledge but also in investigating, transforming and extending it. Such processes take place, moreover, both in active dialogue with one's students and in active dialogue with oneself and one's colleagues in the whole context of the design and preparation of teaching for students. As such the 'scholarship of teaching' assumes level 4 and level 5 – learning oriented – conceptions of teaching. It is primarily distinguished from research (the 'scholarship of discovery') in terms of the audience it addresses (its 'addressivity') and the methods it employs. It presupposes a conceptual framework of 'dialogue' and shares with research what Clark calls 'a culture of enquiry' (1997: 252).

If research elucidates more precisely those qualities of enquiry and discovery at the heart of excellent teaching, the practice of teaching similarly discloses more clearly the critical issues of learning at the heart of research. Research is a process of learning. It is equally concerned with 'questioning one's own pre-existing knowledge and understanding in light of new ideas and new evidence' (Brew, 1999: 297). It constructs its meanings within culturally and academically established situations replete with their own particular approaches, methods, 'languages' and criteria of success. Both research – facilitating one's own and one's colleagues' learning – and teaching – facilitating one's own and one's students' learning – operate with different methods, in different contexts with different constraints and criteria of achievement. At their core, however, they share the same essential premises and meanings. They are not fundamentally distinct activities but are integral parts of the same academic enterprise.

The two models of the relationship between research and teaching described here provide the basis for distinct categories of conceptions of research which mirror the conceptions of teaching discussed earlier. The first is primarily a content-oriented category, embracing an epistemological approach in which knowledge is viewed as detached from human 'knowing' and as essentially 'discovered'. It regards research as the discovery and extension of knowledge through the 'decoding' of the meanings of 'reality'. Good teaching is the clear and organized 'encoding' of meanings for the transmission of knowledge. The two are very separate activities. The second is a learning-oriented category, embracing an epistemological approach in which knowledge is seen as inseparable from human 'knowing' and as a process of 'narration'. This category regards research in terms of the construction and extension of knowledge through an active engagement with shared social meanings and discourses. Teaching, similarly, rests in facilitating and encouraging the construction of knowledge through the active sharing of complementary academic meanings and discourses. Research and teaching are characterized by the same practice, providing exemplars and models of learning for one another and, notably, for the student. In this development the feeble – typically non-existent – correspondence and 'encounter' between researcher and student is established. The enriched social premises and 'meanings' of learner (researcher) and learner (student) are shared and enhanced (see Figure 3.3).

Together they generate the dialogical conditions for the integration of the 'worlds' of academic practice: for an integrated community of academic practice. As such, they provide the essential conceptual location upon which is based the concept of reflective professionalism developed in this book. The 'professionalization' of learning and teaching in higher education is not limited to learning and teaching. It requires critical reflection on the whole of academic practice, including research and scholarship. It is a challenge that is both substantially in advance of current

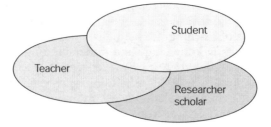

Figure 3.3 The 'worlds' of teaching revisited

practice (Brew, 1999) and at the heart of a broad proposal for reinventing undergraduate education (Boyer, 1998).

Principles of academic dialogue

The above discussion needs to go further than the conceptual and epistemological framework describing the relationship between the key 'worlds' of academic practice within a dialogic or intersubjective model. It needs to begin to describe the academic principles and/or values, which characterize that practice. They are principles and values that, we suggest, are only capable of proper professional expression within that dialogic model. These values and principles characterize academic dialogue, without which the intersubjective development of learning and teaching is impossible. They include but are not limited to the kind of values highlighted by the Institute for Learning and Teaching in the UK, and comprise commitments to:

- *scholarship and research*: in teaching as well as in their own discipline;
- *collegiality and consideration*: with and for all members of the learning community including students, teachers, researchers, those supporting teaching, and so on;
- *equity and opportunity*: to encouraging participation in higher education and to equality of educational and learning opportunities;
- *difference and empowerment*: to respecting, developing and empowering individual students within their common and different learning situations;
- *reflection and improvement*: to continued critical reflection and evaluation of practice and its innovative and creative improvement.

The values underlying these commitments are, however, much easier to acknowledge than to achieve. Superficially, at least, they draw upon the finest principles and interests of academic tradition and are almost impossible to reject. In practice they require as substantial and significant a transformation of understanding and 'being' as those advocated for teaching and research. We may usefully consider these principles in terms of two models of 'being' an academic (or of 'academic being'): the 'autonomous' and the 'relational' (Bennett, 1998). These models condition the relationship between self, others and community in higher education. They also closely correspond to the conceptual distinctions described with respect to teaching and research.

The first model, 'insistent individualism', is lodged in the idea of self as individual and detached. It 'emphasises separation, individual autonomy, privacy, fragmentation and self-sufficiency' (Bennett, 1998: 12). Such a person specializes in 'academic freedom', arguing at its extreme that the scholar's merit is absolute and intrinsic, essentially inaccessible to external evaluation, particularly from other disciplines or even other specialist areas or sub-specialist areas within the same discipline. This model draws upon both the academy's celebration of uniqueness, distinctiveness and independence of mind, and upon its inherent suspicion of the collaborative and the co-operative. It fosters a conception of research and scholarship which is individually designed, executed and aimed, first and foremost, at 'making a name for oneself'. Academic rewards reinforce it: better to author than co-author, better to be first author than second author; better to be distinctive than find commonality. Even students (particularly research students) – through the promotion of student 'followings' and 'cults' suitable to the academic's interests and needs – are regarded and valued in terms of their contribution to this individual mission.

At the heart of this model, is the notion of 'unilateral power' (Loomer, 1976), the power to individually control and shape others while at the same time resisting being controlled or shaped by others. It is a power defined by contest, by 'winning' over others who 'lose', by academic pecking orders and freedom from academic responsibilities which do not contribute to individual academic status, power and reputation. Its primary arena is disciplinary in character, an arena of battles waged over specialized intellectual 'corners' and niches requiring insistent and uncompromising defence. Ironically, the emphasis of this model on individuality, separateness and self-sufficiency is conditioned by social relationships and social constructions of meaning and importance. Indeed, the battle is about meaning, about what we construe as meaningful and important in the community, about what is knowledge. 'Even academic individualism presumes that knowledge is a social achievement, not a private accomplishment' (Bennett, 1998: 21). Its character is defined less by the idea of a private, separate individual than by the quality and practice of social relationships within the academic community. Insistent individualism does not describe an individual (versus a social) model so much as a 'corrupted' social model, one in which conception and practice of social relationship has been degraded towards 'monologue' rather than constructed in genuine 'dialogue'. Its unidirectional character discloses a fundamental 'impoverishment' which – in so far as academic self-identity emerges through such relationships – also describes the individual's academic self.

The alternative 'relational' model of academic self, Bennett (1998) contends, is deeply imbedded in earlier academic traditions defined by a common sense of community and shared purposes. These are traditions receding under increasing specialization, market pressures, the growth and diversity of faculty and their conditions of employment. It is a model that does not regard others in academia as merely means through which to pursue private ends, as competitors for resources, advancement and reputation. It constructs, rather, a genuine dialogue by extending value to others as colleagues, recognizing that self, other and community are not simply intersubjective 'realities' but also locations of intersubjective human value. It requires the recognition of the essential importance and worth of others in the whole academic enterprise. Against 'unilateral power', this model rests in the idea of 'relational power', and 'the notion that the capacity to absorb an influence is as truly a mark of power as the strength involved in exerting an influence' (Loomer, 1976: 17). In this respect, relational power inheres in the dialogical idea of 'active responsive understanding' described in the previous chapter, in a collaborative 'narrative' and the meanings and meta-rules governing its practice.

This focus on the 'other' is not merely an intellectual acknowledgement of the social nature of practice but also, importantly, a concern for 'others'. It is a concern that discloses academic practice as an inherently ethical as well as intellectual enterprise. The principles of academic dialogue are better regarded as virtues than rules, virtues with intellectual significance: 'not mere expressions of feeling, but guides to behaviour that correlate importantly with learning and the increase of knowledge' (Bennett, 1998: 35). Bennett goes on to describe these virtues in terms of the concepts of 'hospitality' and 'thoughtfulness'.

'Hospitality' retains its widespread sense of being open and welcoming to the other, and of listening and accepting, but in a disciplined and rigorous way. It neither suspends critical judgement in the face of inadequate evidence nor enters dialogue with judgements already irrevocably formed. It does not include, therefore, complicity with indulgent, conspiratorial or even simply easygoing practices, but rather of being open to the full potential of the other's experience and thought irrespective of difference, status and privilege. It embraces a willingness to engage with the strange, the different and the uncertain; to evaluate it sincerely and honestly; to enlist and empower this other in the pursuit of learning and knowledge. 'Thoughtfulness' also embodies its commonly understood qualities of being intellectually 'reflective' and 'critical' and of being ethically 'sensitive' and 'considerate'. In both it draws upon the virtues of fidelity and courage: intellectual fidelity to the spirit and rigour of the inquiry and ethical fidelity to the needs and concerns of the others, be they students or colleagues. It similarly recognizes the importance of courage in sustaining responsible and rigorous exchange and discourse. It neither yields intellectual or ethically to abuse of power by others, nor succumbs to the practice of such abuse of power towards others. Courage requires the recognition and acceptance of one's vulnerability and responsibility to the mutually shared freedoms of the other.

This relational model provides the conceptual framework supporting the practices and behaviour described by the interrelated principles of academic dialogue mentioned above. A commitment to *scholarship and research*, for instance, goes beyond a concern for informing one's teaching through ongoing study and learning in one's own disciplinary fields. It recognizes the importance of ongoing scholarship and research of one's own teaching practices, conducted with one's students and colleagues. It is a commitment essentially to integrate the whole of academic practice within the larger context of continuous learning. Such a commitment by definition embraces the other principles. It recognizes, for example, the intersubjective location of academic practice and the ensuing requirement that principles of *collegiality and consideration* govern relations with the whole spectrum of staff, students and all external persons with which one's academic projects are engaged. Such a principle entails an understanding of how we create and express ourselves in academic exchange, of what enhances exchange and of what undermines it:

> ... undisciplined rhetoric is destructive. Polarizing rhetoric, careless and self-indulgent discourse, being candid only when personally convenient, and dwelling in unchecked negative complaining, corrode the very foundation of a community. The collegium disappears when members are too abrasive, when aggressiveness dominates exchange, when learners are abused, or when concepts insisted upon are isolating and obscuring rather than inclusive and illuminating. A constant threat to any collegium is individual insecurity and jealousy – diminishing community and generating isolation and insulation. (Bennett, 1998: 29)

This, it should be emphasized, does not mean conformity, 'group-think' or superficial consensus which would merely substitutes group 'monologue' for individual 'monologue'. The model stresses, rather, a genuinely open, critical and constructive dialogue that draws upon all of its constitutive voices. It sustains both the principles of *equity and opportunity* and of *difference and empowerment*, asserting an active dialogue, which respects and values the difference (as well as the commonality) disclosed by 'others' in the intersubjective situation. It provides opportunities and encouragement to participate in the appropriate academic discourses and learning situations. It appreciates the obstacles to participation that diverse groups may face for reasons such as gender, race/ethnicity, class, age, etc., and it actively works to overcome such obstacles.

It is a model insisting, moreover, that learning and teaching within an integrated conception of academic practice is actively maintained and continually refreshed to ensure both its vigour and to prevent its collapse into a model of insistent individualism. Robust intellectually and ethically informed academic dialogue is characterized by principles of continuous *reflection and improvement* conducted collaboratively with colleagues and students. The relational model of 'being an academic' within a genuine intersubjective or dialogical situation insists, almost by definition, upon reflection on practice and social exchange. It is reflection with purpose: to critically improve academic practice – enhancing and extending learning and knowledge – with and for the 'other(s)' implicit in the socially shared situation.

Conclusion

This chapter has described the 'dialogic' or 'relational' character of academic practice that lies at the heart of our concept of the 'reflective professional'. We have suggested that the three central worlds of 'student', 'teacher' and 'researcher' are deeply and theoretically interrelated. They not only share significant 'overlaps' in their various social and academic roles but also share the essential structures of their associated conceptual frames of understanding. Each is characterized by opposing conceptual frameworks – relational versus individual or dialogic versus monologic – with substantial implications for academic practice. Furthermore, in the dialogic model these worlds converge in the crucial concept of 'learning' – the third 'location' of our conceptual framework. A detailed discussion of the nature of learning and the constitutive role that it plays in our understanding of the 'reflective professional' will be the subject of the next chapter.

Finally, it should be emphasized that this chapter was informed and characterized by an acutely ethical component which is inextricably embedded in the dialogic framework and conceptually entrenched in the idea of the 'other' which defines academic 'being' and practice. It provides the foundation upon which principles of academic dialogue – commonly accepted and cherished by academic tradition and formalized by such professional bodies as the Institute for Learning and Teaching – are established. A concerted effort to ensure that such principles and values genuinely and pervasively characterize academic practice may, indeed, be the most significant factor in bringing about real change in practice and does, therefore, probably represent its toughest challenge.

4

A Critical Matrix of Learning and Teaching

The academic weave

The previous two chapters explored the theoretical and academic locations of the conceptual framework in which the 'language' of the teacher as reflective professional is situated. This chapter will explore the third 'location' of this framework. It addresses the key issue emerging from these two prior 'locations', that of learning, the critical concept towards which our discussions so far have been moving. It emerged in the first chapter as a central feature of the 'knowledge specification' which society is contracting with higher education to deliver. There it mainly focused on student learning and the challenges it presented teachers and lecturers in higher education. Learning was not considered in terms of learning particular disciplines or areas of knowledge, but with issues of meta-learning (learning to learn) and transferable learning (and the development of transferable skills) within an increasingly changing, uncertain and contestable world. Learning in this broad sense challenged the teacher to become a reflective professional.

Chapter 2 explored the 'contructivist' character of learning, drawing out its intersubjective and social features. Learning, like language and self, is essentially 'dialogic', requiring socially shared meanings and understandings. In Chapter 3, this understanding of learning was considered in the academic situation with an analysis of academic practice in terms of two models. These two models – 'individual/monologue' and 'relational/dialogue' – were consistent across the main academic roles. The former, however, contributed to the fragmentation of academic roles while the latter offered the opportunity for their mutual regeneration through an understanding of learning as central to academic being. Learning is not simply the outcome of one practice (teaching) and of marginal interest to another (research). It provides the defining feature of both practices and is central to a comprehensive model of academic practice more generally and the reflective professional in particular.

In this chapter, we shall examine the nature of learning in detail – particularly as it relates to higher education. In so doing, we shall complete the articulation of the conceptual framework we are setting out in this part of the book. Learning is not merely another set of concepts and/or principles which teachers in higher education should be aware of with respect to their students or, indeed, reflect upon in their own professional practice, but rather it is part of the whole of the academic enterprise. The challenge for academics is not simply to help students meet the challenges that they are facing in their formal studies and will be continuously facing throughout their lives, but to ensure the same level of engagement for themselves. The two are not mutually exclusive. In a truly dialogical situation they cannot be. Learning, like self which it generates, is part of the social situation, fundamental to 'life itself' (Jarvis, 1992: 10). It is not simply part of or even the whole of the fabric of our academic life; it is the 'weave' of that fabric, the weave of our academic being.

This, of course, is not good enough in itself. Learning as the social 'weave' of academic existence, however expressive and important to recognize, is not going to help us facilitate or assist in the development of our own learning, let alone that of our students. It does, however, provide a useful location from which to address the sheer complexity and paradoxes (Jarvis, 1992) of learning. This 'weave' of learning encompasses a range of intellectual, personal, social, cultural, ethical, political, practical obligations, interests and concerns which students will need to both address and balance in their lives. These go far beyond the learning demands of specific discipline knowledge or of general transferable skills. They constitute a rich tapestry of learning. Barnett uses Habermas's term 'life-world' to describe 'the total world experience of human-beings' (1994: 178) which higher education must address. He contrasts it with teaching that limits its practice to the intellectual 'academic competence' of discipline-world or to the practical 'operational competence' of work-world.

Teaching needs to address the wider multiple discourses of the 'life-world'. These may include, for example, an ability to respond meaningfully to and critique one's own responses to political debates, health issues, cultural matters, social and family relationships, works of art, diverse social groupings and ways of thinking, voluntary and charitable services, the media, leisure activities and even religious experience. It requires an ability to 'critique' these from multiple frames and perspectives in open, democratic and socially just ways. It even demands the ability to critique one's grounds for critique. While accepting contingency and uncertainty, this calls for the development and construction of a dialogical commitment, solidarity (Rorty, 1989) and action within this multiplicity. Learning so conceived is not a process of individual knowledge construction within a socially and culturally stable situation, but is fragmented, uncertain and changing precisely because it is constructed in this increasingly fragmented, uncertain and changing world.

Faced with the complexity of the 'life-world' alongside its apparent limitless potential for change, it is difficult to describe the nature of this 'learning weave', let alone developing strategies for facilitating, assisting, supporting, fostering and nourishing it. It would, moreover, be a reckless and imprudent writer who suggested that teachers manage the sum of their students' learning. Learning is not entirely or even mostly in the power of the teacher. Teachers cannot substantially change the character and nature of individual abilities and styles of learning, predispositions toward different 'intelligences' (Gardner, 1993), individual circumstances and histories vis-à-vis different educational issues or diverse social and cultural backgrounds. Despite the paucity of their influence on 'presage' characteristics (Dunkin and Biddle, 1974) which students bring to the encounter or the enormity of the challenge, teachers cannot abdicate their responsibility for significant teaching. Good teachers have a huge role and moral obligation in student learning.

Student learning has become a ripe area for research in recent years, developing a productive consensus in many areas. In discussions of student learning, particularly those provided for academic staff looking to develop their teaching, this consensus has often been achieved through a tendency to over-focus on particular aspects of the research on learning, without fully acknowledging the relevance and importance of other related work. While in many respects this is inevitable, it can lead to an uneven representation of the area. We also, of course, make critical choices in this area. In the following discussion, we shall frame our choices within two general structural arrangements. The first is considered within a schema of *'learning gaps'* (Cox, 1992) which characterize the present and future professional lives of our students. It is used for developing a knowledge and understanding of the key issues of learning involved in a wide range of research and scholarship relevant to student learning. The second presents a *critical matrix of learning.* It describes the underlying structure of the learning environment, providing teachers with a conceptual tool for designing, developing and implementing their teaching across the various 'genres' of their teaching practice. Both provide useful conceptual charts for navigating the challenges of understanding and facilitating student learning.

Learning gaps

As we saw in Chapter 3, teachers often see learning as an outcome in terms of a 'state of knowledge' which students achieve as detached selves rather than as an outcome in terms of a 'process of constructing' which they achieve within an integrated social situation. While lecturers may have a sense of what they would like their students to achieve, and recognize it in the assessments, they frequently have a very limited idea of why students are failing to achieve. This situation, moreover, is picked up and acutely felt by students who have no idea of what the nature of the problem is. In such situations the teacher's response is commonly limited to rather unhelpful comments about, for example, their exam results or course work not being up to standard, or suggestions that the student is not working hard enough. A deeper understanding of why learning is not achieved is missing: it remains hidden in a kind of 'shadow' land. Here we explore some of the relevant research and literature in terms of how learning might occur. We do so within a framework of five learning 'gaps'. Briefly, they can be described as being between

1 recall and understanding;
2 understanding and ability;
3 ability and wanting to;
4 wanting to and actually doing;
5 actually doing and ongoing change.

These gaps lie between a continuum of different areas of learning – each encompassing the previous ones – laying out the extent of the professional challenge (see Figure 4.1). At the most basic level, there is a *gap* between the ability of learners to recall or recognize information and being able to understand it. Even if understanding is achieved, however, there can then be a *gap* between that and being able to or having the abilities/skills to actually put that understanding into practice (practical understanding). In subjects like medicine and dentistry, it has long been clear that students may often be able to write reasonable examination answers and yet be very incompetent when faced with real patients. Sometimes efficient learning situations can be devised which result in students with knowledge, understanding and the ability to use that

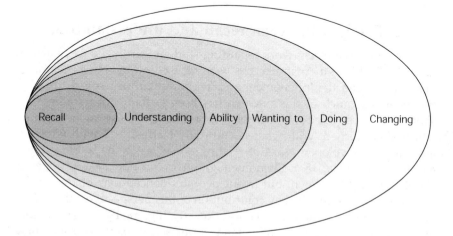

Figure 4.1 Learning gaps

understanding, and yet they end up not actually wanting to use it. The very efficiency of some systems may indeed contribute to turning students away from a real commitment to their subject or their work. An even bigger gap, one that can be quite disturbing for teachers as well as students, occurs when the student understands, is able to put that understanding into practice, even wants to do so, but still does not actually do so. Of course, there are many excuses such as timetabling or pressure of work, but there is often a great deal more to it than this. A final gap – possibly a more postmodern gap – emerges with understanding, ability, wanting to and actual doing coupled with a failure to change as the situation (and the postmodern conditions) of our practice mutate and change. Many of these gaps have more to do with conceptions of self and the anxieties and threats which students (and teachers) perceive about them, rather than ignorance or lack of competence.

In exploring these 'gaps' we shall not review all the relevant literature on learning but look instead at key areas where we believe particular literature is most appropriate. Much of the literature applies across several of the 'gaps'. While the organization we propose provides a holistic, integrated schema for approaching learning-in-practice, it is not intended as an all-embracing model of learning. Indeed, such models often 'get in the way of developing an understanding of the differing strategies necessary to enable diverse adults to learn different things in different settings in different ways' (Hanson, 1993: 107). Competing traditions are offered here with respect to their distinctive contributions for the development of teaching. Individually they allow us to look at the pertinent features of particular gaps. Collectively they establish a rich conceptual framework of learning which teachers might find critically useful in reflecting upon and improving their professional practice.

1 The gap between recall and understanding

Much of the most recent work regarding student learning, particularly in Britain, Sweden and Australia, has been focused on the issues central to this gap. Indeed the 'phenomenography' paradigm of research that has characterized much of this research has been a dominant paradigm for about 20 years. Phenomenography is a qualitative research program which is concerned 'with what is culturally learned and with what are individually developed ways of relating ourselves to the world around us' (Marton, 1988a: 181). Phenomenographers 'do not make statements about the world as such, but about people's conceptions of the world' (Marton, 1988b: 145). The key contribution of this perspective – that learning occurs with 'a change in conception' (Dahlgren, 1997: 34) – is that 'what' we experience and understand of our social reality is inseparable from 'how' we experience and understand it.

Approaches to learning

Earlier phenomenographic research has developed what has now become a widely adopted qualitative distinction between 'deep' and 'surface' approaches to learning. More recently Entwistle extended it to include a category called 'strategic learning' (see Table 4.1).

Table 4.1 *Approaches to learning*

Deep approach	*Transforming by*
Intention – to understand ideas for yourself	
Relating ideas to previous knowledge and experience	
Looking for patterns and underlying principles	
Checking evidence and relating it to conclusions	
Examining logic and argument cautiously and critically	
Becoming actively interested in the course content	
Surface approach	*Reproducing by*
Intention – to cope with course requirements	
Studying without reflecting on either purpose or strategy	
Treating the course as unrelated bits of knowledge	
Memorizing facts and procedures routinely	
Finding difficulty in making sense of new ideas presented	
Feeling undue pressure and worry about work	
Strategic approach	*Organizing by*
Intention – to achieve the highest possible grades	
Putting consistent effort into studying	
Finding the right conditions and materials for studying	
Managing time and effort effectively	
Being alert to assessment requirements and criteria	
Gearing work to the perceived preference of lecturers	

Source: Entwistle, 1997: 19

In a 'deep' approach to learning the student's intention is to understand the subject in a way which is personally meaningful to them and which engages their own experience and their previous knowledge in an interactive (dialogical) process with the relevant content, logic and existing evidence of the subject. The primary concern is to *make* personal meaning with and out of the shared meanings available. A 'surface' learning approach on the other hand is characterised by an intention to *use* the available meanings in an instrumental way to meet the requirements of situation. While used, the meanings are, nevertheless, perceived as 'alien' to the student, and external imposition often simply approached through memorisation. There is no sustained personal engagement with the student's own experience and their previous knowledge.

The 'strategic' approach to learning is sometimes seen as engaging elements of both the 'surface' and 'deep' approaches. The main concern of this approach is to achieve the highest possible grades. As such, an assessment-focused approach organizes effort, time and conditions in an overall 'strategy' to deliver its goals. It *organizes* the meanings of the learning situation to optimum effect. In this endeavour, it may exploit aspects of the other two approaches. 'Strategic'-oriented students are alert and responsive to the cues they pick up about the nature of the tasks and demands made upon them. Even students who are inclined to take a 'deep' approach will at times feel this is less 'strategic' than employing a 'surface' approach if, for example, the assessment methods suggest that memorization of facts will meet the requirements more effectively.

Study orientations

Aspects of these categories of approach to learning correlate significantly with similar dimensions disclosed in other research on student learning (Entwistle, 1988: 100). Collectively they have been linked to describe three general *orientations* to study: 'meaning', 'reproducing' and 'strategic' (Ramsden, 1997: 211). Pask (1976), for example, contrasts 'comprehension learning' which uses analogies to build up meaningful descriptions of topics, emphasizing the outline of ideas and interconnections with 'operation learning' which relies on a step-by-step, logical approach often emphasizing the reproduction of factual details. Biggs (1999) distinguishes between 'intrinsic' (meaning-oriented) and 'extrinsic' (outcome-oriented) motivations in student learning. Students are intrinsically motivated when they 'learn because they are interested in the task or activity itself', and motivated extrinsically when 'they perform tasks because of the value or importance they attach to what the outcome brings (e.g. qualifications)' (ibid.: 59–60). He also identifies an 'achievement' motivation where students 'learn in order to enhance their egos by competing against other students' (ibid.).

Conceptions of learning

The concept of 'conception' of learning grew out of the original research on approaches to learning. It worked at 'a superordinate level of description' (Marton and Saljo, 1997: 55) describing more general perceptions or preconceived ideas of learning from past experiences which students brought to the learning situation. More recently it has developed more individual applications and 'has been used to describe a general understanding of the discipline or subject area . . . for example, a conception of history' (Entwistle, 1997: 17) or of particular practices such as essay writing (Hounsell, 1997) or creative writing (Light, 1995). It has also been used in a more narrow way to describe how students understand a particular topic or idea in a syllabus. We focus here on the wider application of this concept as a key descriptor of more general conceptions of learning and understanding. Table 4.2 presents six learning conceptions divided into two general categories: 'reproducing' and 'transforming'.

Table 4.2   *Conceptions of learning*

1	A quantitative increase in knowledge	
2	Memorizing	*Reproducing*
3	Acquisition of facts and methods, etc.	
4	The abstraction of meaning	
5	An interpretative process aimed at understanding	*Transforming*
6	Developing as a person	

Source: Marton et al., 1993

The contrast between reproducing and transforming conceptions corresponds closely to the above distinctions in both approaches to learning and learning orientations described above: a correspondence demonstrated by Van Rossum and Schenk (1984). It is very difficult to encourage the development of deep approaches to learning in a particular learning situation with students who hold a general reproducing conception of learning. These conceptions also may be seen as constituting a developmental continuum. Students may enter higher education with initial 'reproducing' conceptions but it is expected that they will leave with more developed 'transforming' conceptions. Their more general learning will largely rest in such change. The research describing conception has essentially been characterized by a cognitive perspective. The sixth conception, developing as a person (which was added later), indicates features of conception that go beyond the cognitive to encompass more personal characteristics, although these are not fully developed.

Entwistle and Entwistle (1992) suggest that understanding is best 'seen, not as a cognitive process, but as an experience' characterized by feelings of 'satisfaction', 'confidence', 'significance'. The hierarchy of five 'forms of understanding' (conceptions) they describe begins with category (A) which is 'limited to grasping material presented directly by lecturer or through required reading' (ibid.: 13) and is basically concerned with remembering facts or procedures. It ends with category (E) where the student independently and actively develops his or her own structures and extends the breadth of their material across topic, course and discipline.

It is a useful classification and strongly supports the distinctions above but remains primarily cognitive in its design.

This research on learning approaches, orientations and conceptions enables us to reflect on how our pedagogical strategies, and the teaching and learning environment we establish might aid or hinder students to cross the gap from recall to a more genuine understanding. It reminds us of the considerable role that 'students' perceptions of assessment, choice over subject matter and methods of studying it, workload, and quality of teaching' (Ramsden, 1997: 214) play in the development of learning. Bridging this first gap is a valuable starting point, but it not enough.

2 The gap between understanding and having the ability/skills to practice effectively

Given its emphasis upon meaning making and the relationship to personal experience we would expect deep or transforming categories of learning to be more closely associated with abilities to perform than the surface or reproducing categories. Research, however, has not made a great deal of this relationship, tending to focus on the purely intellectual arena with less importance given to practice.

Experiential learning

Relevant in this respect is the work of Kolb (1984) and others who stress the critical importance of 'experience' in learning. In his classic book, *Experiential Learning* (1984), Kolb develops a comprehensive theory of learning which stresses the fundamental role of experience in learning: *'Learning is the process whereby knowledge is created through the transformation of experience'* (ibid.: 38; original emphasis). Echoing the idea of learning as a 'transformation' in the previous section, experiential learning focuses on a transformation which is both active by definition and explicitly grounded in the concrete social environment in which experience occurs. Experience, here, is described, after Dewey (1938), as a transaction between an individual and what, at the time, constitutes his environment. It is a 'fluid interpenetrating relationship such that once they (person and environment) become related, both are essentially changed' (Kolb, 1984: 36). Drawing on the organizational development work of Lewin (1951) he further argues that learning is 'best facilitated in an environment where there is a dialectic tension and conflict between immediate, concrete experience and analytic detachment' (ibid.). He has concisely illustrated his theoretical discussion in the widely used cycle of experiential learning (see Figure 4.2). In this four-stage cycle, immediate concrete experience provides the basis for observation and reflection. These observations are, in turn, assimilated into abstract concepts and general-

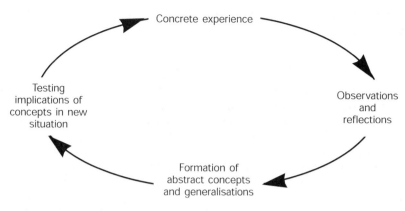

Figure 4.2   Experiential learning cycle (Kolb, 1984: 21)

izations ('theories') from which implications for action can be read and developed. These implications may be regarded as 'hypotheses' that then serve as guides for action, for testing in new concrete situations and, thereby, for generating new concrete experiences.

The experiential learning cycle incorporates a feedback process directed towards active experimentation and the abilities/skills that that requires. In higher education, such abilities will differ according to different curricula but may include such things as:

- writing essays and reports;
- giving presentations;
- chairing seminars;
- engaging in discussion;
- working on a task as part of a team;
- performing experiments;
- solving a group problem;
- engaging in research;
- carrying out clinical duties;
- undertaking projects;
- reading aloud to a group;
- assessing peers;
- writing exams;
- evaluation of learning.

At its most effective, this learning cycle ensures critical and reflective, goal-directed action and evaluation of the consequences of that action. Its main contribution, for our purposes, is the intrinsic space it provides within active learning for the development of the skills/abilities inherent in the generation of new and meaningful experience. Although it should be recognized that the Kolb cycle has been criticized for not fully capturing the complexity of the process (Jarvis et al., 1998: 48) and for leaving out important aspects of experience such as emotions and feelings (Boud, et al., 1985).

Experience and Meaning

An important feature of the effectiveness of an experiential learning cycle is getting the balance right between experience, reflection, theory and the action they lead towards. While one must be careful about reducing what is essentially a holistic cycle to constituent parts, it does provide a way of looking at problems that may be blocking the achievement of learning. Not all experience, for example, is 'meaningful' or results in learning. Figure 4.3 illustrates a series of relationships between experience and learning.

Meaningful experience requires an initial set of premises or meanings – knowledge, skills, attitudes, values, beliefs, etc. – be shared between the student and their specific learning and teaching environment. Learning, paradoxically, requires a 'disjuncture' in the sharing of meanings: 'disjuncture, or discontinuity, between biography and experience of the wider world is a fundamental condition of human learning' (Jarvis, 1987: 80). If there is a full overlap of meanings, while it may be meaningful, it will not result in new meanings or learning; it might, in fact, be so complete, repetitive and unchangeable as to be oppressive and alienating. On the other hand, a full 'disjuncture' between student biography and the situation will render the experience meaningless. We might also add rather importantly that experience can be 'marginalized' by the learning environment. There is an overlap of relevant meanings between the student and the environment but the prevailing 'authority' and 'discourses' within the environment does not accept or permit their use – for

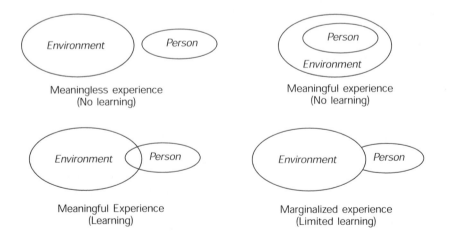

Figure 4.3   Learning: response to experience

a range of social reasons including issues of class, gender, age, ethnicity, etc. (Light, 1996) – and thereby limits the student's learning.

Reflection and experience

Reflection and experience is also a more complex relationship than is often thought. Responses to experience may result in non-reflective as well as reflective forms of learning (Jarvis, 1987). Non-reflective learning includes reproductive practices such as memorization, imitation and the development of rote skills. Reflective learning includes contemplation, experimental learning and the development of reflective skills. Boud and Walker (1998) point out that 'acts of reflection can become ritualised', particularly when they are encouraged, even imposed through prescribed activities within the learning situation. Reflection, like experience, they found is very context dependent, sensitive to the social and political environment in which it occurs. Reflective learning may also occur during action or actual experience. As noted in the introduction, Schon (1983) distinguishes 'reflection-on-action' – which the Kolb cycle suggests – from 'reflection-in-action' occurring simultaneously with an activity or practice. Argyris and Schon (1974; 1978) also differentiate between two theories of action employed in practice: 'espoused-theory' used to explain actions and 'theory-in-use' that actually governs practices and actions. An existing but incompatible theory-in-use may inhibit learning new 'theory'. Although a student may appear to have a new understanding, their actual skills and abilities are not being developed, as they are still embedded in already fixed theories.

Learning environments

The literature associated with the gap between recall and understanding revealed the key role the pedagogical formation of the learning situation plays in relation to student learning. The experiential learning literature linked to the gap, here, between understanding and ability focuses our attention on the role of the learning situation in construing experience, and the students' opportunities for developing abilities and skills to put their understandings into practice. Working through its implications leads to a more complex and differentiated view of learning environments. Kolb analysed four different types of environment (see Figure 4.4).

It is worth noting that the 'symbolically complex' environment (in Figure 4.4) maps closely to the 'content-oriented' teaching conceptions described in the last chapter. The other three, however, begin to map the learning-environment more closely to different aspects of the 'learning-oriented' teaching conceptions. While this experiential learning perspective may aid us in the alignment of teaching and learning environments more conducive to promoting skills and the ability to put understanding into practice, designing learning environments to

i) Affectively complex	ii) Perceptually complex
(a) focus on here-and-now experiences (b) legitimization of expression of feeling and emotions (c) situations structured to allow ambiguity (d) high degree of personalization	(a) opportunities to view subject matter from different perspectives (b) time to reflect and roles (e.g. listener, observer) which allow reflection (c) complexity of multiplicity of observational frameworks
iii) Symbolically complex	iv) Behaviourally complex
(a) emphasis on recall of concepts (b) thinking or acting governed by rules of logic and inference (c) situations structured to maximize certainty (d) authorities respected as caretakers of knowledge	(a) responsibility for setting own learning goals (b) opportunities for real risk-taking (c) environmental responses contingent upon self-initiated action

Figure 4.4   Learning Environments

meet the wide range of learning needs and wants of students is still problematic.

3 The gap between having the skills/abilities and actually wanting to use them

It may be that courses and degrees which are effective in increasing knowledge, encouraging understanding and the acquisition of appropriate skills and abilities will also, almost as a corollary, be effective at developing a willingness, even an aspiration, to go on learning or working in a particular field. Yet, many courses encourage the feeling that, after the certificates and the degrees have been won, the books will be shut for good. And while the accumulation of qualifications and letters after the name might have its own emotional satisfaction, in the present social and economic climate, the experience of learning needs to be a willing part of lifelong professional development. Certainly the immense satisfaction that so often arises in understanding and deriving meaning from almost any aspect of life – from the jigsaw to the most complex questions of nature – is a crucial part of 'wanting to'. This is particularly true of meaning which one is able to integrate with one's own experience and put into practice. Nevertheless, for a variety of reasons this may not be sufficient. Wanting to and a corresponding commitment to act may falter.

Drawing on his long work with students at Harvard, Perry (1970) became very concerned with this question of commitment. He found that very often there is a distinctive developmental process related to students' changing conceptions of learning, teaching and knowledge, which is at the same time part of a more personal development involving emotional issues of personal commitment. He identified a complex developmental process illustrating how the progress of students through higher education is punctuated by a number of important positions and transitions which often have a profound influence on their learning. His widely reported 'scheme of intellectual and ethical development' – depicted here in a simplified version (see Figure 4.5) – describes nine positions in student development.

The first three positions in Figure 4.5 move through a dualistic perspective in which the student regards knowledge and learning as something external and objective, right or wrong. This sort of epistemological perspective is extremely difficult to give up if it is held with any conviction, a conviction that quite often goes back to early childhood and may be strongly invested with emotion. Teachers and the learning environment may have been vested with many of the qualities of parental or childhood authority figures. The difficult transitions from the security of dualism into the insecurity of relativism is not simply a matter of absorbing new ideas or information, but is very much a restructuring at an emotional as well as a cognitive level, and may be accompanied by extreme anxiety. If, on the other hand, the student remains defensive about uncertainty, they may become certain with a comparable conviction that anything goes and that there are no valid reasons for anything! The move into the final three positions can again be accompanied by anxieties where the student recognizes learning as making and balancing commitments within relativism, within ever changing situations. When students make this move, however, commitments may be an extremely important source for wanting to do things. Longer-term and deeper commitments will arise out of seeing that commitments need revising because

Dualism
modified

1 The student sees answers as right or wrong: authority is accepted.

2 The student sees diversity between authorities: some are frauds, the true authorities are right.

3 The student accepts diversity as temporary until the authorities get the truth.

Relativism
discovered

4 Where there are no right answers the student accepts everyone has a right to his opinion. No one is wrong!

5 Student accepts in certain courses authorities are not asking for right answers but for thought.

6 Student sees all knowledge as contextually relative.

Commitment
in relativism
developed

7 Student sees a need for some form of personal commitment within an uncertain world.

8 Student sees need to make several commitments.

9 Student accepts that making, revising, pulling apart and creating new commitments is an unfolding and ongoing process.

Figure 4.5 Intellectual and ethical development (developed from Perry, 1980)

of deeper understanding and new experiences. Wanting to do things becomes part of a new, evolving structure and one which will hold interesting challenges and new perspectives in the future.

Intellectually effective and efficient teaching practices are frequently not sufficient to encourage students to put their understandings into practice. They must at the same time understand and construct the social and emotional context for wanting to make commitments. Paradoxically, much successful teaching does not consist of finding ways for constructing knowledge, but of ways for deconstructing some of the fiercely dualist and even purely relativist positions which students cling to. Such positions constrain them from wanting to make commitments and to put into practice their developing understandings and skills.

4 The gap between having the abilities, wanting to use them and actually doing so

From the previous section, we can see that the teaching environment supporting the development of 'wanting to' involves much more that simply providing knowledge and skills. A genuine 'wanting-to' requires a significant degree of change in many of the ways students perceive and understand knowledge and, indeed, the world in which their intellectual, personal and social commitments must be made. There is a resonance here with the 'developing as a person' aspect of the transforming conceptions of learning mentioned on p. 51. And yet the deeper changes associated with wanting to are often not enough to bring about action, to instigate an actual doing. There can be an important gap between wanting to do things and actually doing them.

There are, of course, very real practical reasons why people do not do things, but quite often these things can be a smokescreen for something else: deep concerns and threats which are felt, for example, in the face of taking on some new role. The problem, here, is often related to issues of self and self-identity. In order to act on new knowledge and skills, it may be that developing a new perspective is not sufficient. A student needs to develop a new self. This requires a deeper transformation of self.

Andragogy

Knowles (1978) originally coined the term 'andragogy' to describe a model of learning that he felt was distinctive of adults. He contrasted it with 'pedagogy' which he felt was more concerned with the learning of children. The main features of the 'andragogical' model (see Table 4.3) focus on the concept of self as being responsible for one's own life, of being self-directed, a concept Knowles initially argued was characteristic of adults (as opposed to children). It attributes to adults a rich social and cultural reservoir of meaningful experience, a readiness to learn charac-

Table 4.3   *Andragogical model of learning*

The concept of the learner
- Being self-directing
- Responsible for own learning

Learner experience
- Being a rich resource for themselves and each other

Readiness to learn
- When they experience a need to know or do something in order to perform more effectively (can be encouraged)

Orientation to learning
- Task- or problem-centred

Motivation to learn
- Internal, intrinsic
- Self-esteem
- Confidence
- Self-actualization

Source: Adapted from Knowles, 1984

terized by a real need to know and do; a life-centred, problem-centred and task-centred orientation to learning, and intrinsic, personal and emotional motivators such as confidence and self-esteem.

While 'andragogy' was originally sharply contrasted with 'pedagogy', the two are better conceived as a continuum. The social context of the learning situation favours or hinders particular experience in such a way that some 'pedagogic' assumptions are more appropriate for adults and some andragogical assumptions more appropriate for children. The term 'adult refers to a social status rather than a biological age' (Jarvis, 1987: 11). The marginalization of relevant experience (noted earlier in the discussion on p. 54) might, for example, contribute to reducing the student's experience and moving him or her towards the 'pedagogical' end of the continuum. This is especially significant for higher education, because of the large number of younger students who are often poised – socially and biologically – between the two ends of the continuum. They can be particularly vulnerable to courses which, however unintentionally, 'demote' them, in the face of the superior knowledge, expertise and confidence of the teachers.

Andragogy does not, then, define a unique theory of learning with respect to 'adultness', but it does raise important issues for teaching practice (Merriam, 1993). This is especially so regarding the development of a 'self-directed' learning self, as opposed to a 'teacher-directed' learning self. To surmount this gap, quality of experience, volume of experience and even transformation of experience in the construction of knowledge are not sufficient. It is the role they play in the transformation of the person towards a critically self-directed and emancipated self that matters. To put into practice their understandings, to actually 'do', may require a critical reconstruction of self within the broader social, cultural and political situation. It must recognize the freedoms (Boud, 1989) that such a reconstruction requires (freedom in learning) and generates (freedom through learning). It encompasses 'conscientization' (Freire, 1972) or perspective 'transformation' (Mezirow, 1983). Mezirow describes an 'emancipatory process of becoming critically aware of how and why the structure of psycho-cultural assumptions has come to constrain the way we see ourselves and our relationships, reconstituting this structure to permit a more inclusive and discriminating integration of experience and acting upon these new understandings' (1983: 4).

The failure of doing, of actual concrete action, is often an issue of whether the student has constructed a learning self which is truly self-directing within the social overlap of his or her experience and the experiences of the learning situation. As we noted above, the experiential overlap is critically important and undermined by courses that ignore or marginalize student experience. The structure of the learning situation itself is also important, particularly the opportunities it affords the student to take responsibility and control of their learning and also of the methods, procedures and activities which structure the learning environment. Encouraging self-direction means not only sharing the social and cultural premises or meanings of the learning environment, but also sharing control of the teaching and learning activities. This constitutes the nucleus of self-direction in learning; 'At the heart of self-directness is the adult's assumption of control over setting goals and generating personally meaningful evaluative criteria. One cannot be a self-directed learner if one is applying techniques of independent study within a context of goals determined by an external authority' (Brookfield, 1986: 19). Self-directed learning occurs when teaching and learning become the same thing, neither leading nor trailing one another. For Rogers this is closely associated with meta-learning:

> the goal of education, if we are to survive, is the facilitation of change and learning. The only man who is educated is the man who has learned how to learn; the man who has learned how to adapt and change; the man who has realised that no knowledge is secure, that only the process of seeking knowledge gives a basis for security. (1969: 103)

The construction of such learning environments is, again, not easy, particularly for young students in the first years of their undergraduate studies. It may also be inappropriate to the learning situation and counter-productive to learning. But the development of self-directed students – students who have not only developed a deeper understanding of their subject and the abilities and skills to put it into practice, but also want to and actually do put them into practice – is one of the key challenges facing teachers in higher education. It is not sufficient to encourage students to cross a limited number of these gaps. Teaching must provide the opportunity for all to be positively addressed. The hidden message at the centre of many learning environments is that if you follow the prescribed programme and methods and work hard you will be successful. But at what cost? Success may simply result in the construction of conformist and dependent selves and self-identities, identities that play an extremely important role in preventing us from doing what we want to do.

5 The gap between actually using the skills/abilities and changing

It appears odd to refer to this as a 'gap' in which one position is change. As the above comment from Rogers illustrates, change has been a crucial theme in all of the learning issues that we have been addressing in this chapter. What is meant here, however, is something more complex. If helping students to cross the other learning gaps has been a key process of change, crossing this gap is also a process of change, but it is a process to a position of 'changing', to a situation in which change is an ever-present and defining feature. This gap is concerned with the integration of continuous change as an intrinsic aspect of learning and practice, of being in the life-world, of 'supercomplexity'.

> The world of the twenty-first century into which graduates will have to make their way is likely to be one of ever-widening uncertainty, challenge and conflict, bearing on the three domains of knowledge, action and self. Criteria of truth, the will to act and the sense of one's identity will be relentlessly tested and will be subject to continuing change. (Barnett and Hallam, 1999: 149)

Yet, even this articulation is not fully sufficient to describe the 'supercomplex' condition for which we are preparing our students and ourselves. The issue is not simply facilitating the capacity for change *over* time – and the reconstruction of knowledge, action and self which this entails – but also facilitating the capacity for change *within* time. It requires the ability to operate with and switch between different synchronous perspectives and frames of thinking and action. Students need to develop the ability to make a series of ongoing commitments and challenges, as well as the ability to shift between them, to cope with change within the 'synchronous' demands of multiple perspectives. This condition of 'changing' requires capabilities for:

1 the construction of multiple identities and selves which can be sustained simultaneously;
2 the practice of these multiple frames of knowledge-action-self to critique one another;

3 the management of this multiplicity and synchronicity of thought, action and being within the appropriate present and future situation;
4 the continuous integration, critique and development of this synchronous multiplicity in future learning.

The challenge is to construct a 'curriculum of the future' (Young, 1998) which is not simply for the future but of the future.

Being of the future, this curriculum must reflect in its vision, design and implementation the 'uncertainty, unpredictability, contestability and challengeability' (Barnett, 2000: 159) which the 'future' increasingly and more pervasively injects into the present. It is this escalating overlap of the future with the present that defines the nature of the 'supercomplex' condition. Our teaching and pedagogical structures need to reflect this condition in our own understanding, the students' understanding and the learning environment shared. He describes such a new conception of higher education as having three key objectives: to create epistemological and ontological disturbance in the minds/beings of students; to enable students to live at ease with this perplexing and unsettling environment, and to enable them to make their own positive contributions to this supercomplex world (ibid.: 160).

The overall challenge for teaching and learning which this fifth 'gap' discloses, is to prepare our graduates to be no less than 'riders of the storm', a condition mirroring exactly the teacher's own professional challenge. It is no less an important teaching challenge for being shared with our students. It means that ownership of the learning environment that we design and construct should not only be shared with our students but with ourselves as well. Our responsibility for designing and structuring the learning environment is focused on both our students and ourselves. As teachers with personal learning responsibilities (involving knowledge, action and self) within a range of academic (disciplinary and institutional) structures and traditions this structure must go further than simply the traditional teaching situation. It must as we saw in Chapter 3 incorporate other academic practices and will include the ability to reframe one's teaching and learning within, for example, the multiple frames of research, management, consultancy and service. Our own professional development as academics is, thus, implicit in our own teaching.

The learning situation: structures of meaning

The boundaries between many of the different theoretical perspectives on learning discussed in the above schema of learning 'gaps' are not intended to be precise or definitive. Overlaps and vital interrelationships abound. Many of the issues relating to the achievement of learning in one 'gap' are of central importance in others as well. Despite their different approaches, these theoretical perspectives provide a useful basis for reflection on the complex issues characterizing the achievement of student learning – issues which teaching can successfully address.

> Students will not suddenly switch to being the model of holistic, deep and epistemologically sophisticated learners ... Teaching must create a learning environment ... at every level of description of the learning situation: i.e. conceptual structure, actions, feedback and goal must relate to each other so that integration can work. (Laurillard, 1993: 93)

In this section, we develop a model of the structure of meaning characterizing the teaching/learning context. It is intended as a conceptual 'tool' to assist practitioners to address the above learning 'gaps' while exploring their own teaching responsibilities and practices. The above discussion touched on a wide range of pertinent issues and themes, but the central concepts throughout were 'meaning' and 'context': meaning constructed within the discourses (or 'meta-contracts') of the social context in which the learning encounter occurs. The key to traversing each 'gap' is an active 'construction' and integration of meaning in the social situation. Learning is not concerned with decoding and recalling information but rather with the process of social and practical understanding. It is an active and meaningful construction of facts, ideas, concepts, theories and experiences in order to work and manage successfully in a changing world of multiple and synchronous contexts. It goes beyond the intellectual to encompass the personal, practical and social dimensions of students' learning life.

If the multidimensional nature of learning is a product of the social context, its character, development and practice are also substantially shaped by the nature of the learning dialogue offered to the student. The 'modes' of this learning dialogue – the methods and procedures by which the 'learning situation' exercises and realizes its meanings – have a significant role in assisting (or hindering) the student through the gaps described above. Such modes have sometimes been regarded as categories of strategy. Gibbs and Jenkins (1992) refer, for example, to 'control' and 'independence' strategies which teachers may take. These strategies or modes are closely related to the learning contexts from which they arise and which they help to create. Biggs (1999) refers to such contexts as climates and distinguishes between 'X and Y climates'. Teachers forming 'X' climates assume students 'need to be told what to do and what to study' (ibid.: 62), whereas teachers operating in 'Y' climates 'assume students do their best work when given freedom and space to use their own judgements' (ibid.). Teachers will generally operate with combinations of the two but individual teaching 'philosophies' or conceptions may incline us towards one more than the other.

For the purposes of this discussion, we refer to three general contexts: support, independence and interpersonal. In contexts described by *support*, the principal modes of meaning (e.g. course content, purposes, objectives, methods, assessment, evaluation, etc.) and their implementation are entirely or primarily dependent on the teacher. The modes of meaning

DIMENSIONS

CONTEXTS	Intellectual	Practical	Personal	Social
Support				
Independence				
Interpersonal				

Figure 4.6 Teaching and learning environment: a critical matrix

in *independence* contexts, on the other hand, are given over to the individual student to independently specify and enact. Finally, the *interpersonal* context and associated modes of structuring meaning are specified, developed and implemented 'among' the students and with the teacher. Because these contexts inform the different kinds of meaning prevalent in the learning situation differently, we can relate them to the four dimensions of contextual meaning – intellectual, personal, social and practical referred to earlier (see Figure 4.6).

In Figure 4.6, the intention is not to suggest that certain contexts align more closely to specific dimensions, but rather (a) that these contexts relate to and subsume all four dimensions and (b) that they may usefully overlap within the learning environment. In thinking about how to address the issues raised in the 'gap' schema, teachers might wish to think about the general context(s) of meaning they will be using and the most appropriate dimension(s) to focus on, given the learning issues they want to address. There are an extensive range of options and possibilities and those that are the most appropriate will depend upon an array of variables. These will consist of the nature of the discipline, student numbers, student composition, academic background, degree level, and will include a variety of academic, institutional and even national constraints. There is no prescribed 'right way'. Experience generally suggests that a balanced approach is the most effective. 'Balanced', of course, means different things to different professionals in different contexts.

None of the learning theories considered actually advocate a strong controlling environment. Such an environment might encourage a debilitating form of intellectual and personal dependency that would make crossing the individual 'gaps' difficult, and probably impossible. On the other hand, at certain points in the learning process, carefully controlled and managed environments may also be extremely 'supportive' and encouraging. Indeed, the development of self-directed learning depends upon an element of risk-taking. An emotional context that is perceived as independent, cold and aloof may be personally threatening and one in which risks and the development of positive qualities of intellectual independence are avoided. While students might need support in discovering and locating the intellectual material and practical experiences from which they will learn – and are to that degree dependent on teachers and the learning context – they do not need to be told how they should learn from those experiences. In certain situations, considered confusions, contradictions and discrepancies have also been effectively used to encourage students to examine their own assumptions and to make them more aware of habituated ways of perceiving, thinking, feeling and behaving.

The forms and levels of 'balance' teachers should strive to achieve will vary enormously. At this stage, the learning matrix is intended as an 'instrument' for exploring and reflecting upon the general issues and problems about learning raised in this chapter. It will be extensively referred to in the next part of the book, providing teachers with a range of different ways for thinking about and achieving their teaching – specifically relating the elements of the matrix to the different 'genres' of teaching practice. It addresses the area between developing a conceptual framework for a professional language and the more particular use of that language. The next part of the book, then, will take the idea of the reflective professional into the terrain of exploration. It will look at a series of 'genres', which he or she will need to 'map' out for him or herself according to the constraints and possibilities of their actual teaching situation. In the final part of the book, we shall suggest how this 'language' might be more fully realized.

Part 2: GENRES OF TEACHING IN HIGHER EDUCATION

5

Designing: Course and Curriculum Design

A curriculum is more than its knowledge components; much more. Interpreted broadly and correctly, curriculum embraces the students' engagement with the offerings put before them ... It represents a prior identification of worthwhile knowledge, albeit in particular epistemic fields. The ordering and presentation of those knowledge elements in a curriculum reflect a sense on the part of the educator as to what counts as a genuine act of knowing. Further, the pedagogical relationship that the educator determines for his or her curriculum itself acts as an epistemic framework. (Barnett, 1994: 45–6)

Introduction

Course and curriculum design is changing. As we observed in the previous chapter, there are increasing social and economic pressures on higher education to generate a wider range of knowledge, skills and attitudes for coping with the demands of our 'supercomplex age'. The current pace of technological and social change is impelling teachers to think in terms of educating students not for today's problems but for those of tomorrow. We demand greater flexibility and imagination in educating for the future and want our students to develop learning skills and the ability to transfer what is learned to new and more complex situations. In the process our very concepts of learning – and teaching – are also changing. Learning is itself regarded as a process of change, change not only in relation to intellectual reconceptualization but also, as we emphasized in the previous chapter, encompasses personal, social and practical transformations.

There is now a broad consensus on the need to engage with a more diverse range of experiences in the design of courses. We have conceptualized this diversity in the idea of 'the learning matrix' described in Chapter 4. In this chapter, we shall explore course design in terms of the critical dimensions raised in that matrix. We shall do so in three sections. In the first section we shall draw upon three decades of experience providing courses for faculty development in learning and teaching – across the whole spectrum of higher education disciplines – to examine a particular type of course: the workshop or intensive short course. It will provide a case study of what we refer to as the learning and teaching genre of 'designing', and offers the opportunity to address a wide range of the broad design issues arising from the matrix. Indeed, the rather unique qualities of the workshop/short-course design raises course design in a manner which will permit us to explore just how far the design of courses might actually go in addressing the multiple learning issues raised by the matrix. In the second section of this chapter, we draw upon the case study to elucidate more concisely some of the essential underlying principles and issues of course design. Finally, in the third section we shall draw upon the more general lessons to consider these ideas with respect to some of the central design choices – course objectives, course content and course structure – that teachers will make in designing their courses.

There are similarities between the workshop/short-course approach to design explored here and, perhaps, the most important revolution in course design in the last 30 years; the change from topic-based to problem-based learning (PBL). A complete restructuring of courses along PBL lines would require extended study and consultation, but many of its central tenets – echoed in this chapter – may be useful in implementing less drastic design changes and revisions. Many courses are already drawing upon this approach, specially designed sessions with teachers linked by independent study supported by set tasks and resources. Many new academic faculty are now experiencing similar ways of learning – in courses provided for the development and accreditation of their teaching. A second essential feature of the case study presented below is that it will chiefly focus upon a range of workshops and short courses developed to assist academics and faculty in developing their teaching. Reflecting on this example, then, will we hope assist in our understanding of teaching more generally as well as course design more particularly.

Finally, course design is, in many ways, the core 'genre' of the language of learning and teaching, the 'genre' every teacher has to master. It raises the most fundamental issues of learning and teaching, drawing together its diverse elements into a comprehensive and coherent whole, informed by a substantial body of knowledge and conceptual understanding of learning. It fully embraces the work of the reflective professional.

Course and curriculum design: a case study

Learning, innovation and multiple intelligences

We are not attempting here to extensively review work on design or to give a comprehensive guide to all the issues relevant to running effective short courses. While these can be helpful (see further reading at the end of this chapter) a large number of 'dos' and 'don'ts' runs the risk of missing out on the active learning which is central to workshops themselves.

It often avoids the more reflective professional challenge of understanding why many of the tips and 'prescriptions' are suggested – of personally working and thinking it through from key principles and research findings. In this respect, we suggest a rationale for developing strategies in course design that may be used across a variety of courses in a diverse range of subjects and disciplinary contexts.

There are three major areas of development in recent thinking about course design which are central to our exploration of this case study. The first is research on how students learn. This, as we have seen in the previous chapter, has increased substantially in the last 20 or so years and is beginning to impact widely on learning and teaching in higher education more generally. Second, this case study of course design will draw upon the work on multiple intelligences (Gardner, 1993; 1999) and its lessons for our consideration of teaching. Gardner's work extends the more general concept of 'intelligence' beyond its rather narrow focus on the intellectual dimension – the linguistic, spatial and logical/mathematical aspects of our thinking – to include other 'intelligences' including the interpersonal, intrapersonal, musical, visual, bodily/kinaesthetic and most recently, existential concerned with wider issues of being and purpose, and naturalist, concerned with classifying. The third area concerns developments in innovation theory and is concerned with understanding processes of organizational change. Most of this work has been focused on change in business and industry (Anderson and King, 1995), but more recently has also been applied to higher education (Berg and Ostergren, 1977) and the development of teaching as a process of change in particular (Hewton, 1982; Kolb et al., 1994). Table 5.1 presents the relationship between the key ideas in these three areas with respect to the four dimensions of the learning matrix.

Understanding courses in terms of these three areas will not merely assist us to improve courses which have a substantial element of workshop or short course in their design, but will also contribute to our understanding of the essential principles of teaching and our ability to improve more traditionally delivered courses. In the following discussion, we shall consider the role of the three theoretical areas in terms of the four central dimensions of the learning matrix – the intellectual, the personal, the social and the practical – which can be served particularly well by workshops/short courses. In addition, achieving balance in these four will be set within the broader matrix contexts of providing support, encouraging independence and developing the interpersonal. Rather than provide a detailed theoretical description of these three theoretical orientations here, the following discussion will explore them through their relationship to a range of ideas, activities, resources and environmental conditions central to our case study.

Table 5.1   *Workshop design: the learning matrix in relation to learning theory, innovation theory and multiple intelligences*

Matrix dimensions	Learning theory	Multiple intelligences	Innovation theory
Intellectual	• Deep/transforming • Relational • Relativist/committed • Task/problem centred • Reflection-on-action	• Verbal/linguistic • Mathematical/logical • Visual/spatial • Naturalist	• Gain/loss • Empirical/rational strategy • Openness to new ideas • External changes
Emotional/ personal	• Personal change • Active • Personal experience (valued) • Reflection-in-action • Adult self-directed • Learning in response to readiness/need • Committed viewpoint • Self-actualization • Identity • Confidence • Sharing verbalizing • Alternative perspectives	• Interpersonal • Intrapersonal • Bodily/kinaesthetic • Musical • Visual/spatial • Existential	• Ownership • Unfreezing • Deskilling • Normative strategy • Environment • Trust
Social		• Interpersonal • Intrapersonal • Bodily/kinaesthetic • Musical	• Unfreezing • Linkage • Normative strategy • Leadership • Power • Environment (informal)
Practical	• Active • Practice • Emotional context for remembering	• Linguistic (practice) • Mathematical/logical (practice) • Visual/spatial • Interpersonal • Intrapersonal	• Gain/loss • Ownership

The intellectual dimension

The design and practice of short courses comes closest to good traditional teaching in the intellectual 'dimension'. In terms of innovation theory, it essentially employs an 'empirical rational strategy' (Hewton, 1982) concentrating on giving evidence and reasons as the basis for initiating change. It is an approach that draws upon the more traditional 'intelligences': verbal/linguistic, mathematical/logical and visual/spatial. In relation to learning theory, these courses work towards developing deep approaches and transforming conceptions which, as we saw in the previous chapter, emphasize meaning, purpose, seeing in a different way and relating one's own experience and the wider context to the course material. Learning and teaching strategies draw on alternative perspectives and explore the relative strengths and weaknesses of these in different contexts. Adult learning theory and the concepts of reflective practice inform the course activities. These are essentially task or problem centred rather than topic or content centred.

Background readings/formal lectures   The courses essentially exist to help people develop their knowledge and solve the practical problems they face in their working lives. The requirement for new ideas and information needs to be met by different means than merely through more formal and didactic input common to traditional courses and/or conference talks. We try to meet the need for new information in rather different ways. We suggest that initial orientations be made through 'background readings' rather than through introductory lectures. The inclusion of formal talks are rare but can be helpful to enable participants to meet people whose work they may be reading. Interactive ways of engaging with these talks are, however, encouraged, as it is naturally frustrating if there is little opportunity to discuss their ideas with them. A need to discuss formal input from hospital consultants on a general practitioners' course, for example, was addressed by providing a break for group work to formulate comments and questions to raise at a second session with the visiting consultant.

Syndicate or peer-managed learning   Early attempts to present theoretical material and research evidence on teaching in higher education through formal inputs were generally unsuccessful. Current courses have transformed these lectures into 'syndicate' or 'peer-managed' learning activities. These consist of providing groups of four to six with resource packs of the material and the task of reading it to find out what is relevant and helpful to their own teaching. They work as a team to look at and cover different aspects of the information, which is then discussed in the small group and reported back to the larger plenary sessions. This has generated a positive approach to addressing relevant aspects of theory and research for practice, rather than the previous intellectual detachment of the two, which was often the response to lectures. Participants begin making use of the information to see how it helps them become better teachers.

Handouts   Much of the intellectual stimulation generated on courses may be lost in returning to an environment, which is not always supportive. This is regularly addressed through the provision of extensive handouts, packaged to have a useful 'shelf-life'. These handouts go beyond what has been covered and enable people to feel they are taking away resources, which can help them follow up the frequently brief acquaintance with complex ideas.

Project groups   The sense of intellectual continuity to learning is often difficult to generate in short courses, particularly those trying to acquaint participants with a wide range of issues. We find it is often useful and important to take thinking beyond the extended discussion and carry over work on particular themes across two, three even five days. While syndicate work can provide this focus to some extent, the teacher usually chooses tasks. On our longer workshops, we frequently set up project groups focused on themes chosen by the participants. They are used as a focus for integrating learning on a topic into a more coherent framework, which is then shared with the larger group through presentations and/or posters. This type of learning is associated closely with approaches taken in problem-based learning (Boud and Feletti, 1997).

Triads   Within these workshop courses, general reflection and discussion on the relevance and use of ideas, concepts, is supplemented by frequent meetings which take the form of 'triads' where it is easy for everyone to speak. These triads consist of groups of three people where personal reflection is encouraged on what is being learned and how it applies to the individual problems.

The personal dimension

The intellectual is never purely intellectual, and with courses which have a more practical orientation there is a need to see that energy is generated to enable the intellectual changes actually to translate into action. Many traditional courses can be reasonably effective at encouraging students to remember and even to understand but are not so effective in giving students the ability to act. This is often the result of deeper inhibitions and anxieties as well as a mismatch between what we have learned and profound concerns about the sort of people we are and/or wish to be. In the previous chapter we looked at learning theory which draws on much more than our intellect, stressing the importance of the emotional and personal side of learning – particularly that which emphasizes the importance of adults being self-directed and working towards self-actualization. This is dependent upon giving students a stronger sense of identity and confidence, which can generate an important sense of responsibility and commitment extending beyond the confines of a discrete educational event.

Ownership and 'deskilling' One of the essential concepts of innovation theory is 'ownership'. Without a general feeling that this is something which we all have a part in, innovations can often fail. This sense of ownership can be undermined by the 'deskilling' of participants through an overpowering emphasis on the teachers' (or other contributors') expertise. The sense of inadequacy can lead to withdrawal, alienation or simply leaving all the serious thinking to the experts. Innovations which stress 'normative strategies' focusing on changing attitudes and approaches, rather than empirical/rational ones focusing on change through the strength of the ideas or content alone, can be more truly educational. Ownership is often dependent upon creating the right environment, feelings of support and a sense of trust.

'Unfreezing' and 'ice-breaking' Another interesting concept of innovation theory is 'unfreezing'. Where current thinking is unyielding and/or even complacent, there is little hope of change succeeding without a prior 'unfreezing' of the existing position. An important feature of workshops (such as ours) is the use of techniques for emotional 'unfreezing' – ice-breaking activities to enable people to get to know each other and feel more relaxed and less inhibited – and for challenging some of the intellectual assumptions behind resistance to our general aims. Quotes such as that by the nuclear physicist Edward Teller – 'confusion is not a bad thing: it's the first step towards understanding' (Teller, 1991) – critically probing the view that teaching is essentially about putting across our knowledge in a clear and interesting way – have been very effective. If this 'unfreezing' is too aggressive it can set up resistances, but it is as important as a general principle of design to think about the assumptions and resistances which may block the courses aims.

The environment: music, space and the visual The 'intelligences' which this dimension mainly addresses are the intrapersonal and the interpersonal, but we also think about the relationship of the workshop to the bodily/kinaesthetic, musical and spatial/visual 'intelligences' as well. We often use music as an aid to welcoming participants, for example. While some people do not notice, others appreciate it as an expression of our recognition of them as more than intellects. Spatial/visual intelligence is a highly important part of many people's ability to learn and using it in the form of visual diagrams and written words is generally highly developed. An aspect which is less common in more traditional teaching is engaging them in the process of constructing their learning in terms of posters, more 'creative' use of overheads, flip charts, boards, and so on.

In workshops this is often integrated with the soliciting and recording of participant views. The latter is particularly effective with the use of 'brainstorming' in which producing ideas and solutions is separated from the often limiting impact of immediate intellectual criticism. Visual expression and 'intelligence' can be engaged in many other ways – as a stimulus constructing complex relationships for example – and gives a sense of contribution and ownership as well. Finally, in the movement of individuals between groups, or in recording discussion and/or making presentations, workshops even engage bodily/kinaesthetic aspects of the learning environment.

Problem contribution　　If emotional needs and personal needs are to be met, then the general atmosphere needs to be one where participants feel welcome and part of an event. This is partly a matter of style and activities, but the general atmosphere is also generated out of the environment. They need to feel that their own personal problems are acknowledged and progress is made towards actually coping with them. Asking them to contribute concrete problems in advance as well as during the course can often address this. Running particular sessions early on in which the ideas and problems participants bring are acknowledged, discussed in small groups and put up as reminders for the teachers or leaders to deal with throughout the workshop, can enhance this feeling of ownership. In this way the participants can feel a sense of belonging and of responsibility for the way the workshop progresses rather than leaving it all to the teacher. This sense of responsibility enhances learning in many ways and leaves people with a sense of ownership of the course.

Performance and role-play　　Another important part of personal and emotional learning is to include activities that conclude with some sort of outcome and provide a 'performance' challenge to participants. Role-play sessions on lecturing and small group teaching, for example, where participants give short lectures or take a small-group leadership role which is video-recorded and followed by group analysis can engage the emotional side of learning as well as enhance self-criticism. If it is repeated, with improvement, there can be an important sense of achievement as well. Even where role-play is not the theme, participants can be encouraged to take active 'performance' roles, reporting on the results of group work, or formally describing professional or work-based problems that have been difficult for them. They have the potential advantage of engaging the emotional and personal aspects of the 'performance' itself and the personal content of the performance.

Reflective pairs and triads　　Quieter students and participants can even find groups of five and six difficult to speak up in. Pairs and triads (see above) frequently provide an opportunity for students to express some of the more emotional problems common in their learning. To build up confidence and trust, it is often useful to keep these groups constant over the duration of the course, providing extended opportunities to talk about the relevance of what has been happening with respect to the course, their learning and its relationship to their working and personal lives. A useful focus for the final meeting may be a discussion (and planning) of what they are actually going to do as a result of the course.

The social dimension

Of course, personal and emotional life is strongly bound up with social relationships and many of the issues already discussed are highly relevant to meeting social needs. The frequency and variety of tasks and group sizes and leadership within the activities of the course are important, as the occasional session labelled 'group work' may not be particularly effective. People need time to begin to work well together. Indeed, groups often go through a period of 'storming' or hostility after the 'forming' stage (see Chapter 7). Even if this is not outwardly expressed, they may, nevertheless, go through a period of intense emotional turbulence. Generally, such turbulence is considered something to be avoided at all costs but, in fact, crises can be extremely effective in the development of deeper learning and feeling. Provided they do not become destructive, they can lead to radical change (Cox et al., 1981). (This is, of course, a common feature of many therapies.) Unfortunately group work in many courses is often too intermittent for group forces to be particularly valuable, and change and reconceptualization rarely comes from very intermittent events.

Leadership and ownership The role of leadership and power is an extremely important issue in encouraging change. In a workshop format, power is typically relinquished as much as possible to the group – whilst realizing that responsibility for structuring activities cannot be completely delegated. For the most part, the form of leadership is informal and fosters a general sense of ownership. Frequent peer discussion and 'buzz group' discussion can encourage more easy social relationships, as do the layout of the furniture and indeed the type of furniture. Introducing various levels of formality and informality within the various workshop activities is also instrumental in establishing a balance between leadership and ownership on the course. Balancing 'brainstorming' contributions, for example, from the group – acknowledging and writing them up on flip charts or boards – with the formal instructions and rules of the activity specified by the leader can encourage that sense of 'ownership' – of both the process and what is produced – at the centre of innovation theory. The various alternative participant perspectives disclosed in such group activities and tasks also reflect important features of learning theory noted in the previous chapter.

Sharing meals and a drink   The workshops also encourage the social aspect of learning through providing coffee, teas and lunch whenever possible. In the evening we often provide a departing drink. Many stay despite being very tired, and more than a few often continue talking for many more hours. Sharing refreshments and meals together has long been recognized by the Oxbridge colleges, for example, as an important feature of education. Indeed, this is a much valued part of our general social interaction, but within higher education is an increasingly rare part of student-teacher interaction.

Follow-up meetings   An essential feature of our courses is the negotiation of follow-up meetings, which are quite often valued for the social relationships that are developed. Many participants are genuinely interested in the brief friendships that develop and in what others are doing. Indeed one of our groups has continued meeting for over 20 years!

The practical dimension

Workshops are places for working not just listening. Our workshops for teachers, for example, are essentially about meeting their practical 'needs'. These, however, are often not the same as their 'wants'. Seeing learning as change, for example, has profound implications for teaching and some of the most satisfying outcomes can be from participants realizing that they now see teaching and learning in a different way.

Practical skills are not all straightforwardly instrumental. Typically, they will represent underlying personal needs and social needs, which can have a very practical dimension to them. Asking participants to think about specific practical problems and issues before the course and then bring them to the course can be extremely useful. The time set aside on the course to specifically look at these accentuates the practical outcomes of the course in a context that is relevant to practice. On some of our workshops, for example, participants are asked to bring a teaching design, which is then developed with contributions from tutors and other participants. Other courses include exploration and development of practical designs for course evaluation, student assessment processes and even departmental guidelines for implementing learning and teaching reforms.

On some of the workshops, many of the practical outcomes result from considerable time spent in actual practice. This is particularly the case, for example, with the lecturing and small-group workshops. Here repetition – which usually results in clear improvements – is especially important. Many exercises can result in feelings of inadequacy and so wherever the opportunity to repeat a practical exercise and improve on it can be introduced, this can result in a substantial gain. In addition, frequent use of our linguistic 'intelligences' in small group work, for example, can lead to reinforcement of our practical learning and raises the possibility of future practical changes, as too can an emotional attachment. The integration of many 'intelligences' rather than relying too much on the verbal/linguistic or the logical/mathematical can make practical outcomes much more significant. Use of our visual intelligence can help to consolidate learning and the interpersonal intelligence can give it a strong sense of personal commitment. Perhaps the most important, however, might be the much less frequently considered intrapersonal intelligence through which we begin to better understand ourselves and re-evaluate our own behaviour. This may not only provide a sense of gain and ownership but also a better understanding of who we are, the way we learn and how we might be capable of changing.

Learning contexts: balance and structure

Support and independence While the above discussion has focused primarily on issues concerning the dimensions of the learning matrix, those dimensions were disclosed and described with the range of the matrix's learning contexts. Much of the discussion centred implicitly on, for example, the balance between giving support with a workshop and encouraging independence. Too much support – either in the form of being told too much information or working within tight and controlling structures – and students may feel they are not taking part, that they have little ownership of what is happening, that it is not relevant to their lives. Too little support, on the other hand, and they may feel too anxious to take risks and/or too inadequate to have much to offer. Support from teachers (and fellow participants) needs to be matched by challenging tasks, the opportunity to take risks with new ways of working and the opportunity to rethink many of the assumptions which have served well in the past but raise serious doubts for the future. Achieving a better balance of support and independence is often mediated through specific tasks but can be helped by experiencing a wider range of specific roles. Overall, traditional teaching does not require students to engage in very many different roles. They mainly listen, read, complete exams and other assignments and occasionally do some practical work. This limited range of roles, however, does not parallel what they will have to cope with when they become independent professionals. It certainly does not address the students' future need to develop 'transferable skills' nor their ability to engage in 'meta-learning' and learning how to learn (see Chapter 1). An essential issue in developing these skills includes more emphasis on the interpersonal context of learning.

The interpersonal The interpersonal context stresses the need to develop abilities through which students are able to contribute to the learning of and to learn from others. It is the basis for strong relationships and requires a great deal of sensitivity about the way students are understood by one another both at an intellectual and a personal level. Within the interpersonal context, they will need to be supportive but, to avoid conformity and to ensure the success of the interpersonal situation, they will need to make distinctive and independent contributions. Many students, even on workshops, do not always expect or even want to learn in such an interpersonal context. They believe they are coming to hear experts tell them what is right and what the best course of action is. On the other hand, one of the most common and positive features of workshop evaluations is how much they appreciated the opportunity to meet and discuss with colleagues from other departments or institutions.

Structure   Short courses are often very concentrated, so the structure in terms of beginnings, middles and ends needs to be thought out carefully. Common 'ice-breaking activities' for getting to know one another are important but, as suggested above, this must also be an 'unfreezing' time in terms of beginning to recognize that some basic ways of understanding and behaving may be serious obstacles to learning new ideas which may be worth trying. If learning in general is more a question of change than assimilation then courses need to recognize that change processes can be difficult. The structure needs to reflect this, not only within the days of the workshop itself but in its preparation and, if possible, within the time during which the learning is applied after the course. It may even include future reunions and reflections upon the problems and success of that application. Innovations often fail because the implementation is too difficult and the training and the sense of ownership of the innovation are not highly developed. Perhaps the processes were only intellectual or the unfreezing was superficial, leaving in place many of the ways of thinking which later under stresses of the old environment undermined the new ideas and practices. New ideas and information are essential issues in designing courses but they are easily diminished by a lack of deeper integration with behaviour and feelings. Even on the workshop itself! Variety in presentation, activities and relationships are not there simply to prevent people from getting bored but are critical ways of integrating what is learned into a firmer network of reinforcing influences. For some people chatting over a drink at the end of the day may be a more important element of consolidating learning than the more formal consolidation activities.

Evaluations   The evaluation of a course is, too often, tacked on as a bureaucratic feature. If, however, we see evaluation as part of the process of becoming reflective professionals, it needs to display many of the features that characterize the course as a whole. Evaluations should not, for example, simply reflect what participants liked and disliked but how they felt it affected them, why it affected them that way and how their fellow students or colleagues responded. Simple questionnaires can be helpful to tutors for improving their courses but they are rarely sophisticated enough to engage participants in very serious reflection and are quite often seen as a rather peripheral event. Much deeper reflection and evaluation needs to be built into the learning activities themselves. On the workshops, for example, deliberations and reflections arising from 'triad' groups provide a rich source of material for evaluation. They develop a continuity of personal reflection which can be integrated into an action plan which can give participants a clear sense of gain (or loss) but also a clearer sense of personal understanding about how they themselves have begun to change and adapt to a range of new perspectives. Asking participants to contribute written qualitative statements of their individual or group reflections during one of these sessions or to bring them to a focus discussion can enhance their learning and improve the workshop.

Conclusions

We hope that the relationships to the theoretical and conceptual frameworks raised here are helpful in contributing to a broader understanding of design. Such relationships are often made in terms of learning theories but rarely in terms of innovation theory, and they offer reasons for broadening the lessons from workshop design to more traditional forms of teaching. Short courses highlight the need to relate to participants as whole people rather than intellects. Traditional teaching has generally suffered from separating off the lecture and seminar room from the social dialogue and engagements of a concrete world; where human intellect functions within the rich and substantial context of social relationships and personal conceptions of who we are and what we want to be. These broader issues of personal and occupational identity can dramatically affect our learning in all contexts. Their significance is, however, easily overlooked or ignored by traditional teaching, and yet they frequently become the most important and relevant components to student success.

Course and curriculum design: principles from the case study

In this section, we shall begin to draw out more formally some of the features gained from the case study. In the first instance, it is worth noting that short course design as described above engages with the fundamental issues and principles raised in the earlier chapters. These include:

- the requirement for a curriculum of transferability and the development of the student's higher level meta-learning abilities (Chapter 1). They are in tune with the important new emphases on developing wider professional skills and with demands of super complexity;
- the construction of an environment/community in which communication, learning and knowledge are understood and practised as 'dialogue' with students and not monologue (Chapter 2). They make it

more difficult to acquiesce in the transmission model while providing strong incentives to move towards the engagement model of teaching;

- the potential extension of the social context from ones solely focused on the learning of students to one which encompasses the mutual learning experience of the teacher as well (Chapter 3);
- the integration of research/theory and practice and an understanding of the nature of the potential 'gaps' of learning which they describe (Chapter 4);
- the full range of dimensions – intellectual, personal, social and practical – and contexts – support, independence and interpersonal – of the learning matrix (Chapter 4).

Depending on the nature of the particular programme, discipline, institution and/or professional bodies concerned, these courses will have different interpretations and stress different aspects of the above, but there are likely to be general features concerned with all of them. Some we shall suggest are general features that all design needs to address; others we acknowledge may be difficult for more traditional courses to entertain.

Central features

Students as whole people   Short courses encourage teachers to see students as people rather than simply as intellects. This needs to be a feature of any course design which is seriously concerned with the needs of students within the complexity of today's professional life.

Change   There is no point in running a course if it does not bring about a significant change in knowledge in terms of approach, conception, attitudes and behaviour. This is an important requirement of traditional undergraduate teaching, but where the 'transmission' model predominates, the focus is frequently on remedial work and the assimilation and accumulation of basic knowledge and skills. It is difficult for significant change to occur if the process is simply regarded as one of assimilation. Many of the short-course techniques for encouraging change can be relevant even within those more purely knowledge and skills based courses of undergraduate teaching.

Motivation   There is a great deal of emphasis in short courses on making them active, enjoyable, reflective and challenging. Developing an intrinsic motivation and real engagement is not always easy to bring about unless there is more emphasis upon the active and more enjoyable aspects. This sense of ownership, however, generated by active participation techniques such as triads and brainstorming, and processes for jointly coping with course crises can be an important part of any course.

Such motivation needs to be understood in contrast to extrinsic motivation of success and failure in traditional exam-led assessment. We need to be aware of the short-term aspects of such motivation and supplement them with more intrinsic aspects integrated with a developing sense of personal and occupational identity.

Transferable skills   While the short-course is not the only way of addressing transferable skills, more traditional approaches often attend to them as isolated skills to be 'bolted on' so to speak. Under such circumstances, their prospects for being developed long-term and becoming an important feature of professional life are diminished. Problem-solving, learning to learn, interpersonal and social skills, interdependence and communication skills, and the intelligent use of resources are essential features of short-course design which are focused on change, and these need to replace the formal tokenism which can be the way they appear within unintegrated skills courses.

Community   An important feature of short courses is the creation of a learning community. Longer courses should have much more scope for developing this, although it is often not given substantial emphasis and the pressures of overloaded curricula often make it difficult to provide the necessary space for its development. The emphasis on group work and learning from colleagues which, as we have seen, is a feature of workshops/short courses, is an important lesson for traditional courses. While many are already successful in developing such communities, others are frequently little more than a collection of individuals who learn little from their peers and contribute less.

Self-evaluation   Finally, evaluation is often practised as a bureaucratic imposition, adding little to the quality of learning or, ironically, even to course improvement, and opportunities for self-evaluation are generally overlooked. The integration of serious educational reflection with social interaction and the development of learning skills is a key part of many workshops which does not yet appear to have been successfully extended to many undergraduate courses. Time for reflection, diaries, commentaries and group follow-up meetings can both enhance student learning and provide opportunities for them to develop reflective practices over the long term.

Working with difficult features

Some of the features described in the case study are clearly going to be difficult – even impossible – to use in the context of expanded staff–student ratios that proliferate on courses that are more traditional. Creating a learning community, for example, with 200 students may seem unachievable, and providing active practice sessions with teachers providing analytic feedback may seem entirely out of the question. If these are seen entirely as the teacher's work, this will, more than likely, be perfectly true. In an 'engaged' situation, however, teaching like learning is not entirely the province of the teacher.

Broadening responsibility   The focus on developing abilities for learning how to learn, for internalizing a 'lifelong learning agenda' requires students to take a great deal more responsibility for their own learning earlier on: both as individuals and as members of a group. In Germany, for example, students on courses with extremely high staff–student ratios have spontaneously formed working groups to compensate for the lack of faculty attention. This can provide substantial opportunities for reflection and comments from peers. This creation of active peer learning communities is essential to developing a sense of individual and group responsibility in students. Some medical education programmes focusing on problem-based learning approaches to their curriculum are already encouraging the development of such peer groups. There will be a role for teacher support in initiating such groups but certainly not in terms of the teacher doing the work for them.

Student contributions   Perhaps the most prevalent feature of workshops, which may be problematic under high staff–student ratios, is their capacity to address specific problems, concerns and interests of the participants. Splitting larger groups into smaller groups to help them interact more easily can enable them to formulate problems and issues that are more directly related to their own experiences and concerns. Such groups may start, for example, with individual thinking extended through contributions from others as the groups expand. Again, this offers opportunities for more students to contribute, but also provides a key route for exploring solutions to common problems. The teacher role in such sessions is less focused on transmitting a higher concentration of material but rather on facilitating and bringing together material and issues for discussion in the larger groups. They will focus on commenting on and comparing the different issues and solutions arising, contributing material where there are substantial gaps, and adding more sophisticated and critical perspectives on the topic.

In many cases such groups offer students an opportunity to go away and do extensive reading of their own which is shared within the group in later sessions without direct or immediate involvement of the tutor. This can mean that students have a far greater opportunity for choice than is usually the case. Unfortunately, the more courses become excessively burdened with required work the less scope there is for student choice. As content overload is one of the most significant pressures towards surface learning, reducing the content or, perhaps, distinguishing between 'mastery' content and 'acquaintance' content may give students the time to develop their own thinking and, indeed, extend their own knowledge of the topic.

Balancing support and independence This provision of space for student contributions highlights what may be the most serious feature to incorporate into undergraduate teaching: establishing the optimum balance between support and independence. Students are often very ambivalent about needing support from staff. They often want to be told the answers and be directed, especially in conditions of high anxiety, but if this becomes the dominant experience of the course, it can have a very serious effect on motivation. This ambivalence is a crucial aspect of even those students who appear the most submissive. It reflects a need to become independent of the pressures of family and school life and to become fully adult. Acquiescing in a state of dependency may be unacceptable to both the student and teacher. It is as important in science and technology, which often requires a great deal of conformity to extensive curricular demands. The opportunity for choice and challenging independent work should be introduced early and not left to later years.

Problem- and task-based learning The development of specific skills is another area where it is difficult to adopt the teaching-intensive pattern characteristic of workshops or short courses. Problem- or task-based learning is an approach where highly structured resource-based and computer-based learning can be acceptable and appropriate. Teaching staff may not need to be heavily involved; it is essentially a question of setting up processes and enabling students to go through them at their own pace. They will, however, need to receive formal feedback mediated either by senior students, mentors or through computer generated responses. Within some contexts this may be quite difficult but in others such resource-based learning approaches are very effective.

Follow up and follow through Finally, the opportunity for follow-up sessions, which are a feature of many short courses, is typically difficult to arrange with large undergraduate courses. With support and encouragement from teachers, this, again, might be something students could organize. Teaching staff could play an important role within such an initiative without being overly directive and without it becoming a unreasonable demand on their time. It can also become an important source of information to draw upon for course evaluation, particularly as it relates to student career progression following the completion of their studies. Inviting previous course students back for a session – as in the general practitioners' course mentioned earlier – can become a regular and effective feature of a course. Current students can gain useful insights with respect to their learning and teachers can acquire interesting perspective on the impact of their course.

Issues of course and curriculum design

The focus on workshops/short courses in the previous two sections of this chapter has drawn attention to a critical range of conceptual ideas that are easily ignored or not given sufficient attention in more traditional approaches to course design. In this section, we shall explore these ideas with respect to some of the central design choices – course objectives, course content and course structure – that teachers will need to make in designing their courses.

Course objectives

Objectives, aims and outcomes 'Objectives' have long been a key aspect of course design and in recent years have been the focus of renewed emphasis from national agencies such as the Quality Assurance Agency in the UK. They are usually distinguished from course aims in that aims refer to what one is trying to do whereas objectives refer to what the students should be able to do having successfully completed the course.

Aims are best thought of as *general statements* of educational intent, seen from the *student's point of view*.

Objectives are more *specific* and *concrete statements* of what *students are expected to learn*. (Ramsden, 1992: 130; emphasis added)

Objectives have often been used interchangeably with 'learning outcomes', suggesting a rather linear and causal relationship which needs to be critically addressed. Rigidly constructed objectives described – even prescribed – in detail and linked to learning outcomes offer little space for student involvement in the development of their own learning. They need to be carefully considered and explored with course teams, previous students and, if possible, scope provided for negotiation within the course. The issue may be compounded if the teacher is, as is increasingly the case for new faculty, taking over a course with previously defined aims and objectives. The lack of such a critical exploration may encourage a superficial understanding of what the course is about. An existing course, continuing with the same syllabus – but with new teacher(s) with new perspectives and ways of interpreting and translating it into teaching and learning practice – constitutes, as Pring (1995) notes, a new 'curriculum'.

Course ... refers to a set of arrangement procedures and college *syllabus* which meet the relevant criteria (standards) ... The *curriculum* refers to the learning experiences (planned for the most part by the teacher) through which that course is put into practice ... Teaching and leaning styles are part of the curriculum. Curriculum is a richer concept than that of syllabus or course ... The same syllabus can be taught in different courses, the same course taught by different teachers – in each case producing different curricula. (Ibid.: 81)

Sources of objectives   The development of course objectives is to a large degree conditioned by the overall educational and/or ideological perspective of the course including the institution and disciplinary context in which the course is situated. Warren Piper (1975) describes 'three plus one' general educational perspectives in which objectives may be embedded (see Figure 5.1). The first three are the 'cultural' in which education is essentially regarded as a process of passing the richness of our culture on to the next generation; the 'functional' which views education as a way of creating an educated workforce to ensure national development and global competitiveness; and the 'social service' perspective focused on providing opportunity for citizens. The fourth is the 'course' itself; it has more local 'facilitative' objectives to ensure students are learning successfully and happily on the course.

These sources of educational objectives are not necessarily mutually exclusive but, as Toohey (1999) suggests with respect to a similar categorization, they need to be carefully considered. They will often draw upon different epistemological understandings of what 'knowledge' is, what content should be included, how they are best assessed, and so on. The current concern in the UK for the development of transferable or key skills, for example, has been very much informed by the functional view, but this does not mean that objectives which consider such skills cannot draw upon service or cultural perspectives and the engaged 'facilitative' approaches which we have stressed in the previous parts of the chapter.

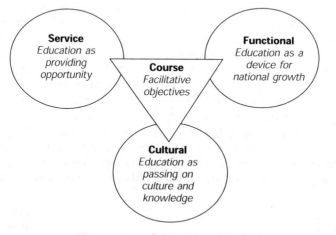

(adapted from Warren Piper in UTMU 1976: 115)

Figure 5.1   Sources of Educational Objectives

Approaches to objectives: rational v. reflective   The course team's decision on where to situate course objectives will, to a large degree, be related to their stance to two different approaches to the use of objectives: the rational and the reflective. The more formal objectives are closely associated with behaviourism and the associated 'rational' view suggested earlier that courses are designed to provide uniform outcomes in a linear and causal way. Precise and strict definitions of what the course is trying to do are important and they should be measured by formal standardized procedures to determine how far these prescribed outcomes have been achieved. Diversity, while not eliminated, is nevertheless reduced and standardization is a high priority. In the second, more expressive or 'reflective' approach to objectives, courses are not designed to produce uniform products but rather to provide a rich environment of learning experiences to which students will respond in different ways. These include the kind of valuable experiences – including developing creativity, flexibility, open-mindedness, complex understanding (Eisner, 1994; Stenhouse, 1975) – addressed in the case study. The teacher is not subject to a prescribed 'rational' system but will 'reflect' on the objectives in terms of the ongoing changes of the course and make professional judgements-in-action. Although this approach will provide more diversity and independence of student response, it does not entail, as some fear, that standards are jeopardized. It simply provides a means for more fully engaging students in the various aspects of their learning environment, offering some degree of choice in what and how they study and, even where appropriate, in how they are assessed.

While these two approaches are diametrically contrasted here, they should not be regarded as exclusive. They are best understood and practised as occupying the two ends of a continuum (see Figure 5.2). Different courses within different disciplines will be working with different constraints and need to make professional choices as to where on the continuum they wish to locate their course and programme. Within the constraints of formal professionally accredited courses based on formal specifications of objectives there is still considerable scope for increasing opportunities for choice and independence through different ways of learning and the use of additional more diverse outcomes. Similarly, even within very radical project-oriented courses encouraging creativity and flexibility and living with the consequences of that creativity, structures and standards are important. Ironically perhaps, the recent emphasis on 'prescribing' objectives for transferable skills – encouraging independent

Figure 5.2 Approaches to Objectives

meta-learning – calls for a substantial review of highly structured courses offering little scope for independent work in which students become technically proficient but lack flexibility and creativity.

Categories of objectives   The discussion has tended to focus on 'horizontal' aspects of objectives, comparisons between different sources, approaches and so forth. Objectives also have what might be called a 'vertical' dimension: differences of complexity and standard. The most often cited taxonomy of higher education objectives in this vein is that of Bloom (1956). While he distinguishes between kinds of objectives – relating to knowledge, attitudes and skills – his key contribution here concerns his six-level classification of objectives by complexity. More recently Biggs (1999) – through his 'Structure of the Observed Learning Outcome' taxonomy (SOLO) – has also usefully classified objectives by complexity and level. While both taxonomies take a different approach, there are close parallels between them. Figure 5.3 compares both, presenting associated verbs that identify what students are being asked to do with respect to each level.

Teachers will wish to consider carefully at what level they are 'pitching' their course and/or individual teaching sessions. Courses that often purport to be emphasizing the higher levels of these taxonomies, nevertheless, deliver material and construct assessments aimed at and eliciting significantly lower levels of attainment. Assessment systems, in particular, indicate to students at what level they should be aiming their learning and are, therefore, a useful way of encouraging students to take these levels seriously (Chapter 10).

Course content

Criteria for devising a syllabus   Exploring course objectives will inevitably involve choices concerning course content. In some cases the content will suggest specific objectives, in others objectives may indicate appropriate content. It is a close, at times almost dialectical, relationship which will vary substantially between disciplines and topics. Specifying content will always be necessary in course design, but teachers need to avoid simply thinking about content in terms of lists of topics to be covered. Emphasis also needs to be focused on the tasks the student should be able to perform which may form an essential part of their education. Table 5.2 provides an overview of the criteria that might be considered when deciding the content of a course.

Quantitative phase	Bigg's SOLO	Associated verbs	Bloom's classification	Associated verbs	Simple
	Pre-structural	Misses the point	*Knowledge*	Write; state; recall; recognize; select; reproduce; measure	
	Uni-structural	Identify; do simple procedure			
	Multi-structural	Enumerate; describe; list; combine; do algorithms	*Comprehension*	Identify; illustrate; represent; formulate; explain; contrast	
	Relational	Compare/ contrast; explain; analyse; relate; apply	*Application*	Predict; select; assess; find; show; use; construct; compute	
	Extended abstract	Theorize generalize; reflect hypothesize	*Analysis*	Select; compare; separate; differentiate; contrast; break down	
			Synthesis	Summarize; argue; relate; precis; organize; generalize; conclude	
			Evaluation	Judge; evaluate; support; confront; avoid; select; recognize; criticise	
Qualitative phase					Complex

Figure 5.3   Cognitive objectives and associated verbs

Content overload   It is worth concluding these remarks on course content with a brief note on the issue of content overload, which is, perhaps, the most significant problem confronting course design in higher education. It is at the centre of 'transmission' approaches to teaching (Chapter 3) which judges teaching by content transmitted, quality of teaching by content chosen and challenge to the student by the quantity and volume of content transmitted. Courses where student contact (transmission) time is

Table 5.2   *Criteria for choosing course content*

	Criteria
Philosophical	• Enhances intellectual development of students – not an end in itself. • Raises moral, ethical and social considerations. • Goes beyond technical matters. • Contributes to a deep and critical perspective of knowledge.
Professional	• Addresses the appropriate theoretical and practical experiences of accreditation/registration. • Addresses professional principles, values and ethics.
Learning	• Avoids overload; distinguishes 'mastery' from 'acquaintance' content. • Avoids excessive fragmentation. • Provides opportunities to develop higher-level intellectual skills in reasoning, problem-solving, critical thinking and creativity. • Addresses the development of appropriate attitudes and values.
Resource	• Draws on accessible and/or suitable alternative materials. • Is linked to relevant and available teaching resources (library, computer equipment, labs, people, patients, environments, etc.).
Student	• Reflects needs and interests of the student group. • Is matched to the intellectual and maturity level of students. • Addresses the diverse life experiences, backgrounds of the students.
Teacher	• Is appropriate to the teacher's level of knowledge and understanding. • Is interesting, engaging and ethically acceptable to the teacher.

Source: adapted from Newble and Cannon, 1989

high, and content overload is a pervasive feature, are associated with surface learning outcomes and a propensity for teachers to focus their teaching on knowledge reproduction, basic comprehension and application at the expense of the higher levels of analysis, synthesis and evaluation.

Ironically, such a focus – and the typical method of delivering it, lectures – is not even an effective way of ensuring basic comprehension and knowledge recall (Bligh, 1998). Students rarely 'know' more than a third of the content at the completion of a course and substantially less six months or a year later. Emphasis on such low-level objectives also contribute – as a department of mechanical engineering reported (Cox, 1987) – to substantial issues of demotivation. An overloaded course is experienced as mere conformist grind instead of an opportunity for challenging exploration of key issues within the subject and the development of a sense of occupational identity that is often an important issue in attracting students to the subject. One possible solution to overload is to distinguish 'mastery' content from 'acquaintance' content. What is it essential to master in order to achieve the course objectives? Making those choices and reducing course content is, however, much easier said than done. There is much truth in the saying that changing a course is rather like moving a cemetery, there are many emotional attachments even after expiry.

Course structure

Course length There is no ideal course 'length'. The 'length' of a course is typically related to bureaucratic guidelines and regulations on the length of courses, themselves constrained by trends and changes in wider academic and professional requirements. Length is also crucially related to its objectives and content. Short courses are by definition short, but depending on their overall objectives, content and location in the wider academic/professional context, they may be too long or, as is often the case, too short. 'Length' is ultimately dependent on learning. The volume of content, which a teacher covers over the length of a course, may not be related to the speed with which students can cope. In this respect, reducing the length of the course and/or class time, while extending external opportunities for study and learning through study groups, peer groups, problem/task-based activities, the use of the new technology, and so on, may extend the educational 'duration' of the course without increasing its 'length'. Such opportunities should not generally be seen as times to introduce more content but rather as opportunities for consolidation, application and higher levels of understanding – for getting the contexts and the limitations, not simply the essentials. 'Over-learning' is a useful psychological concept here, it means going on learning even when you feel you understand. We have suggested, moreover, that change is a critical aspect of learning. This generally occurs over longer periods than are required for the simple assimilation of new ideas and information.

Modularity The modularization of courses into discreet units of study has recently become a widespread feature of curriculum development. It is regarded as an effective way of providing students with more choice and flexibility in their study. It offers students increased versatility to structure their courses in combinations that interest them, at times that fit their schedules, in sequences that suit their learning and in overall time frames that are more appropriate to their lives. Although it certainly has many advantages, it also raises its own problems. Without careful consideration and guidance, modularity often leads to both intellectual and social/personal fragmentation. The integration of the different 'modules' into an overall coherent programme of study can be difficult for students, particularly with respect to making and understanding key relationships and links between the modules. Students also frequently experience a lack of continuity in developing social and personal relations as a result of constant changes in peer groups. Staff, too, may have less frequent contact with other teachers as well as a diminished sense of the rationale of the course as a whole. The opportunity to share teaching experiences more widely and discuss the concerns and understanding of students is also frequently curtailed. Some of the problems of fragmentation are difficult to solve, but modules can be designed around enabling students to integrate their understanding of the separate modules in relation to each other. Project work may provide an essential element in such integration but has not traditionally been important in this respect. Some universities use examinations for relating different modules but students can see this as being asked to do what their tutors have failed to do. Peer study and support groups may also help students to avoid some of the intellectual fragmentation as well as providing opportunities for social and personal development.

Sequencing Sequencing is closely related to modularity. It is an important principle of teaching that student learning is closely related to what they already know. This is not to suggest that sequencing is simply concerned with a simple linear addition of blocks of knowledge. From one perspective, it is crucial that modules or units of study which require previous knowledge of the subject should be sequenced after the student has had the opportunity to develop that knowledge and understanding. From another perspective, however, sequencing is concerned with achieving a more holistic approach to a subject. This concept of sequencing considers how course design might develop multiple dimensions for approaching material. In a 'spiral curriculum' approach, for example, students revisit themes and concepts which they have considered earlier but in revisiting them they come from a different perspective, developing both a facility for handling multiple conceptual frameworks but also for confronting and/or integrating them to construct new perspectives. Problem-based learning, as we have seen, reverses the usual sequence of giving information to students first and asking them to apply it to problems later. Designing interesting and engaging problems that encourage students to think and solve problems, rather than being told answers, becomes an essential part of course design. While the nature of the problem will diverge widely across disciplines, much in the way of significant teaching innovation will rest in how creative and imaginative teachers are in constructing relevant, appropriate and stimulating problems or tasks for their students.

Projects   Projects and project work provide another significant dimension to sequencing. Generally they are situated at the end of a course and in some respects this can be sensible and certainly logical. It can also mean, however, that students may go through years without working in a way which seems to be directly related to their life, the career they hope to enter or even their conception of what the course is really about. Project work can be the focus for a great deal of commitment and personal expression. If this is postponed for a long period it can result in students becoming disillusioned and failing to see the relevance of the course to some of their main concerns. Sequencing projects earlier in the course would help, but it does suggest that there should not be just one project. There should be earlier projects aimed at involving students and developing their initial learning as well as introducing the basics of managing projects. Later projects could then be more in-depth and more capable of being integrated with their earlier learning on the course.

Resources   It goes without saying that the design of courses will need to be structured and delivered within the constraints of the available resources. Table 5.3 gives some of the areas that will need to be considered. These include but are not limited to:

Table 5.3   *Course design: resource considerations*

Resources	
Staff	Academic faculty, support staff, administrative and managerial staff, visiting staff
Library	Library, media and computing facilities
Reprographic	Printing and publication facilities
Space	Classrooms, lecture theatres, laboratories, clinics, studios, field trips, etc.
Materials	Course packs, key texts, equipment
Guidelines	Course directories, handouts
Training	Computer, library, equipment, health and safety, etc.

Methods, assessment and evaluation   The teaching methods, by which the course will be taught, the assessment methods, by which the students will be assessed, and the evaluation methods, by which the course will be reviewed and improved, all play an essential role in course design. A design that did not encompass these areas would not be a design. Course objectives, course content and course structures may, for example, convey a great deal about a course to the student. How the course engages them, how it is assessed and even to some degree how it is evaluated are, however, much more revealing. They are so fundamental that we shall spend the next six chapters discussing them at some length. It is worth remembering, however, that the same considerations raised in Part 2 of this book – and drawn out in some detail through our discussion of the case study – are also at the heart of our discussion of the following genres of learning and teaching.

Conclusions

In many ways, course design is the integrating 'genre' in the language of learning and teaching. In this respect it may be regarded as a kind of 'meta-genre' in which the other 'genres' dwell. Such a perspective has the advantage of emphasizing the core feature of 'design'; its role in 'integrating' or 'aligning' (Biggs, 1999) the various aspects of learning and teaching into a comprehensive and coherent practice informed by and drawing upon a substantial body of knowledge and conceptual understanding of learning. We have suggested that a useful way of engaging practice with this body of knowledge is through the learning matrix, a conceptual tool which we shall be referring to throughout the following chapters. The following 'genres', however, dwell within course design only so to speak 'on paper'. The practice of design is not the practice of assessment nor the practice of lecturing. However intimately they are linked, these 'genres' are distinctive and can be usefully differentiated for separate consideration. Nevertheless, their mastery as a 'language' – to return to our opening quote – yields that professional 'pedagogical relationship that the educator determines for his or her curriculum' and which *is* the 'epistemic framework' at the heart of the concept of the 'reflective professional'.

Further reading

Anderson, N. and King, N. (1995) *Innovation and Change in Organization*. London: International Thomson Business Press.

Berg, B. and Ostergren, B. (1977) 'Modes for description and analysis of innovation processes' in *Innovation and Innovation Processes in Higher Education*. Stockholm: National Board of Universities and Colleges.

Biggs, J.B. (1999) *Teaching for Quality Learning at University*. London: Open University Press.

Boud, D. and Feletti, G. (1997) *The Challenge of Problem Based Learning*. London: Kogan Page.

Chopra, A.J. (1999) *Managing the People Side of Innovation: 8 Rules for Engaging Minds and Hearts*. West Hartford, CT: Kumerian Press.

Gardner, H. (1999) *Intelligence Reframed: Multiple Intelligences for the 21st*

Century. New York: Basic Books.

Kolb, D., Osland, J. and Rubin, I. (1994) *Organizational Behavior: An Experiential Approach*. New York: Prentice Hall.

Rowntree, D. (1985) *Developing Courses for Students*. London: Harper & Row.

Rowntree, D. (1994) *Preparing Materials for Open, Distance and Flexible Learning*. London: Harper & Row.

Stenhouse, L. (1975) *An Introduction to Curriculum Research and Development*. Oxford: Heinemann.

Toohey, S. (1999) *Designing Courses for Higher Education*. Buckingham: Open University Press (SRHE).

6

Lecturing: Large Group Teaching

I was in a state of panic throughout the lecture. I never looked at a face in an audience for fear it might smile, or frown or yawn. I've always lectured to the top right-hand corner of the room. I spoke very fast in order to get to the end. It was rather like crossing a narrow bridge over a causeway with lions on the right, tigers on the left. At the end of the lecture I always felt 'Now they can see through me and I'm no good'. (Isaiah Berlin, in Ingrams, 1997: 2)

Introduction

When one thinks of teaching and learning in higher education, one invariably thinks of the lecture. The lecture and lecturing is almost synonymous with what higher education is about, particularly for undergraduates. It is what higher education teachers do; indeed, in the UK, it describes the title of the profession – lecturer. Significantly, it also describes a way of human communication that would not be acceptable in most other forms of social interaction. The statement 'you are lecturing me' in almost all other social situations would not be a positive statement. It would be regarded as dehumanizing and unnatural, if not condescending and offensive. Yet, as a method of communication aimed at large groups of students (even in small groups), it thrives in higher education. The 'large group' context makes the lecture an acceptable form of addressing others, just as it makes the speech or the sermon acceptable. In addition, the 'efficiencies', which the 'large group' context is purported to provide higher education, support its continuing and increasing institutional popularity. Assuming adequate space, voice and technology, the lecture can 'teach' the student multitudes. Even as burgeoning student numbers have given the lecture this larger role in the teaching repertoire, however, it has also been increasingly and severely taken to task. Some commentators have even called for its total abandonment (Barnett, 2000: 159).

There is certainly a growing quantity of research literature supporting this educational assault on the lecture, particularly in its traditional or conventional form which Bligh describes as 'more or less continuous periods of exposition by a speaker who wants the audience to learn something' (1998: 6). In his now classic review of the extensive research literature investigating the achievement of the lecture, Bligh found that lectures are:

- no more or less effective than other methods in transmitting facts and information;
- not as effective as discussion methods in promoting thought;
- relatively ineffective for teaching values, inspiring interest in a subject or for personal and social adjustment;
- relatively ineffective for teaching skills.

In terms of the 'gap schema' presented in Chapter 4, the research evidence suggests that traditional lectures are as effective (but no more so) than discussion-based and other teaching methods in helping students reach the acquisition/recall of information stage in 'gap' 1. It is, moreover, less effective in aiding students to overcome the other gaps. Given the strength of this research it is not surprising that educational scorn has been heaped upon the lecture and questions as to its continued use raised. Biggs (1999) suggests that it does have significant advantages over both group work and books, for example, which rest in the lecturer's unique scholarly mind and integrates their role as teacher and researcher/scholar. The lecturer can bring to the lecture both their own critical perspective or 'angle' on the subject and the most recent developments which books may not have had time to provide. In this, the lecturer becomes both a facilitator for helping students transform and construct knowledge but also in the very practice of the lecturing can model that transformation for them. While these are admirable objectives for the lecture and necessary, they are not of themselves sufficient to justify the use of lectures. Such approaches and objectives can be achieved (and usually are achieved) more easily in small group teaching situations.

If lecturing is to be justified educationally it must be done in terms of the one overwhelming advantage it has over all other methods of teaching: that unique combination of incorporating both live, face-to-face contact with large-scale student numbers. The former feature, of course, is common to most teaching and learning sessions in higher education, be they seminars, tutorials, workshops, clinical work, etc. The latter feature is common to much distance and open learning where technology and media can aid in large-scale teaching projects. Only the lecture, however, combines both. If it is to be seriously justified it needs to exploit this combination. Unfortunately, this combination has been traditionally and rather feebly justified as being (a) a good way of delivering content to (b) a large number of students (c) cheaply. The first point is mainly true for the teacher as 'encoder-transmitter', much less so for the student as 'decoder-receiver'. The second and third points probably provide the main reason for the lecture's longevity, but they are not integrated with the educational issues implicit in the first point. And they do not address the critical aspect of the lecture as a method of live human contact, cost and numbers potentially achieved more effectively by new technology. Both the justification for and description of the lecture, here, are couched in the linear (or monologue) model of human communication. Lecturing is fundamentally a one-way traffic of information in which the live human quality of the situation is an historical accident soon to be taken over by technology. Understood and practised within such a model, lecturing has little educational justification. This chapter, however, looks at how the practice of lecturing might be repositioned within an intersubjective (or dialogical) model and, in doing so, take advantage of the tremendous potential of the live plus large group experience.

Being where the action is

Higher education is full of exceptional lecturers who inspire, provoke, stimulate and fuel the mind with new ideas, thoughts, feeling and the desire to learn. It is a very unfortunate student who has failed to be enthused or stirred by at least one lecture. These lecturers achieve with a wide range of styles and approaches, sometimes employing a wide range of techniques and other times captivating with the very simplicity of their methods. Most experienced lecturers will probably be able to recall at least one lecture which they gave where the combination of material, presentation, location, audience and so on seemed to come together into a wonderful shared experience of mutual learning and appreciation. Where it worked! It is possible. The problem is that these occasions are too rare and they are extremely difficult to repeat.

This quality is also the quality of lecturing which is generally regarded as somewhat mysterious and 'unknowable'. Some lecturers can inspire others cannot. It is a form of 'artistry'; something you either have or do not have, a quality of birth, so to speak, which can neither be taught nor learned. Consequently, it is often simply noted in discussions of lecturing with no serious attempt to understand it. The best that one can do for the lecturer unfortunate enough to lack such qualities is to smother him or her in a range of tips, hoping that some will stick and be of benefit to their students. It is an 'additive' approach. The lecturer remains essentially unchanged. While there are lecturers who undoubtedly take to lecturing more easily and successfully than others, it is not because they have added 'bits' to their lecturing behaviour and personality, but (whether instinctive or learned) is primarily a consequence of a different way of thinking about lecturing and 'being' a lecturer. Moreover, what is probably the case in the vast majority of occasions when 'it worked' is that the vitality of the achievement was grounded to a large degree in the situation being live, large and engaged.

The wider experience of dialogue

Being 'live' provides a wonderful opportunity for engagement and dialogue. Being 'large' gives that dialogue the potential for a tremendous sharing. This should not be underestimated nor devalued. That feeling of sharing in large numbers can provide a wonderful feeling of intellectual security and exhilaration, of being part of a broader dialogue, a higher intellectual conversation that extends substantially beyond me into an extensive and inclusive network. It is the same feeling enjoyed at huge sports events, or cultural events or festivals. It is the feeling of relevance and of 'being where the action is'. 'Being where the action is' is a feeling often most fully enjoyed in large numbers. It can be enjoyed in smaller number but normally only when such numbers enjoy the authority and support of large numbers, such as being with social, political and/or cultural celebrities. A few lecturers enjoy such status and their very presence is often enough to engender such feelings.

For students, however, the experience of 'being where the action is' may simply rest in the opportunity to participate within a 'larger' higher education community, sharing with academics and a large number of their fellow students the various aspects of a new 'academic' language and new ways of thinking. This may consist of sharing the lecturer's comments about a reading list, or indications about what is central in a particular topic, or a new use of particular terms and vocabulary, or key remarks about the assessment/examination procedures or hints about how to approach their studies in this discipline. More extraordinarily, it will include the shared experience of being on the threshold or at the entrance to a new conceptual framework, a network of new ideas and concepts along with the opportunity to explore them and test them out. In all of these the authority and weight of larger numbers can increase confidence and facility in new ways of thinking, understanding and practising. 'Being where the action is', of course, has its potential dangers. Numbers and authority can amplify confusion and insecurity, even become a form of intellectual tyranny, if badly managed, facilitated and/or directed.

All too frequently, however, lectures are neither directed nor facilitated. They are avoided. For reasons that we address below, the lecturer is often not fully engaged as a person. The result of such a lack of engagement is the opposite of the feeling of 'being where the action is'. It is the feeling of being where the action is not: of being in a remote, impersonal situation replete with the feelings of irrelevance, anonymity, insignificance and disorientation. Many students frequently realize that they can miss the lecture without missing anything of critical import. Others suffer on in the vain hope of relevance and meaningful connections, often yielding to what Carbonne (1998) refers to as 'internal noise' – those internal dialogues and mental tangents which transport them out of the lecture situation. Without a break, the maximum attention span of students in such lectures is about 10-15 minutes, after which learning drops off dramatically (Bligh, 1998). The student is, at best, in reception of 'unmediated' content in which the lecturer's personal presence is almost invisible or even unhelpful. For some students, the better students, it is just about adequate. For most students it is not, and it certainly does not justify the lecturer's presence. While necessary, content is not in itself sufficient.

The experience of relevance

In an innovative study of students' experience of the relevance of lecture content, Hodgson (1997) found that students experienced relevance in qualitatively distinct ways. For some students their experience of the relevance of the lecture content was 'intrinsic', expressed in terms of their understanding of it and the meaning it has for them personally and linked to deep learning. The experience of others, however, was 'extrinsic', expressed in terms of assessment or even in terms of a merely hoped for potential use and linked to surface learning. Her main finding, however, was of a third kind of relevance, a *vicarious* experience of relevance which she describes as a 'bridge between extrinsic experience and intrinsic experience' (ibid.: 171). This vicarious experience, moreover, is related to the lecturer, to the way they lecture, to their enthusiasm, their use of illustrations, the ways in which they engage students.

Content is, then, not the problem, it never has been. It is the use and 'context' of content that is the problem. There is nothing inherently wrong with $e = mc^2$ or the idea that Hamlet suffered from an oedipal complex or that Thatcher came to power in 1979 or the theory of evolution. Whatever one's view of them, the existence of facts, ideas, concepts and theories to talk about is not inherently problematic – challenging perhaps, but that is not the point. It is how we talk about them that is problematic. In lectures, we rarely talk in the way they first made sense to the teacher but rather in ways that often do not make sense. As the stuff of human dialogue, content reigns supreme. As the stuff of monologue it clatters on deaf ears and disengaged minds and vanishes. When this happens, the lecture as a method is blamed.

Models of lecturing

The issue here is not so much lecturing but rather, as suggested above, the way in which it is envisaged and realized. As a practice with the potential to ignite that sense of 'being where the action is', the traditional lecture needs to be re-envisaged as a dialogue in which the lecturer is genuinely engaged. Table 6.1 notes some of the characteristics of such an 'engagement' model, contrasting them with those of the more traditional 'transmission' model of lecturing. The two models closely echo the general distinctions observed with respect to both the models of communication and the conceptions of teaching described in Chapter 3. The models are divided into three categories describing how the lecture is conceived. The first category describes features of the general structure of lecturing. The second describes the character of the lecture's essential method. The third describes the nature of the lecturer. They are not meant to be mutually exclusive but rather descriptive and shall become clearer when we describe the practical aspects of lecturing.

Table 6.1   *Two models of lecturing*

Transmission	Engagement
Structure	
• Lecturing 'causes'	• Lecturing as 'by-product'
• Linear structure	• Non-linear structure
• Information	• Understanding
• Monologue	• Dialogue
Method	
• Lecturer agenda	• Learner agenda
• Transferring information	• Engaging minds
• Surface lecturing	• Deep lecturing
• Concern to get material 'out'	• Concern to get material 'in'
• Lecture as truth or opinion	• Lecture as narrative
Lecturer	
• Head and body	• Head, body and self
• Severed persona	• Engaged persona
• Cognitive focus	• Interpersonal focus
• Objective or subjective	• Human (intersubjective)

Transmission   The first model focuses on the information/material of the lecture almost exclusively. The lecturer is generally viewed as an instrument for transmitting information: head to 'carry' the material, body to physically transmit it. The approach is essentially prescriptive: improvement consists of performance techniques and tips being added to the lecturer like fiddling with the antenna and the knobs of a television set to adjust the picture, sound, colour, etc. until the quality is sufficiently loud and clear. Lecturing consists here of little more than the surface reproduction of objectively established tips and techniques to transmit the material. Its aim is to get the information 'out' clearly: to send it. The implicit assumption is 'monologic' and linear: that given the lecturer can be properly heard, lecturing causes a transfer of information (and hopefully understanding) and will be remembered on the strength of the information.

Engagement The second model focuses on the lecturer as a person committed to engaging with other people in a dialogue concerning particular material. This approach considers the lecturer/person as the pre-eminent 'instrument' for communicating to other people. It regards issues of voice, body, movement, use of technology, etc. as aspects of the lecturer's personal engagement with the audience and material in the situation. It aspires to a deep integration or transformation of both the self and the lecture material in terms of the audience (students) to which both are directed. Its aim is to engage the audience: to get the material 'in'. The view here is 'dialogic' – that lecturing (and, indeed, being 'heard') is the 'by product' of learning and understanding and will be remembered on the strength of the engagement as constitutive of the whole situation.

In the rest of this chapter, we shall look at the practical issues of lecturing in terms of moving away from reliance upon the 'transmission' model and towards the development of an 'engagement' model of lecturing.

Designing the lecture

Designing a lecture from the perspective of the above 'engagement' model is essentially a question of designing a human encounter. In this respect, it is a professional performance addressing a range of issues with respect to both external and internal conditions. By these we mean, respectively, the overall teaching and learning context and design to which the lecture is contributing and the conditions or parameters of the specific lecture(s) itself. Designing the internal aspects of the lecture needs of course to take into consideration the reasons why the lecture is being employed and what its role is within the overall learning and teaching context in which the lecture is situated. What general aims and objectives is the lecture method addressing? What contexts of meaning are appropriate and what dimensions are to be addressed? How does this relate to the other methods of teaching used, to the forms of assessment being employed, to the issues of evaluation being raised? In other words, it needs to be designed within the overall context of the course and curriculum strategies that we explored in the previous chapter, including the appropriate context and dimension of meaning.

The three primary features describing the internal conditions of the lecture are (a) the lecturer, (b) the student group to whom the lecturer is lecturing and (c) the material which the former is 'sharing' with the latter. (We shall come to the environmental situation in which the lecture is taking place in a moment.) In the traditional 'transmission' model, the commonly regarded configuration of these three features is given in Figure 6.1. It is, as suggested earlier, linear and monologic in structure, placing substantial constraints on all three features. The positions of the lecturer and the student group are essentially detached from one another. Their relationships are primarily defined with respect to the material that

Figure 6.1 Restricted lecture

is privileged to the neglect of the other two features. It is, moreover, privileged in a textual format – knowledge as written – reducing its potential with respect to both the lecturer's presentation and the students' reconstruction of it. As such, in terms of the structural matrix describing the teaching and learning environment, the conventional lecture has generally tended to focus on the intellectual context of student learning, drawing primarily on this material feature at the expense of the social, personal and practical. In addition it has primarily been constructed as a method of support to student learning, the material chosen and structured with respect to what discipline 'knowledge' students should have at the appropriate level; support, however, often that is conceived and delivered as a stream of facts, concepts, theories, etc.

The lecture does not have to be so constrained, either in terms of the roles of the student and lecturer or in terms of the structure of the learning matrix employed. In order to diminish some of these constraints the three primary features need to be reconceptualized without a centrally privileged or dominant feature. Figure 6.2 depicts the underlying structure of an engaged model of lecturing in which the material neither defines the relationship between lecturer and student, nor remains aloof to change as a result of the relationship between lecturer and student.

In the reconceptualized structure in Figure 6.2, the lecture integrates the three features equally. The relationship between the lecturer and the student group is a human relationship potentially capable of addressing a much broader range of the aspects of the matrix describing the learning situation. It will also have repercussions on the way in which the content of the material is chosen and structured. From this perspective the design of the particular lecture or series of lectures is not simply a question of designing a lecturing 'text' – determining and structuring the material to be presented – but rather designing a lecturing 'voice' or

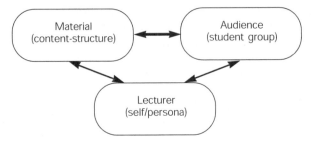

Figure 6.2 Open/Engaged Lecture

'mode of being' which integrates material, students and self. By this we do not mean the actual speaking voice but rather the way in which the individual lecturer is engaged with all the elements making up the lecturing situation. It encompasses the nature of the general learning matrix being used as well as more specific issues of lecture preparation, performance and management.

Expanding the learning matrix

As noted above, lifting the constraints on the relationship between the lecturer and the student group allows the lecture to address a much wider range of the learning matrix. Where, for example, a passive relationship almost by definition eliminated the potential for developing the social and practical dimensions of learning and commonly the personal dimension, a more active or interactive approach opens up the possibility for developing these learning dimensions. It goes beyond the few minutes for questions at the end of a lecture, providing time and a structure for students to become actively engaged throughout the lecture. The following activities illustrate the increasing range of such interaction:

- Provide time during the lecture for students to reflect upon the material presented, to digest it and begin to construct their own personal knowledge from it. This may consist simply of a few minutes out for reflection. It might be focused around a question posed by the teacher verbally or on a transparency such as: 'What is the main point of the lecture so far?'
- Provide time for students to share the main ideas and points of that part of the lecture with a neighbour. Again, this may be focused around a question or even a problem they address together. They may be asked to think of a pertinent question for the teacher or the class. They may, moreover, be encouraged to keep the same partners from lecture to lecture and share out of class as well.
- Provide time for students to form small groups of four to six people in which to take the material raised in the lecture further. This may range from a free-flowing discussion to a set task or problem that they address together. Groups may be asked to elect a chair/spokesperson to feedback questions, points and concerns raised by the group to the teacher and/or to the main group plenary. Such groups may also be asked to work together outside the lecture.

These activities for encouraging interaction can, of course, be used separately or together, one leading to another in a 'snowball' fashion. They may be used several times during the lecture depending on time and can be effectively linked to a series of pre-readings as well as the lecture material. Students need some preparation in the acceptance and development of such interactive techniques. Teachers need to develop and practice their own practical and creative skills in initiating them and managing them within the constraints of the lecture hall. They can be extremely effective and successful for even very large groups of students in a wide range of spatial configurations.

Managed well, it offers opportunities for students to develop the social dimensions of learning with others and opens up the potential and time for practical learning in the form of task- or problem-focused group work. In addition, it goes a long way towards addressing key problems associated with traditional lecturing, chief among those the student's lack of engagement with the situation and material and the distracting internal dialogues ('internal noise') disrupting their concentration and attention. It permits the development of focused and pertinent dialogue, dialogues which, moreover, can be internalized and developed into active and constructive approaches to the content and material. In this respect interactive techniques of lecturing encourage the development of the 'double-arrow' nature of the relationship between the lecturer and student group in Figure 6.2 above, extending its dynamic and potential. Such techniques, moreover, also sanction the personal dimension of learning and at the same time extend the relationship between 'student' and 'material' in Figure 6.2. In providing the space for students to contribute their own personal material to the lecture situation, material from their readings, personal experience, reflections in the form of ideas, concepts, illustrations and so forth, the interactive lecture is able to enrich the material/content aspect of the lecture immensely.

While the lecture is generally regarded as primarily a method for supporting student learning, the open/engaged model permits the possibility of developing the lecture as more of a process for facilitating an interpersonal context of learning. Here, interactive learning techniques are extended to overall leadership of the lecturing session. Individual groups of students or the whole group itself may be given the authority and role of deciding the content/material, the objectives and the learning methods of particular lecture sessions or even series of lectures. Structured guidelines for such student-led sessions and training in their operation may be necessary but they have been found to result in wider ranging discussions and more complex learning outcomes (Tang, 1998; McKeachie et al., 1986). Lectures might also be used to encourage the development of such peer-run groups outside the classroom.

The lecture, moreover, need not confine itself to supporting learning or facilitating interpersonal learning. Lectures or substantial parts of lectures might be designed to encourage independent learning. This does not simply mean devising innovative methods for interactive group work. It requires methods by which they are encouraged to develop independent curriculum in certain topics, with guidelines and strategies for self-direction in their out of class reading, use of the library, exploration of computer-mediated resources, electronic bulletin boards and so forth. It may include – particularly for more mature students and part-time students

– sessions that encourage critical self-exploration of appropriate social, cultural and work-related activities. Each provides potential access to the range of intellectual, personal, social and practical aspects of their learning.

The context and dimensions of student learning are here intrinsic to the lecture, guiding the development and complexion of the matrix on which the lecturer will develop their design. How that matrix is structured will ultimately depend on the overall course matrix (Chapter 5) and include subject matter, the level and experience of the student group, the learning objectives for the lecture sessions, the other teaching and learning activities and methods, and so forth. It will also have significant implications for preparing the lecture, its performance and management.

Lecturing preparation and performance

Preparing for a lecture is both more important and more multifaceted than is often imagined, particularly if one is preparing an 'open/engaged' lecture. All too frequently lecturers have regarded themselves primarily as the writer of a lecture and sometimes, albeit reluctantly, as an actor delivering the lines. In truth, they are writer, actor, director and producer, responsible for all aspects of performance and its preparation. The main function of these roles is to ensure that the key links between the lecturer, the students and the material shared between them are integrated, aligned and working together. In this respect, preparation should focus on the development and relationship between six key areas (see Figure 6.3).

The arrow in Figure 6.3 suggests that decisions and consequent links will tend to go from left to right although this is not strict. There is typically a recursive aspect to preparation which entails a back and forth movement across the features. Limits and constraints in the resources and space available will have repercussions on what can be effectively accomplished. Generally, however, it is useful to decide on the shape of the learning 'matrix' which the lecturer wishes to address and then design the specific objectives and content/structure for the lecture in light of that shape. Much of this part of the preparation may already have been undertaken in the overall course design (see Chapter 5). The precise teaching and learning activities that the lecture will employ, the nature of the resources used and the personal style or approach which the lecturer adopts will, ideally, be 'composed' to realize these objectives.

Matrix shape	Lecture objectives	Content & structure	Teaching & learning activities	Resources space & technology	Self-persona

Figure 6.3 Key areas of preparation

Lecture matrix and objectives

In designing the shape of the lecture matrix, one has to be realistic and take into consideration the overall shape of the course matrix and associated objectives (Chapter 5). While the lecture can address more issues of learning than generally acknowledged, it cannot achieve everything. Nor should it be expected to do so. Within these parameters specific objectives should be realistic and achievable for the students, and may even be negotiated with them.

Content and structure

The main question here concerns the relationship between the specific content of the lecture – which needs to relate coherently with the overall general topic/subject of the course or lecture series – and the structure of its presentation. Lecturers routinely take a linear and/or textual approach to the structuring of lecture content, an approach often derived from their own experience, from the textual nature of their own engagement with the material and from not reflecting on the alternatives. Lectures, however, are primarily an oral experience providing the opportunity for a range of more non-linear structures. Table 6.2 presents just a few options which lecturers may wish to consider.

Table 6.2   *Lecture structures*

---

1   Traditional – linear
2   Problem oriented
3   Comparisons
4   Thesis
5   Sequence – development
6   Network
7   Concept map
8   Case studies

These alternatives illustrate just a few possibilities for approaching material in ways designed to facilitate student learning. They include helping students make connections, challenge preconceptions, relate the material to concrete problems and/or real cases and critically analyse hypotheses and interpretations. They can also aid students to develop higher level conceptual tools – models, maps and networks – for exploring and developing ideas, concepts, facts, skills, attitudes, personal and social interactions, and so on. Choice of structure will, crucially, include how the material is introduced and concluded, be that with a problem, an illustration, a quote, an object, a picture or even with an explanation of an unfamiliar structure itself; all of which might be used as introductions or conclusions.

Teaching and learning activities

Opening up the possible lecture structures that can be used also opens up the range of teaching and learning activities, as indicated above (see also Chapter 5), which may be employed. Ideally, the structure and activities will be developed together, complementing one another. A problem-oriented structure may, for example, begin with a demonstration: concept maps with group discussion, case studies with role-play, and so on. The design of this relationship between lecture structures and activities provides the key location for creativity and innovation in lecturing. Even given the usual academic constraints of what is 'permissible' as well as those of space, time, resources and so forth, the permutations and possibilities available to the lecturer are limited primarily by their imagination and confidence.

Resources, space and technology

Preparing for the lecture also requires an imaginative examination of the technological resources available and their integration with the lecture structure and specific activities. In the first instance, this might entail what the space will look like for both lecturers and student group. Lecturers exist in three dimensions but often stand or sit in a one-dimensional spot and deliver in a straight line out to a student body. What possibilities exist for movement: both among students and in front of them? Can they be developed? Can the students easily move or slide into groups? Has the lecturer positioned him or herself in front of a lectern or next to an overhead projector so that movement is inadvertently (or even intentionally) limited? Is he or she maximizing the potential of the space?

What resources are available: overhead projectors, slide projectors, Powerpoint equipment, video equipment, laboratory apparatus, pictures, maps, objects, whiteboards, blackboards, flip charts? Are they familiar with and able to use the equipment? Can it be configured in ways that will help, not hinder the lecture? Can personal resources augment available resources? These questions need to be carefully addressed and integrated within the overall preparation. How, what, when and where might resources be effectively exploited? It is not a good idea to become overly complex and technical just for the sake of it but, on the other hand, it is unwise to avoid using resources that may add significantly to the lecture out of fear, unfamiliarity or lack of skill in their use. Good preparation will include becoming skilled and innovative in the use and deployment of relevant and appropriate space and resources, ranging from ensuring that slides and transparencies are interesting and easily read, to 'reconstructing' the space to encourage movement, interaction and alternative learning activities.

One useful way of preparing for a lecture is to write out a lecture script. Figure 6.4 gives a simple example setting time guidelines against content and structures, teaching and learning activities and resources to be used. Such scripts provide a guide to making effective relationships between these areas and permit the lecturer a quick guide/summary of what they are doing. They may be drawn up in a variety of different ways, experimented with, expanded, condensed and could even provide a useful resource for students.

Time	Content & structure	Teaching & learning activities	Resources, space & technology
0–10 mins			
10–30 mins			
30–50 mins			
50–75 mins			
75–90 mins			

Figure 6.4   Lecture script

Self-persona

So far, we have primarily been discussing the lecturer in their role as the writer, director and producer of the lecture. Lecturers, of course, have a critical role as actor or performer – a role often neglected to the detriment of both themselves and their students. The area most often neglected is what might be called their inner self or persona. The lecturer's intellect is called upon, as too is their physical presence, but their inner self often is not. This is understandable and underpins the general performance dilemma that Isaiah Berlin describes as being 'in a state of panic throughout the lecture. I never looked at a face in an audience for fear it might smile, or frown or yawn'. Box 6.1 describes an embellished version of this dilemma.

This, of course, is an exaggerated version of the lecturer's worst nightmare. The solution is rather simple, if requiring some practice and preparation to implement. Bring yourself into the lecture! More accurately, do not let yourself depart. Maintaining a lecturing self or persona in per-

---

Box 6.1 *Lecturing performance: The dilemma*

Nervous and anxious, the inner self does not actually enter fully into the situation. It leaves the self's presence up to its intellect and body. This is the key problem. Without a self to regulate it, nerves get in. There is an empty 'place' for them to inhabit. From this position, they begin to manipulate the situation rather mischievously. They begin to play with the voice: too high, too fast, too breathy, too laboured. They begin to play with the hands: in the pocket, by your side, behind your back, crossed arms, etc. They begin to play with movement: pacing repetitively, entirely static, back to audience, shuffling, rocking, etc. They begin to play with eyes: not looking at anyone; skidding away; looking over top; trapped on one person. They begin playing with time: too fast, too slow and with objects. They fiddle with pens, combs, paper, glasses, watches, and rings. They play with machines: switches do not work, slides and transparencies appear upside down, and screens wobble. They begin playing with the space: tables, chairs and lecterns suddenly surround and constrain or, alternatively, look miles away; the floor is a menacing void. Not content to simply play with these aspects of the lecturer's actual performance, nerves then rather maliciously begin to make the lecturer hyper conscious of what is happening setting off a debilitating succession of feelings of panic, fright, alarm, dread, frenzy, terror and hysteria. The intellect all but collapses and the body all but freezes. The tiny fragment of the self that may have been there has long ago fled.

---

formance is the key to developing a lecturing 'voice' and the secret to cultivating an encounter 'where the action is'. It requires the lecturer to decide the kind of person they wish to be for the lecture. This should not be something counterfeit or insincere but, rather, should be informed by positive and appropriate aspects of the lecturer's personality and extended for the engagement with students. It might, for example, consist of being:

- open and friendly;
- expert and authoritative;
- emotive and enthusiastic;
- relaxed and dry;
- reflective and analytical;
- unpredictable and challenging.

Such selves or personae are best tailored to particular times and audiences. A matrix shape concerned with support for example may be open and friendly whereas a matrix shape focusing on encouraging independence might be more analytical and dry. They are, of course, not mutually exclusive. Such selves should normally also incorporate a willingness to enjoy oneself within the central concern to engage students. Preparing the self adequately, moreover, usually requires a degree of 'rehearsing' with the material, space and resources, particularly if they are unfamiliar. Even two or three minutes spent preparing both the lecturing self and the space can be immensely effective. Finally, it is worth remembering that a lecture is not a monologue starting from nowhere but rather a dialogue responding to a tangible comment or question or expression of interest evidenced by the very presence of the student group. The nature of that interest is precisely that which the lecture is addressing and is embodied in the lecture's objectives. Preparation, however elaborate, is then preparation for a response. The degree to which one prepares will depend on the lecturer, the lecturing style he or she develops, the environment and so forth, but providing time for preparation can make all the difference to both the students' and the lecturer's learning.

Delivering and managing the lecture

Lecturing 'tips'?

How the lecturer delivers his or her lecture will depend largely on how the above issues have been developed and prepared. The idea of an 'engaged' encounter focused on dialogue and student learning addresses a wide range of key delivery issues often provided as communication 'tips' in a rather 'additive' way. These include:

- taking care that you can be heard by everyone;
- making eye contact with the whole student group;
- ensuring that your visual aids and handouts are clear;
- using humour, anecdotes, illustrations;
- stressing important points;
- being prepared to be flexible and change/add/delete aspects of the lecture.

Such general 'tips' are important but must make sense to the lecturer and not be slavishly implemented for reasons the lecturer is not sure about. All of the above points are largely common sense and, in each case, their effective use is a result of an 'engaged' lecture. If, for example, a lecturer genuinely wants to engage and communicate with his or her students he or she will naturally want to find ways to ensure his or her voice is heard (using microphones if necessary), to make eye contact and stress the important points. This is not simply a question of raising one's voice to the minimum required of a monologue or staring at students or underlining points for the sake of it. Similarly, the design and clarity of visual aids and handouts is to enable engagement not simply clarity itself. Humour, anecdotes and illustrations, moreover, may be prearranged but their use is most effective when it arises naturally and is not merely inserted for the sake of it. Be prepared not to use them or to use others where appropriate. Likewise, be willing to ad lib – to change, delete and add material – if this encourages engagement between lecturer, students and material. Lecturing tips and communication advice should not be simply add-ons followed for the sake of it but, rather, integrated within the lecturing 'voice' or 'way of being' and practised only in so far as they promote engagement and learning.

Management styles

If the range of 'lecturing voices' behind the delivery of lectures is broad and diverse, there is also considerably latitude in the general management styles employed in lectures. They range from the complete 'laissez-faire' to seeing the classroom as the 'sacred temple of learning' (Carbonne, 1998: 77–8) with many shades in between. They each have their respective responses to such issues as attendance: arriving late/leaving early, reading the newspaper at the back, side talking and so on. Some lecturers will accept just about anything, others will accept very little. There is no right or wrong as such. What is appropriate when and where will be a decision for individual lecturers but should develop from the relationship between their lecturing self, the nature of the student group and the material. Behaviour which is disruptive to other students or offensive for a range of social and equity reasons will need to be addressed. It is unlikely that one set of 'rules' will be appropriate for all situations. The key issue will be the effect of the behaviour on the quality of the engagement and student learning and this may, in many cases, be effectively shared and negotiated with the student group.

Evaluation

Finally, developing and improving one's lecturing is an ongoing process. Moreover, in so far as it is so to speak a 'public' practice, it allows for feedback from a variety of sources other than one's own reflections and judgements (see Chapter 11). These will primarily consist of colleagues and students and may include the use of student evaluations, peer observations, video recordings and so on. Evaluations and feedback will provide a wealth of data and useful comments, information and suggestions. Reflecting and implementing the results of this feedback needs, again, to be considered within the context of the full scope of lecturing as a process of engagement. A small number of teachers will, for various reasons, be unable to develop lecturing approaches in which they are engaged with their material and their students. These teachers should, if at all possible, look to alternative methods of teaching.

Further reading

Bakhtar, M. and Brown, G. (1988) 'Styles of lecturing: a study and its implications', *Research Papers in Education*, 3 (2): 131–53.

Barnett, R. (2000) *Realizing the University*. Buckingham: SRHE/Open University Press.

Biggs, J.B. (1999) *Teaching for Quality Learning at University*. London: Open University Press.

Bligh, D. (1998) *What's the Use of Lectures?* Exeter: Intellect Press.

Brown, G. and Atkins, M. (1988) *Effective Teaching in Higher Education*. London: Methuen.

Carbonne, E. (1998) *Teaching Large Classes: Tools and Strategies*. London: Sage.

Cryer, P. and Elton, E. (1992) *Active Learning in Large Classes and with Increasing Student Numbers*. Sheffield: CVCP Staff Development and Training Unit.

Gibbs, G. and Jenkins, A. (eds) (1992) *Teaching Large Classes in Higher Education*. London: Kogan Page.

Goodlad, S. (1996) *Speaking Technically: A Handbook for Scientists, Engineers and Physicians on How to Improve Technical Presentations*. London: Imperial College Press.

Habeshaw, S., Habeshaw, T. and Gibbs, G. (1984) *53 Interesting Things to Do in Your Lectures*. Bristol: Technical & Educational Services.

Hodgson, V. (1997) 'Lectures and the experience of relevance' in F. Marton, D. Hounsell and N. Entwistle (eds), *The Experience of Learning*. Edinburgh: Scottish Academic Press.

McKeachie, W., Pintrich, P., Lin, Y-G. and Smith, D. (1986) *Teaching and Learning in the College Classroom*. Ann Arbor, MI. University of Michigan, Office of Educational Research and Improvement.

Tang, C. (1998) 'Effects of collaborative learning on the quality of assessments', in B. Dart and G. Boulton-Lewis (eds), *Teaching and Learning in Higher Education*. Camberwell: Australian Council for Educational Research.

7

Facilitating: Small Group Teaching

Of a good leader when his task is finished, his goal achieved, they say, we did that ourselves. (Lao-tse, *c.* 600 BC)

Introduction

This often quoted example of wisdom of the past resonates with many contemporary ideas in teaching in higher education. We discussed in Chapter 5 the importance of innovation theory in course design, and a key aspect of this is encouraging participants' sense of ownership. Linked into this is the view that learning is considered much more a process of change rather than one of assimilation. In other words learning is innovation. In the new millennium, however, we are sensitive to certain undertones of manipulation in the quotation. Are we setting up students to do what we want them to do rather than developing in them a strong sense of responsibility for their own learning and the feeling that their programmes are a joint venture with their teachers rather than an imposition by them? The reality, however, is that we have to be sensitive to our own tendencies to lecture, or transmit in group work, a process which hardly enables them to feel that they did it themselves.

The opportunity to come together in small groups to change conceptions and explore theories and insights provides students with one of the most important learning experiences higher education has to offer. Traditionally this has been considered one of the most central and historic functions. Certainly the Hale (1964) report indicating that there is a strong student demand for teaching through tutorials and seminars still appears to be true (Bligh, 2000). If anything, students have become more interested in learning in small groups. Not all students are, however, happy with the experience. It is a demanding form of teaching where lack of skill can mean that it is not merely done badly but that it is not done it all! Students either do not attend the class or it is transformed into a lecture.

'Classes are purgatory for staff and purgatory for us. They're boring because everyone just sits there and everyone else's silent and I feel it's incumbent on me to speak but I don't like to unless I am sure of myself. I don't like to express half-formed ideas' (UTMU, 1976, Cox: 40). We might say that expressing half-formed ideas to develop in dialogue with others is an important part of the whole process. There could be some timid students who find this difficult but in fact this particular quote is from a strong student. She had done Voluntary Service Overseas (VSO) work abroad, was president of the students' union and later gained a first class degree. Such problems are not uncommon. Teachers experience a wide range of them. They involve such issues as domination, lack of trust, hidden agendas and private aims that can subvert what the group is trying to do. They also include distractions that may be much more than a healthy form of testing out and/or 'scapegoating', which can not only ruin the atmosphere of a group but also prevent any understanding of the underlying problems (Douglas, 1991).

In this chapter we shall first explore some of these general problems and issues and consider the roles and purposes of group work. Then we shall give the practical dimension in terms of how they apply to the different areas of the matrix and what might be done to improve teaching in these areas.

Unfortunately reading some useful advice, even if it is fully understood, does not easily solve problems with groups. Changing behaviour in this context involves some deeper assumptions, expectations and, even, values that do not change easily through acquiring a little extra knowledge. A serious difficulty is the discrepancy between expectations and what actually happens. Usually when we come together in groups, as distinct from crowds or audiences for instance, we do so either to seek pleasure in other people's company, in a pub or at a party for example, or because we need to join together to do something or to produce something. Learning within groups, although it can prove to be productive and satisfying, often does not clearly intend either and can become highly threatening to the participants. The resulting experience is both emotionally unsatisfying and unproductive. Where a group is really nothing more than a collection of individual learners, some learning may take place, but the expectation in small groups is that there will be a sense of belonging and enjoyment, and sharing of ideas and experience. If individuals feel that they have not actually contributed something to the group, they are likely to feel a sense of frustration.

Purposes

Figure 7.1 presents some of the very purposes of group work. There is a great deal of skill and determination needed to see they are achieved. In lectures, we may notice the subtle (and not so subtle) indicators that students are not learning well or enjoying the experience, but with group work the difficulties tend to be much more obvious and urgent.

Some staff may feel that the emotional welfare of their students really

Intellectual	Personal
• Cognitive understanding • Appreciating other perceptions, points of view • Changing conceptions • Questioning assumptions • Developing oral skills • Feedback to staff	• Providing opportunities for practice in self-expression • Developing self-awareness Encouraging autonomy • Encouraging commitment • Weakening defensive attitudes • Improving attitudes to the subject
Social	Practical

• Encouraging co-operation and a awareness of others
• Developing a sense of social identity
• Developing a sense of belonging and community
	• Develop teamwork skills
	• Solve practical problems
	• Carry out specific tasks:
	  • Create artefacts or designs
	  • Write reports
	  • Collect samples
	  • Describe environments

Figure 7.1   Some purposes of group discussion

does not have much to do with their small-group teaching. The essential purpose they say is to make sure that students have really understood what they have been trying to get across in lectures. Careful questioning, they argue, can bring out the major misunderstandings and difficulties and many of these can be dealt with by the teacher in a way in which he or she can be sure that the students have really understood. Under the extreme pressures often felt both by students and staff to cover the ground effectively, such a view of the main purpose of group work is understandable. Although if this purpose is pursued vigorously it may mean that other purposes will not merely be ignored but will be actively discouraged. Strategies which may produce effective learning within the highly structured formal education system can leave students with little ability, or even desire, to cope with learning and relearning when they leave the formal supportive structures of higher education behind them. Nevertheless, at work there will be structures of a different kind. Many professionals, for example, now find themselves working in teams and an important function of group work in higher education is to enable students to know enough about themselves and about others to enable them to work independently and yet co-operatively within a team. Such teams may or may not have formal leaders. The style of leadership, however, is likely to be very different from that of the more traditional seminar leader who controls the activity of the class in such a way that students learn to feel little responsibility for what happens in the group beyond doing required background reading.

The group experience can, in fact, be extremely important in achieving freedom from dependency if the students learn to play a variety of roles in the group and begin to develop a sense of responsibility for its success or failure. In the process of learning these roles they will need to develop more acute self-understanding, to become aware of their own inhibitions, defences and assumptions, and be able to recognize the difficulties which other students experience and begin to help them to overcome these difficulties. In learning to become more sensitive to different points of view and ways of thinking and to work co-operatively with others using the varied skills of the group, they may begin to develop a surer sense of social identity and a feeling of belonging and commitment. This can not only encourage enthusiasm in the subject but a willingness to reveal abilities, which are frequently hidden, even from themselves. Students' oral skills, moreover, are unlikely to develop very highly simply in response to probing questions.

There needs to be a genuine sense of opportunity for self-expression and this may be very difficult in a context where the main object is to increase understanding and correct misconceptions and faulty reasoning. Such a restricted conception might limit other important uses of small-group work such as enabling staff to understand more about how students respond generally to their educational experience. Most staff would agree that it is important for them to know why their students are taking their courses, and what sort of deeper satisfaction and disappointments they are experiencing. This will be very dependent on the quality of the personal relationships established with the students but, if the roles played by the students and staff in their group work are highly restricted, it may be difficult for good personal relationships to develop.

Roles

The traditional role of the teacher is that of a leader or instructor where he or she may initiate proceedings with a short statement or summary and then try to draw out students' thoughts, periodically linking them together and redirecting the content of the discussion as appropriate. Dependency problems can arise out of this and an increasingly popular term for the role now is 'facilitator' (Brockbank and McGill, 1998) which suggests encouraging interaction without dominating the group. Other roles might include 'devil's advocate', 'chairperson', 'consultant' and 'counsellor', the latter indicating a concern for the social and emotional needs of students. In addition, the teacher may sometimes need to be an observer or commentator, at other times, if the group is divided into subgroups, even a 'wandering minstrel'.

A useful role in times of stress for staff is that of absent friend! These varying roles are suggestive of a range of teaching behaviours or strategies which teachers/facilitators might display in small-group work.

Figure 7.2 presents such behaviours in terms of Heron's 'six category intervention analysis' (Heron, 1976; 1981). These may be arranged along polar axes from teacher-centred behaviours in which the teacher informs and tightly prescribes and directs the discussion to more student-centred behaviours where the teacher uses discussion to elicit and support students in the development of their own knowledge and contributions. The significance and importance of 'ritualizing', which often takes the form

Inform

The teacher can:	Related verbal behaviours
PRESCRIBE	Provide a topic/raise an issue; re-route the discussion.
INFORM	Summarize/interrelate/clarify; give knowledge and information.
CONFRONT	Challenge by direct question; disagree with/correct/critically evaluate student statement.
RELEASE TENSION	Arouse laughter.
ELICIT	Draw out student opinion/knowledge/problem solving; facilitate student interaction.
SUPPORT	Approve/reinforce/agree with/affirm the value of student contributions.

Elicit

Teacher-centred

Student-centred

Figure 7.2   Teaching behaviours in groups (adapted from Heron, 1976: 1989)

of predictable greetings indicating mutual acceptance, etc. has been highlighted and Bligh (2000) suggests that the omission of these latter behaviours in discussion groups can contribute to the persistence of interpersonal barriers. Another important role/behaviour which teachers can use is 'imagining', an essential activity for creativity and criticism which is often restricted in academic work.

Leadership

Student roles have frequently been described in general terms that look something like personality characteristics: the 'friendly helper', the 'tough battler' and the 'logical thinker'. Their respective worlds might be described as mutual love, affection, tenderness and sympathy; conflict-flight, assertiveness; and understanding, logic, knowledge and systems. They will have different task-maintenance behaviours, different ways of evaluating others and different methods of influence and suffer from different personal threats (Kolb et al., 1984). Many student roles will, in this respect, be dependent upon the leadership styles that teachers adopt, so it is especially important for teachers to recognize the different leadership styles they might effectively employ. They need also to recognize that they are not limited to any particular styles but may use a range when and where appropriate. In a now classic study (Lippet and White, 1961), for example, teachers were asked to run groups by employing three very different leadership styles – autocratic, democratic and laissez-faire. Each teacher was asked to run these groups each employing the three styles so that the focus was not on teacher personality but was, rather, one of leadership. The teachers, it was found, were each capable of operating very effectively in the three styles. In this respect, student ratings often offer detailed analyses of behaviour within groups (see Chapter 11 on evaluation) which can be very helpful in enabling both students and teachers to learn more about their behaviour within groups.

The styles of leadership, which a teacher might employ, are closely related to the kinds of teacher roles and behaviours described in the previous section. Combinations of supportive and directive behaviour can indicate to a teacher a general style they may wish to employ within group work or at different stages of group work. Figure 7.3 suggests the different configurations.

Phases in groups

It can be important for teachers to realize that groups like people have life stages. Some group behaviour can be very worrying for a teacher unless they realize it is normal for it to be happening at various phases or stages. There is considerable agreement on how to describe these phases with some interesting differences (Jaques, 1991: 38–9). Smith (1980), for example, describes these phases as: (1) testing dependence, (2) intra-group hostility, (3) group cohesion/co-operation, (4) functional role relatedness and (5) mourning. Rowan (1976) has a more memorable classification: forming, storming, performing and mourning. Bramley (1977) describes them as dependent, rebellious, co-operative and mourning. The mourning phase is sometimes described as encompassing a number of possible reactions to the groups end: regression, denial and avoidance. While groups may intend to work towards more co-operative and functional way of operating, they can get a fouled up on the way. They may even break up if the hostility, storming or rebellious phase is too dominant. Some groups do not experience storming or a great deal of hostility, but it certainly seems to be the case that there is an important time

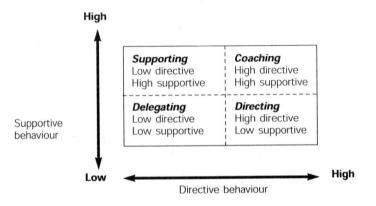

Figure 7.3 Group Leadership Styles

of greater emotion which may come about a quarter of the way through the expected life of the group. With a group which is together over a long period, this might come much nearer the beginning. On a course for general practitioners, which lasted for a week, for example, we found that on the second or third day participants were more emotional. The course leaders capitalized on this by introducing the more emotional-oriented learning activities of the course – such as role-play and dealing with patient hostility or bereavement – at this time. While it did result in some very emotional interactions and even tears, the activities would not have been so engaging and useful in the learning process if they had come on the first day or even on the last.

It is important that the earlier dependency phases are not prolonged. It is also important that the opening phase, where it appears to be necessary to give a great deal more direction, does not set a pattern for the rest of the life of the group. Expecting students to be independent when they are uncertain both about themselves and the group might create serious difficulties. On the other hand when a teacher is very directive at the beginning this can be a learning phase for the group indicating that their role is to sit and listen. Setting ground rules for the group at the beginning may be particularly important where there is a danger that students might develop the wrong expectations about how they should proceed and behave.

Ground rules

If the ground rules are neither written nor discussed, students are likely to imagine their own. They may, for example, begin by assuming that they should leave it to the teacher to fully lead, direct and summarize the discussion; that it is the teacher's job to determine the objectives and procedures; that one should not express one's feelings openly; that one should not interrupt someone making a presentation; that a period of silent reading for the whole group is inappropriate and, even, that breaking into smaller groups or writing is disruptive. Ground rules, which are simply imposed, on the other hand, may have little influence on group behaviour. If the group has a relatively long life, working them out with the students can be helpful and can encourage commitment. They might be less inclined to endure 'purgatory' and feel they have responsibility for modifying rules and developing them during the life of the group. Sometimes individual students may become overly preoccupied with their own behaviour and the group processes, which can distract them from the main group activities. This will need to be carefully considered by the teacher. On the other hand, where it is of particular interest for the group to understand better how groups function, learning from direct experience of the group can be much more effective than being told about it or simply working it out intellectually.

This introduction has briefly raised a number of key general points about group teaching. In the following discussion these will be developed further – in terms of the learning matrix – in order to consider in more detail how different approaches can be related to the different purposes of working in groups.

The intellectual dimension
Providing support

We have suggested that groups primarily concerned with covering the ground, increasing understanding and correcting misconceptions and faulty reasoning may well limit other important uses of small group work. This is important since working in small groups is not the best way of covering the ground in terms of basic knowledge but this does not mean that supporting students intellectually plays no part. Exploring and understanding student problems in coping with difficult parts of the course is difficult in large groups. Although there is feedback in the form of written assignments, small groups offer teachers an opportunity to learn more why students may be having the problems and how they might help solve them.

The first of our intellectual purposes might be approached through essentially supportive teaching, selecting tasks for the appropriate level and exploring where students have misconceptions which prevent them from progressing. We suggested, however, that if this is the dominant pattern it might result in intellectual dependency and a failure to develop as creative, independent learners and productive team members. Teachers can be quite directive in terms of group processes and enabling students to understand these, however, without telling students what to think or doing their work for them. Criteria can be clarified and resources indicated in a way to support their independent and interpersonal learning.

We suggested in Chapter 5 that prior reading could be a very important way of covering the content without wasting the learning potential of interacting in small groups. In many disciplines lecturers have expanded their lecture notes to cover the content and used lecturing time for groups to solve problems associated with these notes. Other groups and the lecturer can look at the strengths and weaknesses of the solutions and so generate the active learning that is the justification for being together rather than learning independently with the help of today's more sophisticated resources.

Encouraging independence

Traditionally, small-group teaching in Britain has been designed to enable the student to 'think for himself (*sic*) and work on his own' (Hale, 1964: iii). But in the new millennium not only would the issue of gender be treated more sensitively, co-operation and teamwork are given a great deal more prominence. There may have been an encouragement for students to talk but this was mainly in terms of expressing their ideas and responding to probing and often challenging questions from the teacher. It was not seen particularly as the time for students to talk to each other nor develop a sense of responsibility for the group nor for producing group reports. Scholarly criticism was very much to the fore but only in the sense that the teacher would model it and encourage students to respond constructively. Generally the teacher or a student would initiate group work and this would be followed by general discussion. Very occasionally a debate between two students might be initiated but a simple structure of introduction and discussion was the general rule. The role of the teacher was not merely to have modelled scholarly activity and challenge ideas but included making sure that one or two students did not dominate the discussion and that more students had an opportunity for self-expression. The focus was on understanding and in the sciences on solving particular problems.

In this context, a wider range of techniques is used to ensure that alternative perspectives arise and students learn to evaluate these without the assumption that they will thereby find the right answer. But fear is still an important characteristic of much group work: 'people ask questions and this stimulates the group. I feel we don't mind if the friend asks a question but if a lecturer asked you'd dry up . . . The member of staff will always have the answer at his fingertips and I've always resented making an idiot of myself' (UTMU, 1976, Cox: 45). We are now realizing that changing the size of groups can be one of the best ways to encourage independent expression. An interesting but still not very common way of achieving this is by progressive doubling or pyramiding or snowballing. This is where a problem or task is introduced and before entering into any discussion individuals jot down their own thoughts. These are not then opened for general discussion but only to pairs where quieter students are able to talk more easily. This is followed by two pairs joining up so that still the groups are only four. The ideas of individual students then are more likely to be followed through on their merits rather than through personality and domination. Students can gradually be introduced to alternative ideas and have the ability to compare them with their own and perhaps see a gradual development of these within the group. The change process, which we have emphasized in earlier chapters, can become a real practical possibility.

Such activities can, in addition, address the concern that academic interaction is frequently conducted in an adversarial style, in which ideas are perceived as being in perpetual competition. De Bono (1994), for example, criticizes this style of academic interaction and the overly critical ways of thinking it often inspires. He points out that this style does not always allow us to arrive at the best of different perspectives and suggests that discussion will be enhanced by engaging in processes of 'parallel' thinking, keeping open a range of parallel ideas and drawing from them. The progressive doubling structure is also particularly help-ful in creating a more personal and co-operative atmosphere and so enabling us to integrate ideas into a wider understanding rather than only progressing by eliminating the apparently weaker ideas. It is often effective to put the ideas of the four or sometimes eight onto flip charts and spend part of the session trying to understand these different solu-tions and integrate them into a richer and more complex approach. This process can not only allow time for ideas to be developed but enable them to be consolidated into new ways of thinking.

A somewhat less developmental way of introducing independent thinking is to ask for a 'round' where the teacher goes around the group encouraging students to express their ideas and comments individually. This can be threatening unless it is made clear that there is no obligation on the students to say something every time. They may simply pass which is, generally speaking, completely acceptable. Both 'progressive doubling' and 'rounds' are useful methods of enabling quieter students, especially students whose first language is not English, to contribute. They can offset the limitation of otherwise stimulating and lively dis-cussions in which there are often no pauses between contributions which, again, can be particularly difficult for those students who are less assertive or less sure of their own linguistic and intellectual abilities.

Developing the interpersonal

Encouraging interdependence can still be focused on ideas and the intel-lect. Enabling students to interact within groups of different sizes is important both for intellectual expression and for learning to appreciate the way people can interact and collaborate productively. Figure 7.4 illus-trates how participation might be much more a function of a group's size than of personality.

Bales's work with leaderless groups indicates that while the distribu-tion of talk in a group of three is not shared equally, it is not particularly wide. This distribution remains similar in a group of four but above that number the gap between the most talkative and the next most talkative begins to grow until, even with relatively small groups of eight, there is a long tail of participants whose participation is very small. The dynam-ics of this finding are addressed rather easily. The simple process of divid-ing groups into smaller groups of three or four will guarantee that almost all the participants will have a good opportunity to contribute. For the teacher, this can also be a much easier task than continually trying to encourage reluctant students to participate in the larger group or pre-venting more talkative students from dominating the discussion through a range of gestures or even direct verbal intervention.

This division can be spontaneous, in response to a very animated dis-cussion, or it can be deliberately planned as syndicate or peer-managed learning where a task is introduced and materials are either provided or

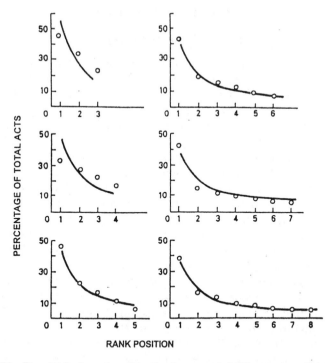

Figure 7.4 The distribution of participation in groups of different sizes (Bales, 1970)

referenced for students to explore themselves either in libraries or electronically. The tasks for these groups can be designed to cover areas of the syllabus in which the selection of materials is central. They are, however, more effectively presented through individual and group processes than directly transmitted by the teacher. The group, then, has a responsibility for planning peer activity, for sharing individual reading and for communicating and initiating discussion of the results of this individual work. The final communication can be given in written form or presented orally in a presentation. As with the 'progressive doubling' it can be an excellent way of enabling students to work on alternative solutions and learn to combine different perspectives and develop the skills of working together.

The use of carefully constructed games and simulations can also be used to address much of the material a teacher may wish to cover in a course. It is not only highly motivating but can also introduce ways of dealing with a changing dynamic context. It is very difficult to teach students the ability to make decisions in the context of change and uncertainty without enabling them to actually be in these situations. Merely telling students about how others have coped may not actually develop the flexibility required to live and work in our changing world.

The personal dimension
Providing support

The most important issue here is for the teacher to establish a support-ive and secure environment. We spoke earlier of the fear many students experience in apparently friendly peer groups and this is not usually reduced by simply saying 'we are friendly' and 'please feel free to express half-formed ideas'. It is often important to challenge some students' con-tributions but if this is a common pattern it may mean that avoidance is a common response. With many groups, the emotional learning might take much longer than the intellectual learning. (William Perry in a lec-ture has described the general problem as 'gut lag'.) Paul Valery has expressed this rather more poetically: 'Long years must pass before the truths we have made our own become our living flesh'.

Intellectual change is often delayed or prevented by emotional resis-tances and these can be associated with early experiences. Teachers can find themselves being treated as parent figures where independence becomes the issue rather than an intellectual problem. Students can be very anxious and ambivalent about both control and support, and many students feel that university life is impersonal and would welcome a closer relationship with staff similar to that they had with their teachers in the sixth form at school (Cox, 1987). University students, however, are adults and part of being an adult at university is relating to the teachers as equals in a way not possible at school. This does not mean that intel-lectually students are on the same level as their teachers but it does mean that in talking about more personal matters it can be a more balanced relationship.

Geologists and botanists often comment on how they get to know their students better and relate more fully on field trips. Although it is more difficult for teachers in other subjects to do this in the same way, there are, nevertheless, ways of relating outside the seminar room. Given the pressures on staff, doing this in coffee bars and pubs may be difficult but changing the atmosphere in the seminar room may not be quite so time-consuming. Coffee might actually be provided and in an engineering department this actually did make a very friendly atmosphere. Eating and drinking are important influences on social bonding. These might be combined with visits to exhibitions, museums or even outside lectures and for arts students theatres and galleries can be obvious ways of com-bining intellectual with personal interests. Some programmes include res-idential short courses and these can be especially useful in breaking down barriers.

In Chapter 5 we mentioned reflective triads which can help students to personalize what they have been learning on their courses. Heron's empathetic building can contribute to this too. This is where the teach-ers build upon a student's idea without taking it away and making it purely their own. Empathy is the key characteristic here. It can give students the sense of real participation in a very personal way. Similarly, asking students questions, which they can actually respond to, might help. Often students are intimidated by questions that may seem appropriate to the teacher but require both conceptual levels of thinking and broad range of knowledge which are inappropriate. There is the example of first-year students being asked to respond to the use of language in a difficult Samuel Beckett play in relation to Hegelian theory of tragedy! The silence that ensued was predictable. On the other hand, asking questions, which simply require short, right or wrong answers, may appear to them more like being interrogated than taking part in an intellectual discussion. Asking open-ended questions can enable students to reply in a way that is more closely related to their personal concerns and not be so clearly wrong. Gentle encouragement to continue, moreover, can help them to take more risks especially if they are not immediately corrected when they make a mistake.

Encouraging independence

One of the elements of the deeper approach to learning is relating what we have learnt to our own personal experience but sometimes students feel this is not a legitimate thing to do within a serious seminar, so it may need to be encouraged. An important aspect of learning is that experience is valued and this is especially true with more mature students who can feel rejected when this is ignored. Independent thinking can be more risky in larger groups and the opportunity to talk in pairs or threes, as we have stressed, can be particularly important for beginning to explore ideas that are more independent.

Encouraging self-knowledge is an important feature of group work and reflecting on the impact of our words on the people in the group can be very helpful. Time-out activities in which the topic is dropped and issues of process addressed are still rare but can be useful in supporting learning. It is also emotionally risky or difficult for the teacher, but as it becomes part of the normal way of working in groups, supported by ground rules, it can be an important aid for developing student independence.

Role-play is another activity where students can take risks in expressing other aspects of themselves, often those which are guarded and concealed. It is a form of teaching which is often used in subjects which are concerned with personal relationships, but as such skills are become increasingly important in all courses, the activity could be incorporated more generally. When students take risks in this way it is important to have debriefing sessions which enable the students to work through any embarrassing anxiety they may have had as well as relating role-play to the learning issues. Role-play can be very enjoyable as well as challenging and, if students enjoy learning, they are likely to become more independent as well as more highly motivated.

Developing the interpersonal

Discussing interdependence within the context of the chapter on small-group teaching could include almost anything that makes the group function more effectively. We want to emphasize, however, that such a heading involves developing self-knowledge. This is a general aim of education but it can be particularly helpful for developing effective group work. One way of encouraging this is to set aside time for individuals or groups to observe the group as it works. For group observation a 'fishbowl' arrangement is useful. This is one in which a group is divided into two, an inner group doing task-orientated work related to the course, and an outer group focusing on the process, observing the way the group is working. Providing students with an observer rating form can be useful (see Chapter 11). As observers, students will begin to see the nature of their own role in a learning session, how far, for example, they may be serving themselves rather than the needs of the group. The reports on them as the 'observed' in the group activities, on the other hand, can assist them in becoming aware of qualities and ways of working – blindspots – which they were not aware of in themselves. These areas have been referred to in a renowned framework for classifying group behaviours – the Johari window – as the 'blind' group behaviours (Figure 7.5).

In the 'blind' category, other members of the group can help individuals see things about themselves, which they did not know about. At the same time there is an opportunity for hidden behaviours, known to themselves but not to others, to become more public and offer the opportunity for constructive learning. The area, which is both unknown to the self and unknown to others is normally not the province of group work in higher education and is best left to a different, perhaps more thera-

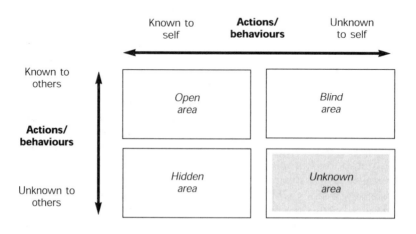

Figure 7.5 A classification of behaviour in groups (adapted from the 'Johari window' in Luft, 1984)

peutic context. This cultivation of self-knowledge together with understanding how groups function might also be encouraged by watching videotapes of the whole group in action. Another way of encouraging students to develop self-knowledge can be provided through opportunities to peer teach, with feedback from the group and a chance to reflect. This may be effectively accompanied by watching videotapes or listening to audio recordings of the session.

The social dimension
Providing support

The beginnings of group life are often very important for establishing the supportive atmosphere. Traditional introductions with a simple round of each participant giving a brief self-description can be somewhat tense and perhaps boring. But where individuals are asked to talk to their neighbour and then give a short introduction of their neighbour this can be both more engaging and more useful as a way of introducing each other since it involves both listening and talking. These functions are important in group work and this way of beginning sets up expectations about the way the group will be run; participants will be expected to both talk to and listen to their peers and not merely listen and respond to the teacher.

Some groups enhance this form of introduction by combining it with making and drinking coffee or tea, although this is not always possible or appropriate. What is appropriate, however, is to organize the layout of the room carefully. Eye contact is very important in ensuring good interpersonal communication and yet we still find groups run in rooms that do not permit everyone to see each other. Often it maybe difficult to avoid this, particularly if poor staff–student ratios mean that seminars have more than 20 students in them. This is one of the less talked about side effects of poor staff–student ratios. Breaking into smaller groups can help significantly here.

Eye contact is not the only issue. Everyone might see each other but the teacher might be seated behind a big desk – an indication of distance and/or of a detached authority relationship that can inhibit student participation. The relationship between students that are more talkative and quieter students is also a feature in encouraging and enhancing more even participation within groups. In a broad discussion about group participation, Bligh, for example, reports research indicating that students across from one another are more likely to respond to one another and those side by side less (2000: 176–7). A teacher sitting opposite a talkative student may make it more difficult for others to participate. Abercrombie (1966) describes another expression of the importance of environment. Two groups were working independently in separate rooms and one group had red chairs the other green. When they came together in another room a circle of chairs was set out with alternating red and green chairs. When the two groups came together, without realizing it each group sat on its own colour chair but talked to their own group across the other group. This rather surprising finding illustrates how sub-conscious influences can be important within groups, in particular when bringing smaller groups back into a larger-group discussion.

Finally, the supportive side of the social dimension may also be enhanced through generating enjoyment on the one hand and a lack of anxiety about what might be happening on the other. It needs to be said, however, that while the lack of clear group guidelines might generate anxiety, a degree of confusion or puzzlement, as we suggested earlier, is often a good starting point for the achievement of understanding. The issue here is that guidelines should not become a straitjacket and clear expectations not a recipe for dullness.

Encouraging independence

A sense of ownership in the group may, indeed, be generated out of working this sense of confusion through into constructive co-operation. We saw in discussing phases in the groups that effective working is often preceded by intra-group hostility but confidence is often a condition for independent work. Overcoming difficulties is frequently important in achieving a sense of ownership of one's learning. The autocratic style did not leave much scope for this but neither did the laissez-faire. Democratic and/or coaching styles of leadership can be important in generating a real sense of independence within the group.

Developing the interpersonal

Here peer teaching may be the best way of encouraging interpersonal and social skills. Lecturers often say they have learned things most effec-tively when teaching but rarely give their students a chance to learn by teaching. Problem- and task-based learning approaches to teaching involve both teaching by students and the need to work in an interde-pendent way. It is important, however, to give our students the range of different tasks and structures so that what they learn in this respect is more easily transferable to new situations. Again, what is learnt may be reinforced by serious reflection on the process.

One learning activity which may have more general application is the 'consultants and assessors' game (see Chapter 10 for a full description). Briefly, a task/problem focused on the course or session topic is given to different groups of students who act as teams of consultants developing solutions. They will need to draw upon course materials as well as using their own initiative to hunt down others which they share with 'col-leagues' to produce a solution. These are presented to a student group of assessors who devise criteria for judging the quality of the solutions and decide how to apply these to the consultant's reports or presentations. This can raise interesting issues of inter-group and intra-group relations in conditions of success and failure. In the process it also raises issues of giving and taking criticism in the context of developing their own assessment and evaluation abilities. It has the important advantage of directly addressing substantial areas of course content.

The practical dimension

Much of what has been said already is in fact about the practical dimension of encouraging students to work effectively within groups. It was suggested that field trips and other practical work can provide a very good context for exploring teamwork and inter-personal skills and the quality of the relationships can often be very much better than that in the seminar rooms. Beyond this what is actually possible will very much depend upon the different disciplinary contexts. The rich variety of ways of relating in practical work needs to be exploited. This is best done by a combination of quiet individual reflection, often with reflective diaries and in the sharing of these with the help of teachers who can encourage students to integrate these experiences into a coherent framework. Within this dimension, a balance needs to be achieved between helpful direction and freedom to explore, to take risks, to fail and to learn from these experiences. Strenuous attempts to avoid risk and failure may undermine independent and deeper, long-lasting learning.

The nature of the practical task given to a group, Bligh (2000) reminds us, will have a significant influence on the dynamics of the group. Members may, for example, have serious differences about how to proceed, or conflicting values guiding their decisions. These plus a sense of urgency, which may be imposed from the outside, can play havoc with group performance. He suggests that students need to be aware in such practical groups of the difference between the group task goals and the group maintenance goals, and spend time addressing both: 'groups that spend longer on group maintenance achieve more. That is to say, discussions about group processes accelerate achievements on content. Why? Because groups that don't maintain themselves spend much longer disagreeing' (ibid.: 121).

Conclusions

Small-group teaching in the past has often promised much but achieved far less. It is popular in theory but often unpopular in practice, even if not universally considered 'purgatory'! It can be difficult, however, for teachers who have been appointed primarily for their ability as thinkers and writers to develop interpersonal skills and understanding of complex and often disturbing group processes. Part of the problem for teachers is that many of the social conventions, which can have a deep-seated influence on our behaviour, are contrary to what teachers need to do to achieve efficient practice. If we were to suggest that a dinner party split into groups of three or four to record interesting points of conversation on a flip chart or to reflect on a video-recording of their interacting, we would probably have to find new guests for our future parties. If on the other hand we prevented our guests from forming small groups of two or three, again future parties would be rare. Similarly, if our seminars have absolutely nothing of the friendly smiles, the sensitive introductions, the attention to the importance of values, beliefs and diversity, they, too, might begin to dwindle and disappear, especially as there is rarely anything to eat or drink, and absolutely no music!

In other words, groups are groups wherever they come together. Mere collections of individuals may learn something together but may lack the personal involvement that can be both memorable and lead to a change of behaviour. In their social lives outside the university, teachers are generally very sensitive to behaviour that can enhance social relationships as well as behaviour that can create bad feeling, hostility and withdrawal. It is not always clear that these skills are actually being transferred into their teaching.

If we want to transfer some of the important features of our enjoyable and interesting social lives to our group teaching, we need to be aware of not only the intellectual dimension but of the personal and social activities and relationships which can make this possible. Parties are not obvious models for seminars but they do have features from which we can learn. Academics do not need books to tell them the key topics, skills and even attitudes which are all-important in their discipline, but they may need to be reminded of the personal and emotional problems which can get in the way of students' learning. Young people, and mature students too, want to feel they are in a community of adults who relate to them as adults and not as parents or a remote intellectual elite that can undermine their own identity as adults or as developing professionals. Creating the conditions for them to engage in the variety of roles that are the context of adult life today is itself important for the role of lecturer. Group work has the potential to enrich the different roles that stimulate engagement and learning. They can give students a wide range of experiences, provided we are willing to go beyond the usual boundaries and encourage students to learn how to learn from observing the group and comparing the reactions, ideas and feelings generated by these experiences. The integration of content tasks with process tasks is often difficult and keenly resisted but, with encouragement, can itself become a valuable group task.

Further reading

Bligh, D. (2000) *What's the Point in Discussion?* Exeter: Intellect Press.
Bramley, W. (1979) *Group Tutoring*. London: Kogan Page.

Brockbank, B. and McGill, I. (1998) *Facilitating Reflective Learning in Higher Education*. Buckingham: Open University Press.

Goodlad, S. and Hirsh, B. (1989) *Peer Tutoring*. London: Kogan Page.

Greenblat, C.S. (1998) *Designing your own Simulations*. London: Sage.

Habeshaw, S., Habeshaw, T. and Gibbs, G. (1984) *53 Interesting Things to Do in Your Seminars and Tutorials*. Bristol: Technical and Educational Services.

Jaques, D. (1991) *Learning in Groups*. London: Kogan Page.

Van Ments, M. (1983) *Effective Use of Role Play*. London: Kogan Page.

8

Supervising: Project, Dissertation and Thesis Supervision

(The PhD) changes people, not simply in terms of technical expertise and knowledge in their field, but also in terms of the ways they value themselves and their work ... A self forged through tackling the difficulties of research, especially when stress from other sources is high, is a new self. So is the self that overcomes the doubts about ability to do the work. (Hazel Francis, in Graves and Varma, 1997: 18)

I like the projects because it's me not just reflections from staff. (A student on undergraduate project work, Cox, 1975)

Introduction

In Chapter 4, we discussed research on conceptions of learning. Dividing into reproducing and transforming categories, the last conception was characterized in terms of 'changing as a person'. In undergraduate courses – where much of the research on student conceptions has focused – the aspect of study with perhaps the most potential to change people is the project. The Masters' dissertation offers even greater opportunities for change, and the PhD thesis has the greatest potential. Wherever an educational experience offers great promise, however, there can be great disappointment. Rudd (1986) who has extensively researched the PhD, concluded that most of the problems, in one way or another, involve shortcomings in the supervision. Although interpersonal skills are quite important when conducting seminars and even when lecturing, in supervision (as to a large degree in personal tutoring) a clash of personality or even insensitivity towards the feelings of the student can lead to disaster. A supervisor, who is willing to help with the emotional turmoil of the process, sharing its pleasures and pains, is as important for researchers as is the tutorial supervision of their work. Francis feels that 'most is gained from the research process by finding a balance between individual drive and autonomy and the engagement and support of others' (1997: 19).

In this chapter we shall begin with an overview of the key issues in supervision which we shall then consider in relation to more specific elements of the learning matrix. We then go on to look at some of the issues in assessment before the final conclusions.

Key issues of supervision

We have frequently stressed the importance of achieving a balance between providing support, encouraging independence and developing the interpersonal. In supervising, this is much more than an intellectual achievement on the part of the supervisor. Supervision involves a constant interaction between the supervisor and the student and since this is a one-to-one relationship, crude stereotypes of each other can be very destructive of any deeper learning. With larger groups, to some extent, we have to work with generalizations rather more, even if they do not amount to stereotypes. But with supervising, sensitivity to individual differences, the ability to accommodate these differences and to accept changes in mood, motivation and even intellectual approach are crucial to the developing relationship as well as to the quality of the research.

In many respects the supervisory relationship is a very useful model for teaching in general and is now beginning to be appreciated as such. In supervising there may be some transmission of information but, essentially, few supervisors like to see their students as just reflections of themselves. In other teaching we may well pay lip-service to the contemporary view that we are facilitators of learning but in supervising it is difficult for this to remain simply lip-service. Not only do we not spend most of our time telling, but we are very intimately concerned with trying to understand the problems and learning processes that the students are going through. Getting in touch with the way they see the topic and the way they approach its problems is very important in enabling us to be helpful to students without taking away that sense of ownership which is essential at all levels of research.

Responding to student problems

The kinds of problems which students present to supervisors are numerous and diverse. They vary widely across the areas of the learning matrix described in Chapter 4. There are no right answers in responding to them and each will have to be engaged in its own terms. Teachers will need to make professional judgements with respect to their responses. Figure 8.1 provides a continuum of kinds of approach which supervisors might choose when students encounter problems. They range between taking the problem out of the student's hands and solving it to sympathizing but not addressing the problem at all. Each has its advantages and disadvantages, and each can be appropriate or inappropriate according to the situation.

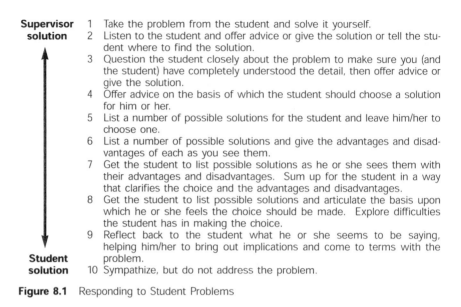

Figure 8.1 Responding to Student Problems

Supervisors may seldom take either of the extremes but on many occasions they will come quite close to one or the other. Some may listen to the student and offer advice, provide the solution or tell the student where to find it. Occasionally this might seem to be a reasonable thing to do, but if this becomes the general pattern of the supervision, then it has serious problems. On the other hand, other supervisors might reflect back to the student what he or she seems to be saying, in an attempt to help the student to examine the implications and come to terms with the problem. While this may be sometimes a good way of encouraging independence, if the meetings are always like this it may actually discourage the student or send him or her on the road to failure. Generally, supervisors feel they should be operating somewhere near the supportive end of the scale, getting students to list possible solutions and suggest bases upon which they feel the choice should be made, and then exploring any difficulties the student might have in making the choice. In practice, however, supervisors find themselves confined to one or two kinds of response, often offering advice and suggesting what the student might do. In their anxiety to retain control lest students make mistakes, they may persist with this approach long after its sell-by date. Supervisors and teachers will better serve themselves and their students by developing and sustaining a wider repertoire of responses to employ as the circumstances require.

Relationships and roles in supervision

Associated with these responses are the more general issues of roles and relationships between students and supervisors. Brown and Atkins (1988) set out an range of roles which the supervisor might take (Table 8.1). At times, most of these can be appropriate but the important and difficult issue is achieving the right balance over the whole supervisory period. Each one relates to a reciprocal relationship on the part of the student. Some of these may not feel like acceptable relationships but they are helpful in reflecting on and reviewing our relationship with our students. Are we are actually operating in a flexible way which is meeting the needs of the particular stage of supervision?

Table 8.1   *Roles and relationships between supervisor and student*

Supervisor	Student
Director	Follower
Master	Servant
Guru	Disciple
Teacher	Pupil
Expert	Novice
Guide	Explorer
Project manager	Team worker
Auditor	Client
Editor	Author
Doctor	Patient
Senior partner	Junior
Professional colleague	Colleague
Friend	Friend

Source: Brown and Atkins: 121

Gardiner (1989) conducted an in-depth research inquiry into the nature of supervision. Much of this concerns placement supervision of practical work but is not restricted to this particular area. He initially focused on trying to understand the relationship of supervision styles to deep and surface approaches to learning. Later he became interested in going beyond these two levels to a reflective level which involves meta-cognition. Gardiner relates conceptions of knowledge to the approaches to learning and styles of teaching discussed earlier (in Chapters 3 and 4). He suggests that it is important to identify the kinds of patterns of interaction and to build them into an interactive model. He developed a complex model identifying three levels of interaction.

The first level focuses upon the content of learning. 'Supervisors believed that the right way to supervise was to reflect the hierarchy casework relationship with clients, and to maintain control, not only of what the student should be learning but also the single right path to achieve it' (ibid.: 131). It is linked to reproductive conceptions of learning. At level 2, the focus is on the process of learning with recognition of diversity and active involvement of the learner in the learning process. There is a shift from the reproductive to the constructive/transforming conceptions of learning. Students take increasing responsibility for setting the agenda, for supervision and for assessing their own work and learning. Level 3 focuses on meta-learning, learning to learn and the demonstration of versatility. Here students and supervisors use their own learning processes as the basis (content) of further learning (process) of a higher order. He feels that this meta-learning can promote transfer of the content and process of learning to contexts other than those in which the original learning arose.

Matching of levels between supervisor and student is very important, especially if the supervisor is operating at level 1. The effect of mismatches, however, is dependent on the level at which the mismatch occurs. If students and supervisors are capable of operating at level 3, they are able to reflect upon and discuss the way in which they are interacting in a mutual engagement which should be able to adjust to any mismatches. If they are not, the potential for dialogue and engagement about both the learning and the interaction is reduced.

Gardiner's work has interesting parallels with Schon's (1983; 1987: 256, 259) two models of interpersonal behaviour. The values of model 1 are, as he says, 'to achieve the object as I see it', 'to strive to win and avoid losing', 'to avoid negative feelings'. Its strategies include unilateral control of the task and the environment and unilateral protection of self and others. It is a very restrictive, 'single-loop' model of interaction where assumptions are not questioned and private dilemmas are concealed. Model 2 is a 'double-loop' model in which the participants are learning about the values and assumptions that drive their own and/or other people's behaviour. In this model learning involves the governing variables that underlie behavioural strategies. Participants are willing to share difficult and sensitive matters that may be getting in the way. In supervising students we need be willing to express disappointment with each other's performance. Both sides need to explore how far it is possible to share issues of doubt and mistrust that can so easily remain private and undisclosed.

'Meta'-skills

Biggs (1999) is also concerned with meta-cognitive learning skills. These focus upon self-management and what the learner does in new contexts – the ultimate aim he suggests of university teaching. Good traditional teaching involves going beyond the information given. Here, direct instruction is followed by thought-oriented activities that challenge students so that they apply, generalize and refine their understanding. Developing learning 'going beyond the information given' goes beyond direct instruction in that students are encouraged by questioning and support to find their own way out as in the best examples of problem-based learning. He suggests, with Perkins (1991), that at this level we are concerned with managing the problems and questions that have not been previously addressed. It involves a reformulation of what the problem is about and asking questions about what further information is necessary and how to try out solutions and test them.

Biggs and Perkins take a more purely intellectual slant on some of Schon's requirements for working effectively within model 2. Schon values the willingness to explore assumptions and inhibitions that we may not know we have. It comes closer to encouraging a more therapeutic approach. And in many respects good supervision requires us to explore what we have called our learning gap 4 where the student may know what to do and want to do it and yet not actually do it. The student may be more worried about it not being good enough, and feel that the risks are not worth taking. On the other hand, the consequences of not taking the risk might be even more damaging in the end to a sense of personal identity. These are important issues in the more creative activities associated with theses, dissertations and even undergraduate projects. The project, as an undergraduate student said, 'is the only real opportunity for your own ideas'.

The intellectual dimension

Providing support

We have stressed, especially in supervision, that support is essentially concerned with helping students to learn and make decisions rather than transferring knowledge and deciding for students. All innovation, change and creative work involves risk-taking but risks are very difficult to take if students are feeling very insecure. At the undergraduate level, projects are perhaps the only area where students may consciously feel they are taking risks. But even graduate students may not be very practised at relating to their lecturer as a supervisor who is not going to do all the explaining and clarifying and directing that they may have come to expect. At all levels, setting ground rules and clarifying them is an important first step. It should not be assumed that because these have been carefully discussed at the beginning they will not be forgotten later under the more stressful conditions of trying to write up the project or dissertation for a deadline. Part of the more supportive side of supervising will be to help students understand a wider range of possible roles and what they actually mean in terms of the supervisor's behaviour as well as their own. It is unlikely that students will initiate discussion about the wide variety of roles and relationships outlined earlier (Table 8.1). And while confronting the student with all 13 possibilities may not be the best way to begin a supervision, it may be useful to make clear in the early stages that coming to terms with a new way of working is an important part of the working relationship.

Roles and relationships are not the only important part of setting the ground rules. It is important to negotiate the actual practical side of what each can expect of the other. In the new millennium these are likely to be set out in course documentation. Although an expectation that these might be read before the first meeting may be reasonable, it is useful to spend time interpreting what they mean and perhaps modifying and suggesting new elements which suit your particular relationship. Now, there are pressures to formalize duration and frequency of supervision meetings but we need to bear in mind that this is an area in which there are important individual differences and working to a mythical average may not always be appropriate.

We should not assume that written ground rules will get in the way of a close personal relationship. It is easy for discussions about processes to be seen as personal criticism. Ground rules, statements of responsibilities, and written criteria can more easily become a subject for discussion than can particular issues troubling the supervisor or the student. Phillips and Pugh describe a set of general expectations which research students have of their supervisors 'regardless of discipline' (2000: 161) which might provide useful guidelines for supervisors (Table 8.2).

Table 8.2   *Student expectations of their supervisor*

	Students expect to be supervised
Students expect their supervisor(s) to:	• read their work well in advance; • be available when needed; • be friendly, open and supportive; • be constructively critical; • have a good knowledge of the research area; • structure the tutorial so that it is relatively easy to exchange ideas; • have sufficient interest in their research to put more information in the student's path; • be sufficiently involved in their success to help them get a good job at the end of it all!

Source: adapted from Phillips and Pugh, 2000

It is also helpful for students to know that other students share their expectations and that they are not expecting too much. On the other hand, these expectations need to be interpreted in context. It may be reasonable, for instance, to feel that their supervisor should have the courtesy not to answer the telephone during a tutorial. Given the pressures on supervisors it is often easy to forget to put telephones through to the secretary or turn them off. If the supervisor were expecting an urgent or very important call, however, many students would agree that this is perfectly acceptable if it were mentioned beforehand. And how much help is it reasonable to expect from a supervisor in finding a job at the end of the research? Guidance, references, contacts, some 'inside' information and so on may be reasonable but pursuing or hunting the job down for the student is not.

All students expect detailed comments on their written work but there is disagreement as to how far these comments should be directed at telling students what they should do and how far they should raise questions and suggest alternatives. Whereas the latter might be the more useful general approach, there are occasions when students might expect straight answers to straight questions. The range of possible responses to students' work (Chapter 10) is not only concerned with the quality of comments. The quantity can also be quite problematic as staff–student ratios deteriorate. Some supervisors write very little and rely upon the tutorial discussion while others write a great deal. Either way extensive feedback is a valuable feature of higher education in Britain and elsewhere.

It can sometimes be useful in reading students' work to have a tape recorder available to dictate our comments as we are reading, with some general reviews at the end once you have read all of it. This is particularly useful if students are working abroad or some distance from the university where the more personal approach of talking might give a greater sense of supporting and caring. E-mail also provides a more personal touch than letters or notes. If the student sends their writing this way as many now do, comments can be interspersed in the text for the reply rather like the tape, but the voice and especially the intonation is lost.

Encouraging independence

Some students, but certainly not all, may begin their research in a state of considerable dependency. Whereas for some students the release from severe time constraints can mean that they feel free to take risks and explore ideas now that they have the time to research and back up their ideas, for others, this open-endedness can be threatening. Fear can be quite a common response to freedom but although more support may be necessary at the beginning, it is important not to set up patterns and expectations that mean that students remain in a state of dependency. On the other hand, in trying to avoid this, we may find ourselves behaving as if our main purpose is to point out all the faults and difficulties to the student and fail to see that this can be very damaging and may make them retreat into even greater dependency. Estelle Phillips has spoken of how students she was interviewing sometimes burst into tears when discussing some of the difficulties they had in relating to their supervisors, even some time after they had actually gained their PhDs. At the time they had not revealed their feelings and felt in retrospect that perhaps their supervisors did not realize just how badly hurt they had been. A sensitive interview provided the opportunity to express the feelings that they had hidden at the time.

Unfortunately, supervisors often get very little help in coping with the more emotional aspects of giving criticism but they may need much more than helpful advice and role-plays can be a very useful addition to supervisor workshops. In encouraging independence the language of alternatives and different perspectives is likely to be more effective than the language of right and wrong or good and bad. Edward de Bono's (1994) approach in terms of parallel thinking provides a useful non-adversarial approach to encouraging more constructive and creative thinking. Different perspectives and arguments need to be kept in mind to see if they might contribute to a richer and more integrated approach rather than eliminating each one because of its particular failings.

Self-criticism can be extremely inhibiting where it undermines self-confidence. Becker in his book on writing for social scientists suggests

> you can, for instance, avoid the curse of trying to get it right first time, and thus not doing it at all, by writing anything that comes into your head for a first draft . . . you know you can clean it up later and, therefore, that you needn't worry about the first draft's flaws. (1986: 164)

Rough drafts can help students to take more risks and be more independent. It can help get past the feeling, as one student put it, that they 'don't like to express half-formed ideas' nor write unless they are sure of themselves.

Another way to encourage more independent thinking is to lessen the threat of criticism by encouraging students to keep an intellectual diary which is not necessarily seen by the supervisor but where they can express guesses, opinions and hypotheses without necessarily immediately having to justify them. This can have some parallels with the very useful device of brainstorming, covered in Chapter 7.

Others might prefer to dictate where there is freedom not only from the constraints of actual writing and typing but from constantly seeing what you have just written. Backspacing on the recorder is always possible but it tends to be used far less than reading back over what you have just typed. This certainly has its own problems but the virtues of speed and fluency are very much appreciated by those who have problems of inhibitions and too much self-criticism. Students may need to be encouraged to try out new ways of writing and being productive as well as new perspectives and alternative solutions.

Developing the interpersonal

Supervision, as opposed to other forms of teaching, is essentially about dialogue. There is a need for constant adjustment to what each participant is saying and the balance between giving and taking, listening and talking, is crucial if the session is not to become a lecture in disguise. Although supervisors can and do learn a great deal from their supervisions, the dialogue is not simply a friendly conversation. Nor is it an interrogation or even a Socratic dialogue. Initially at least there may be a considerable imbalance of power and intellectual sophistication but an important function of the supervision is to reduce this imbalance and to enable the student to become an independent researcher. There may be times when interrogation and serious challenging are appropriate, but if the general pattern is one of unilateral judgement and assessment rather than constructive dialogue it may be difficult to develop the professional skills of self-criticism and critical reflection.

The issue is less one of supervisors not thinking about supervision in these terms, nor that they do not want to develop more reciprocal relationships, than that it is easy to let development not happen. In ordinary conversations we may avoid dominating the discussion but in general if we have interesting things to say we say them and do not see it as one of our aims to encourage the other to say those ideas we feel are our own. In fact, it is easy to slip into either a didactic mode of telling or a conversational mode of enjoying giving our opinions. In supervision, maintaining a subtle balance of talking and listening is not simply a question of letting the other person have their say and listening with interest. There is a more active, searching process involved whereby you become clearer about both the strengths of what the other is saying but also about the hidden assumptions and misconceptions. It is essentially an exploratory process, which can be enjoyable but does not benefit from the self-expression that comes from good friendships.

Supervision is not just about one-to-one interaction, it involves a wider involvement in the student's personal and social life and some of the social life and personal life will be to do with developing their intellectual skills. Loneliness is a dominant theme in many of the books on doing a research degree but, happily, there is now much more interest within universities in creating learning communities not only for undergraduates but for graduate students, too. Science research students have often benefited from being able to interact with their peers and learn from them in the laboratories. Now research students generally are able not only to express their own discoveries and new ideas but also to talk about the problems of their research and its methodology. Sharing perspectives and approaches is an important part of most research students' lives. Perhaps the most valuable part of this is the semi-formal environment of student seminars that are often attended by staff. The more formal courses can also be a new area for students to interact and learn the skills of becoming professional researchers. If these are too remote from the student's own perspectives and approaches then they can appear to be increasingly like being subject to undergraduate control. There is now a wider realization that if these courses are to become part of the transition into professional life they need to become less authoritarian and remote and more responsive to the needs and ideas of the students.

The personal dimension

The influence of personal relationships in supervising is extremely important but it is still rather controversial just how much the relationship should be friendship. Most would now agree that it is important for each to get to know the other and very often this is difficult if the only relationship is in a study or in a seminar room. Although there is very little discussion of this in the literature, many supervisors feel it is important to be able to relate within a more informal social dimension. Supervisors often invite PhD students to their homes, but this is rarer for Masters' dissertation and project supervision. The ways in which groups get to know each other better (Chapter 7) can also be relevant to groups of research students.

Providing support

It is within the more personal one-to-one relationships where boundaries become an important issue. Research students often go through difficult periods of confusion and loss of confidence, not only in the quality of what they are doing, but whether it is worth doing at all. Unlike their undergraduate lives, when they have many areas of interest and many different and quite close relationships, research students find they are very influenced by their view of how their research is going and how the most significant other person in that research, their supervisor, is feeling about it. We saw earlier that undergraduate projects can become a very important focus of students' lives; this is very much magnified for research students. For supervisors, maintaining the balance between support and independence in the personal sphere can be rather more difficult than in the intellectual. With research students, the supervisor is much more bound up with the success or failure of the research and often there is a very strong shared interest in the topic. Trying to make the student more independent might be seen as being uncaring and not supportive.

With the arts and social sciences – and occasionally for the natural sciences – a British PhD can be more of a 'personal journey' (Salmon, 1992) than a process of research training. However, there are more recent trends in the research councils to require a more formal American style 'taught course' element in the research training. Becoming lost on this 'personal journey' can be quite frightening and disturbing for students if they feel more dependent on their supervisor and want to be given firm direction. Helping students find direction is certainly an important role for supervisors but if they become too dominant in this respect then the ownership of the project begins to pass away from the student and towards the supervisor. This might provide some temporary relief for the student but in the long run the question of whose research is it can become in itself quite disturbing. Science PhD students often only meet this problem when they are doing their post-doctoral work; their PhDs are frequently much closer to research training where close direction from the supervisor is expected. With arts and social science students these ambiguities and ambivalence can create tensions which may need an outside professional to help resolve.

Even experienced supervisors often encounter serious problems from having been drawn into personal problems that directly affect the student's work. This can make the more academic aspect of supervision very difficult, and it is important that there should be other academics in the department who have some responsibility for students when supervisors find it difficult to cope effectively. In some departments, it may be difficult for a research tutor to be able to share responsibility for all the research students. Small supervisory committees are, on paper, supposed to be able to cope with this. In effect it is very difficult to take responsibility for another supervisor's students as well as your own unless this is taken account of in resource terms as an important extra responsibility. Supervisors themselves can benefit from being able to share anxieties and pleasures with other supervisors. Some highly stressed professions take care to set up supportive relationships amongst staff.

Encouraging independence

Encouraging independence (in the personal sense) will, to a large degree, depend on the supervisor's understanding of the range of styles and ways in which research may be approached. Supervisors may regard their own approach as the only one and convey it – tacitly and/or explicitly – through the supervisory relationship. Gough and Woodworth (1960) have, for example, identified eight stylistic variations amongst professional research scientists that are still instructive for their diversity:

- the zealot;
- the initiator;
- the diagnostician;
- the scholar;
- the artificer;
- the aesthetician;
- the methodologist;
- the independent.

This is not an exhaustive list and other categories of variations will exist amongst the social scientists and arts. Enabling research students to develop their own appropriate 'style(s)' of research is crucial to their independent development. There are also concerns as to whether a more uniform and formalized system of research training will encourage and further expand such diversity? Such training programmes often justify research methods courses in terms of introducing students to a variety of research approaches. This might help students to discover what sort of researcher they want to be. Supervisors have a key role in guiding and developing individual understanding and confidence in this respect.

Achieving a sense of independent personal and professional identity is an important aspect of graduate education. Many research students do not particularly want to be researchers but see a doctorate as a necessary qualification for becoming a teacher in higher education. With the rapid expansion of higher education throughout the developed world, this may be a bigger problem in the future and it could be that some of the problems which our research students face relate to this issue of professional socialization. Certainly no teachers in higher education should be ignorant of research methodology, and indeed research practice, but it may be that many PhD students should be doing professional or practice based doctorates. Their research is personally important but is not their prime orientation.

The significance for supervising is that we – individually and collectively – need to understand more about why students are doing their research in higher education and how far it enables them to develop a sense of professional identity. Even for students who do want to become research academics, the development of a particular research style can be a crucial aspect of their development. It is not clear, however, that supervisors address this very coherently.

The social dimension

Support, independence and the interpersonal

Although the situation has improved in recent years, social isolation can still be a problem for research students. This is still partly a question of poor facilities for research students (Becher et al., 1994). Science students may be able to identify quite closely with their space in a laboratory but arts and social science students may have little sense of belonging, without a sense of geographical personal identity other than a shifting library seat and the opportunity to use a communal computer. Supporting students in their quest for space within the academic research supervision is important. The issue is now being addressed more seriously and may become less of a problem as graduate students are more integrated into the teaching staff. Cryer (1996) highlights the social dimension of graduate education and promotes the development of more personal student and staff networks. E-mail networks are unlikely to provide all the social contact that students may need, although they can certainly help to reduce isolation and can provide a valuable channel of communication based on the intellectual side of being a research student as well as more personal and social needs.

For a long time it has been common for scientists to work in teams, but now the value of developing interpersonal and teamwork skills has been recognized much more widely both for industry and for social and personal benefits. Many universities now recognize the need to help research students develop their teamwork skills and their communication skills more widely. Conference, poster and seminar presentations are more valued for both content and process. This new emphasis upon the social dimension of graduate studies can make a valuable contribution to developing confidence and independence.

The practical dimension

Providing support

Providing support to students developing their practical research skills may be confined to supporting their practical and technical need for access to equipment/apparatus, appropriate physical spaces/laboratory/clinical/field, relevant services (library, media, computing, etc.). More often than not, it will also include support in the practical use and application of these. Considerable support for the above can be given to students through the provision of:

- clear guidelines, structures and timetables;
- clear support documents/material/equipment;
- clear criteria for the their use together with close supervisor/tutor and technician supervision and feedback.

Encouraging independence

Supervisors will need to be careful in the extent to which they provide such explicit support. There is the danger of undermining the student's developing research independence. As with the undergraduate practical work, there needs to be plenty of opportunity for choice in deciding, defining and carrying out tasks and problems. This may include:

- involvement in planning and decision-making;
- opportunity for students to find and provide support materials;
- involvement in setting criteria for progress and for self-assessment;
- time and opportunity for development and risk-taking.

A difficulty with PhDs in both the sciences and social sciences is that often the supervisor is responsible to specific fund holders for ensuring that a particular research project is designed and completed successfully.

Issues of independence can be difficult to balance with the supervisor's own research responsibilities. Rudd (1985) found that many research students –particularly in the sciences – feel that the research is not their own but rather almost entirely their supervisor's. In those circumstances, it is difficult to develop student independence. Careful planning, however, can help supervisors arrange for both their own needs as project directors and those of their students to be accommodated. Research students are not simply research assistants. They are often engaged in the two equally and both roles need to be recognized in terms of their developing independence.

Developing the interpersonal

Interpersonal practical skills can be developed in the relationship between student and supervisor but it will be restricted. They will be more fully enhanced by being part of either a research team or a group of researchers focusing on mutually beneficial processes of general and specific practices. This will include the negotiations of tasks and roles, setting criteria for progress, and the involvement in peer and group assessment and evaluation of practice. Such activities will be enhanced if group social relations are considered as an integral part of good team working. Many universities also foster professional links, visits and even exchanges which enable students to gain a wider view of research practices and to improve their collaboration and communications skills within them.

Assessing research

Formative assessment

For the supervisor, research assessment is essentially an issue of formative assessment, concerned primarily with feedback and helping students to learn and develop their research rather than with summative assessment that is concerned with the final examination. (See Chapter 10 for a full discussion of assessment.) Supervision may be defined as a process of formative assessment (albeit with a focus on the final examination). In many ways this constant reflection upon the quality of the work the student is producing is a more important feature of the total educational process than it is with undergraduate education. It maintains a much more important role in learning than in ordinary courses since, unlike many aspects of undergraduate assessment, it is constantly integrated into the learning process. The analysis of comments on assignments in terms of both possible purposes and styles of comment (see Chapter 10) is one way of gaining insight into research student assessment. The purpose of enabling students to become more aware of their implicit conceptions of the task is highly relevant. How far, for example, do they understand it as a transformative process, emphasizing in their writing the 'argument' and 'cogency' presented by the material, rather than simply as a telling process with an emphasis on merely the relevance of the material and its textual arrangement?

Sloboda and Newstead (1995) provide a useful analysis of the process of assessing research students, which has been of great use to both research students as well as supervisors. The main interest here is in the criteria to be used for assessing the written submission – central criteria also in giving feedback to students for developing their learning. They divide these into four general attributes and five sectional attributes (Table 8.3). Their appendix contains notes of guidance for examiners concerning the criteria to be applied when assessing each of these nine attributes but with the caveat that they should be considered as indicative rather than definitive.

Table 8.3   *Attributes of PhD assessment*

General attributes	Sectional attributes
• Presentation and clarity • Integration and coherence • Contribution to knowledge • Originality and creativity	• Review of relevant literature • Statement of the research problem • Methods of inquiry adopted • Analysis of data • Discussion of outcomes

Creativity and originality

These criteria say very little about creativity or originality, an important element within all the universities' criteria for examining PhDs. Phillips and Pugh (2000) and Cryer (1996) give interesting reviews of the very diverse conceptions of originality which are currently in use. Originality can be a rather worrying criterion for research students and their supervisor could help them to review the different ways in which a thesis might be considered to be original. Such interpretations as 'saying something nobody has said before' or 'carrying out empirical work that has not been done before' leave a lot unsaid about just how intellectually challenging each needs to be in order for them to count as an original contribution. Designing a new questionnaire, sending it out and analysing the results can be original but a vital question to address is whether or not it is worth doing and whether it has anything important to say. Similarly, making a new synthesis or a new interpretation or trying out in one country what has only been done in different countries, or taking a particular technique and applying it in a new area are all potentially interesting for their originality but by themselves may guarantee very little.

Being very prescriptive about originality may be somewhat contradictory and create new problems. The context and the levels of sophistication are critically important in judging whether a cross-disciplinary study or new methodologies or reinterpretations of someone else's ideas or carrying out original work designed by a supervisor present difficult questions about how far the student really is making an original contribution. Like many other issues of supervision, the best policy is to look at different examples and discuss these with the students. Ongoing discussions with colleagues within individual disciplines and departments are also essential to ensure a critical consensus. This might usefully be covered in research seminars at early stages in the research process. Abstract descriptions of what is required can often be difficult for students who may have different assumptions and expectations from the supervisor and may interpret criteria in a very different way.

Reliability and validity

There has not been a wealth of detailed research on issues of reliability and validity in research assessment, although Johnston (1997) has qualitatively analysed 51 examiners' reports of doctoral theses, searching for common themes. In general, there was a fair amount of agreement amongst examiners, but in some cases the differences are striking. A particular example that she highlights illustrates the disagreements that can occur. One examiner enjoyed reading it and felt in no doubt that it should be passed. Another said 'this is a genuine and admirable doctoral work, well worthy of the degree at any Australian university'. The third examiner, however, recommended it fail: 'It falls short of the key criteria for a PhD . . . I do not think that the idea or the way in which it is deployed in this thesis displays sufficient originality or makes a significant enough contribution to learning to merit the award of a PhD.' Johnston suggests that such cases may arise where there is an ideological incompatibility with the content of the thesis. She feels that there is a need for more openness in the examination process and for more formal induction of examiners.

Supervisors can help to open the process through more thorough going departmental and institutional discussion and sharing of good practice. The organization of mock vivas and providing the opportunity to observe other students going through mock vivas can also be extremely useful and helpful to both staff and students. Like many aspects of higher education, being told about processes or even having them demonstrated might be far less important than enabling students and supervisors to become actively engaged with the process. Past PhD theses can be an important source of information for students. Reading these could be combined with an assessment exercise (however simple) with the supervisor or in the company with other students who have an interest in the area. An interesting feature of Sloboda and Newstead's (1995) report is the suggestion that the students should be encouraged to include a section of the thesis on their learning. This would discuss what they have gained from the research process, personally as well as intellectually, and how they might change and develop their approach if they were to start anew.

In many ways, assessing a dissertation or thesis is more demanding than assessing coursework assignments. Knowledge of the field is reasonably straightforward to assess, but assessing the higher levels of academic work – including originality, analysis, synthesis and evaluation – (often within ideologically incompatible contexts) can be very difficult to reliably assess.

Conclusions

Supervising can be a model for teaching in general. It combines not only sharing and developing a high level of intellectual interest but does so within a very personal and emotional dimension where students' whole lives become intimately bound up with their intellectual expression and development. Many years ago a student was being interviewed in her third year about her response to the assessment system (Cox, 1975). Although initially focused on assessment, the interview soon became an exploration of the changes which students go through in their transition from school to university. The assessment system was seen to be an important element in this transition from dependency to independence. Towards the end of this very long interview, the student said that despite her being in the third year, this was the first time that she had thought seriously about what being at university really meant to her. Her academic work had not been well integrated into her personal life and development. Another student, slightly earlier in her academic life, said 'I'm finding my feet, I don't care so much about the work'. Perhaps today's students think more about what being at university means to them, but often there is no particular encouragement to do this. The process of supervision, however, even at undergraduate level, can provide a much stronger relationship between personal identity and academic work. Francis puts the personal side of supervision strongly:

> Helping to cope with the emotional turmoil, sharing the pleasures and the pains, is as important for researchers as is the tutorial supervision of their work. Friendship helps a great deal – so does the opportunity to bounce ideas and feelings off others also engaged in research. Work with a supervisor is the richer if there is a strong shared interest in the work and in each other's ideas about it; and most is gained from the research process by finding a balance between individual drive and autonomy and the engagement of support of others. One of the most satisfying aspects of the process for both supervisor and student is the emergence or strengthening of a competent researcher, personally wiser

and more confident in their work, and fit to take their place in the research community. (1997: 19)

Even if not everyone wants to take their place in the research community, the experience of writing a dissertation or thesis can be an important formative period in their lives.

Salmon is equally concerned with this integration of the personal with the intellectual. She feels that the PhD process can be a:

> struggle with deep-rooted feelings of personal limits and personal inadequacy: a belief that in the end one is unequal to this ambitious task. Women, in my experience are particularly liable to suffer this personal persistent inner self-deprecation; given the gendered power structure of the social world, including that of academic institutions this is hardly surprising. (1992: 117)

She feels that the often long and difficult inner struggle of PhD work is generally neither smooth nor easy: 'one reason for this is that PhD supervision does not happen in a vacuum. Most students have long experience of academic relationships which are basically authoritarian' (ibid.: 118). Generally, undergraduate education is not a very good preparation for the independent work of the PhD. Moreover, while the 'authoritarian' message – work hard, do as you are told and you will succeed – may be more prevalent in science and technology, it is not confined to it. Many scientists who become independent researchers go beyond their PhD to their post-doctoral research which is much more 'my research not my supervisor's'. Behind this controlling structure is the traditional assessment system which 'has as its criterion the essay or the written exam paper. What has gone into these products, the modes through which they have come into being, are considered altogether irrelevant, of no consequence' (ibid.).

In the new millennium, it is important for supervisors to encourage their students' development as reflective practitioners. With supervision the process is much more transparent and can be seen as a crucial part of the whole process. We often feel that the supervision session should be based upon students' written work and while this may be generally true, Salmon makes the important point that it is often the times between producing field data or writing that are the most important in doing research. The difficulties that a student is having, however, can often generate pressures to offer helpful advice about the directions that might be taken. This urge to step in can be a betrayal of the intention to encourage independent thinking even in undergraduate teaching, where it often seems the most sensible thing to do. Transferring our own learning from supervision into more traditional teaching can be a very valuable development if we are to encourage students in general to cope with the unexpected and the supercomplexity (Barnett, 2000) of modern life.

Supervision allows us to learn a great deal more about the importance of personal relationships in teaching. The end product is obviously of great importance in research but if PhDs were to become a little less concerned with end products and a little more concerned with reflections on learning processes we might learn a great deal more about the nature of graduate studies. Currently the addition of such commentaries are seldom encouraged and not clearly legitimized by the current forms of assessment. Integrating the creation of knowledge with reflection on the technical and personal processes might enable students both to cope better with research life and to produce research with a more developmental orientation which is more in tune with the rapid social and technological changes of the new millennium.

Further reading

Barnett, R. (ed.) (1997b) *Higher Education: A Critical Business*. Buckingham: Open University Press (SHRE).

Becker, H. (1986) *Writing for Social Scientists*. London: University of Chicago Press.

Bramley, W. (1997) *Personal Tutoring in Higher Education*. University of Surrey, Society for Research into Higher Education (SRHE), Guilford.

Cox, R. (1975) 'Students and student assessment: a study of different perceptions and patterns of response to varied forms of assessment in the University of Essex'. Unpublished PhD thesis, Colchester, Essex.

Cryer, P. (1996) *The Research Student's Guide to Success*. Buckingham: Open University Press.

De Bono, E. (1994) *Parallel Thinking*. London: Penguin Books.

Delamont, S., Atkinson, P. and Parry, O. (2000) *The Doctoral Experience: Success and Failure in Graduate School*. London: Falmer Press.

Francis, H. (1997) 'The Research Process' in N. Groves, and V. Varma, (eds) *Working for a Doctorate, a Guide for the Humanities and Social Sciences*. London: Routledge.

Gardiner, D. (1989) *The Anatomy of Supervision*. Milton Keynes: SRHE and Open University Press.

Graves, N. and Varma, V. (eds) (1997) *Working for a Doctorate: A Guide for the Humanities and Social Sciences*. London: Routledge.

Marton, F., Beatty, E. and Dall' Alba, G. (1993) 'Conceptions of learning', *International Journal of Educational Research*, 19 (3): 277–300.

Perkins, D. (1991) 'Technology meets constructivism: do they make a marriage?', *Educational Technology*. May: 18–23.

Phillips, E. and Pugh, D. (2000) *How to Get a PhD: A Handbook for Students and their Supervisors*. Buckingham: Open University Press.

QAA (1999) *Code of Practice for the Assurance of Academic QAA Quality and Standards in Higher Education, Postgraduate Research Programmes*: Cheltenham: Quality Assurance Agency.

Salmon, P. (1992) *Achieving a PhD*. Stoke-on-Trent: Trentham.

Sloboda, J. and Newstead, S. (eds) (1995) *Guidelines for the Assessment of the PhD in Psychology and Related Disciplines*. London: BPS/UCOSDA.

9

Innovating: Teaching with New Technology

Thirty years from now the big university campuses will be relics ...
Already we are beginning to deliver more lectures and classes off cam-
pus via satellite or two-way video at a fraction of the cost. (Peter
Drucker in Lenzner and Johnson; 1997: 127)

As each technological innovation has come and gone, it has left education feeling that something good has happened but that nothing fundamental has changed. (Noss and Pachler, 1999: 195)

Introduction

Innovation is not constrained to teaching with the aid of new communication and information technologies (C&IT). Opportunities for being
'innovative' can be discovered, developed and seized upon in all the
practices and 'genres' of teaching that we describe in this part of the book.
Developing reflective teaching practices that address the wider range of
needs identified in the learning matrix will require more innovative
approaches to teaching. We associate the term with new technologies
here, because the recent upsurge in their use by students provides
increasing opportunities for teachers in higher education to be more
'innovative' in their learning and teaching practices: 'we believe that the
innovative exploitation of communications and information technology
holds out much promise for improving the quality, flexibility and effectiveness of higher education' (NCIHE, 1997: 13.1).

Flexible strategies

This chapter will not examine the scope for using new technology in
terms of creating exclusive, comprehensive 'distance' learning systems
but will primarily focus on its potential for innovative contributions
alongside more traditional lecturing, facilitating and tutoring approaches.

154

Mason calls this 'close-distance education' (1998: 20). Moran and Myringer (1999) describe it as a 'flexible learning' strategy. They define it as one which:

- is applied to teaching and learning wherever they occur – on campus, off campus, cross campus;
- frees up the place, time, methods and pace of learning and teaching;
- is learner centred rather than teacher-centred;
- seeks to help students become independent, lifelong learners (ibid.: 60).

This is not to suggest that fully comprehensive systems of teaching – designed, delivered, assessed and evaluated primarily or fully with new technology – cannot address the full range of 'matrix' issues. Many, such as the Open University in the UK, do so very effectively. Such programmes are beginning to spread in traditional universities, but wholly successful examples are still relatively few. Mason refers to them as still being in the 'cottage industry phase' (1994: 61). Strategies that use new technology as part of a more flexible programme are increasingly characterizing the general evolution of distance technologies (Harry and Perraton, 1999: 9).

This chapter will examine the innovative potential that such 'flexible' strategies offer for exploiting new technology in improving learning and teaching. In the first instance, it will look at a range of frameworks or conceptual dimensions to describe the use of new technology for learning and teaching. Second, it will explore the diverse range of communication and information technologies available. Finally, it will look at how these technologies might be used for extending the learning matrix described in Chapter 4.

Conceptual dimensions of using C&IT

Despite the impact of the opening two quotes, the introduction of new technology in education continues to exercise the educational imagination and open opportunities within more traditional learning and teaching practices in higher education. It draws upon a variety of ways of speaking and thinking about learning and teaching, spawning a substantial and continually expanding body of educational literature. Lecturers have recently been adding a plethora of new expressions to their learning and teaching vocabulary. A selection of these includes distance learning, open learning, flexible learning, dual mode teaching, online education, virtual classrooms, global education, computer-mediated communication, technology mediated knowledge, and so on. The addition of new terms with older ones and the swift ability for writers in the area to develop new permutations of these terms is rapidly increasing this vocabulary. While it is not feasible to keep abreast of the theoretical nuances and implications of every new addition, it will be useful to have a broad conceptual overview of the area. In this section, we briefly sketch out some of the dimensions characterizing such an overview. We do so in terms of some of the important 'polarities' which have come to describe much of the development and discussion.

Figure 9.1 illustrates this conceptual overview in terms of two categories. The first category describes two broad dimensions emphasizing (a) the technology versus human character of this approach to learning and teaching and (b) its critical role in expanding the physical and geographical 'distance' between teacher and learner. The second category consists of a number of pairs of conceptual tensions which have been associated with new technology.

Engagement and dialogue

The use of technology should not necessarily be associated with increases in distance; much of this new technology enhances traditional face-to-face learning and teaching. Recent technologies, however, have been increasingly associated with their ability to achieve effective teaching and learning at a distance, providing access to expanded and more diverse communities of learners. These two dimensions are often erroneously conflated. 'Human' is habitually associated with being physically present and technology is increasingly associated with learning at a distance. It is an association that undermines the essential 'human' quality of teaching. There is no intrinsic reason why the lack of physical presence should be dehumanizing. The telephone, for example, is almost a universal distance technology, and advertized as a 'humanizing' instrument. Take time out to call a family member, a friend, just to talk. Some people also find it easier to 'open up' and 'speak' with the use of technology.

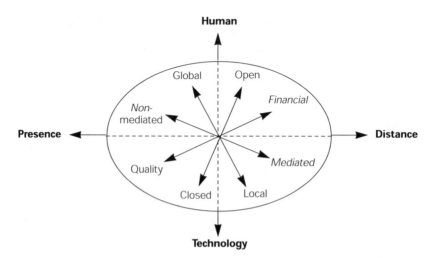

Figure 9.1 Using new technology in learning and teaching: conceptual dimensions and tensions

The conflation of these two dimensions can also easily be associated, if we are not careful, with another pair of terms: 'transmission' versus 'engagement' models of teaching (see, for example, Chapters 3 and 6). It does not take a huge leap of the imagination to see that if presence is conflated with the 'human', human engagement will follow closely behind. Similarly, conflating distance with the technology consigns engagement to face-to-face modes of teaching, linking new technology to transmission modes of teaching. This would be a fatal mistake and undermine its effective use as a mode of teaching. The 'human' aspect of interaction rests ultimately on why and how we use technology. Its effectiveness in improving learning will depend on whether teachers use it to genuinely engage with students in an intersubjective dialogue of shared meanings or whether they regard it as a medium for transmitting content and through which the student can be avoided. The development of genuine 'human-presence-at-a-distance' engagement is the main challenge that the growth of this new technology presents to learning and teaching in higher education. In this, it can support essential aspects of the learning matrix, encompassing the intellectual, personal, social and practical dimensions and their development.

A set of tensions

These two dimensions are supplemented in the framework by a set of 'tensions' that are not confined to the sphere of new technology but are highlighted by its expansion. They include:

- financial v. quality considerations;
- the global v. the local classroom;
- open v. closed learning;
- technology-mediated v. non-mediated communication.

This set of 'tensions' is not an exhaustive or defining list. It illustrates the more general themes associated with the development and use of new technology in learning and teaching. There are other closely linked and more specific 'tensions' – such as synchronous v. asynchronous learning – which we shall discuss later in the chapter. While we shall briefly consider the above themes individually, as we shall see, they closely intersect one another in a variety of ways and in a variety of different social, cultural, political, institutional and disciplinary contexts.

Financial v. quality considerations   Perhaps the most widely and recently voiced arguments for investing in and developing new technologies in higher education have centred on financial considerations. This is the case in terms of the potential for expanding student 'markets' and in terms of achieving efficiency gains within established student 'markets'. 'Financial pressure on institutions of higher education world-wide is probably the most critical factor forcing administrators and policy makers to look to global markets as a way of making up for falling government revenues and falling numbers of traditional learners' (Mason, 1998: 6).

The expansion of student markets does not have to focus entirely or even partially on global markets. They may also wish to address more local markets encompassing a range of different communities and their needs. The development of such 'niche' markets can be expected to develop as students become more familiar and comfortable with an expanding ranges of new technologies and physical presence becomes less of a consideration. Financial and efficiency rationales are often a significant force behind the increasing development of 'flexible strategies' integrating new technology within more traditionally taught face-to-face programmes and courses. It is clear, however, that the use of new technology is not yet as cost-effective as some might wish it to be. There are substantial up-front investments in the technology, course preparation, staff training and support which cannot necessarily be spread over long periods of time as each of these needs to be updated regularly. While it provides opportunities to access new 'markets', real cost savings and/or gains in these areas often come at the expense of educational quality. Maintaining quality costs. Ehrmann (1996) found that programmes employing new technology often increase costs. This is mainly because it is used to enhance both the quality and accessibility of the programme: 'if staff are able to save money in one area . . . the money is reallocated to other pressing needs within the same program' (ibid.: 126).

The global v. the local classroom   The tension between financial and quality considerations intersects here with issues of access at both a global and a local level. While the benefits of new technology – through both its distance and technology dimensions – provides access to both a wider number and diversity of students, accessibility is also paradoxically constrained by these dimensions. They can open the learning and teaching environment and close it down. The very technology itself, for example, excludes those persons with no or little access to the relevant technology. It also excludes those without the relevant technological skills, people who are not technologically literate. This is particularly acute in many third world nations where the technology and the associated training are expensive and limited. This may also be true in the local context, even when used alongside traditional face-to-face courses, but particularly when aimed at students at a significant distance.

Open v. closed learning   If the means of studying becomes highly technology centred – to the point where it is critical to successful completion of the course – more traditional students may also find the course 'closed' to them. This tension of open versus closed learning environments which has been a feature of new technology from the beginning extends also to issues of academic, language and cultural considerations. While new technology opens access to courses previously limited to face-to-face delivery, access is usually only 'open' to those students who have an adequate command of the 'delivery' language and who meet the prerequisite academic standards for entry. This need not always be the case – 'auditors' pursuing open independent study may be permitted access as in many traditional courses – but it requires careful consideration.

Technology-mediated v. non-mediated communication The fourth tension of the conceptual framework concerns the growing distinction between technology-mediated and non-mediated communication and knowledge. The mediation of information and of the modes of human exchange between teacher, knowledge and learner through new technology transforms the nature of both information/knowledge and of human exchange. This does not limit itself to the skills of using new technology but includes closely associated ways of 'writing' to and 'reading' from it – and ultimately of thinking. What is important in mediated communication is 'that intellectual energy must be devoted to the real task at hand. What matters is no longer to massively store facts, but to sort them, integrate them and reveal their relationships' (Moro, 1997: 73). The learner is empowered to choose that 'knowledge' that is relevant, useful and appropriate and is liberated from the necessity of having to accumulate and 'store' it. Mediation in this context contributes significantly to more autonomous and independent learners. 'Work with new technologies invariably involves the delegation of responsibility to learners and successful learning outcomes will depend on learners' ability to work independently and autonomously from the teacher and, increasingly, to take control of the learning process themselves' (Noss and Pachler, 1999: 205).

Such claims, however, need to be tempered by the potential loss attributed to technological mediation. These include suggestions that technology contributes to the breakdown of linear, narrative thinking, of traditional notions of 'knowledge' and 'truth' and associated losses of quality and standards. It also diminishes our sense of community and undermines our fundamental assumptions regarding identity and subjective meaning.

> There seems to be a great difficulty in holding onto the truth – as obvious as it is – that ease and flexibility of switching do not constitute ease and depth in making human contact. Certainly the connectivity makes communication 'easier', but it achieves this precisely by rendering contact more incidental, more shallow. (Talbott, 1995: 74)

In addition, the very global character associated with new technology has been attacked as contributing to a global homogenization of education, undermining local education initiatives and, even, of generating a new version of imperialism and colonization by western values. These potential risks as well as the enormous benefits of using new technology throw down a challenge to teaching in higher education. It is a challenge we should neither ignore nor uncritically pursue. This conceptual overview provides a general map of some of the key issues underlying these benefits and dangers, many of which we shall be returning to later. In the next section, however, we should like to address the kinds and range of available technologies themselves.

New technologies

The rapid developments, adaptations and subtle variations in the range of new technologies are such that it is impossible to do justice to the available diversity in the space available. They are the subjects of continuous research and change. Generally, however, we can usefully group them within three discrete (but broad) categories and one converged category (Mason, 1999). The first three are:

- text-based systems;
- audio-based systems;
- video-based systems.

The fourth is:

- multi-based systems.

Text-based systems

Text-based systems include a wide range of technology for one-to-one, one-to-many and/or many-to-many interactions. These include the use of fax, computer-conferencing, chat-systems, the Web and e-mail. E-mail is by far the easiest and the most commonly used in developed countries where almost all faculty and increasing numbers of students have extensive access to the technology. Teachers normally tend to use it for one-to-one exchanges with students concerning a range of issues and questions regarding a student's individual study. The facility for attaching documents to e-mail messages is also being used more extensively. It is taking over from fax as a way of submitting assignments or drafts of assignments for formal assessment or informal 'feedback' on course work. In addition, e-mail systems afford the possibility of one-to-many exchanges between teacher and students and of many-to-many exchanges and interactions between students. Computer-conferencing systems also provide opportunities for students to develop discussion groups and subgroups on a variety of aspects and issues of the course. These may be formally structured around specific course assignments, individual and/or group projects and tasks or more informally established and free-ranging group discussion including real-time chat rooms. In some cases they may require additional client software, but can also be effectively established within existing e-mail systems (Pincas, 1999). In addition, course web sites and bulletin boards accessed through the Internet provide students access to a range of textual material such as course and programme details, readings, handouts, notices and so on.

Audio-based systems

Audio-based systems extend in this low-tech/high-tech continuum from the relatively straightforward to the complex. At the lower end of the continuum, this technology includes the rather ordinary use of cassette tapes sent through the post that may hold a series of lectures or other audio-focused course material. It will also include the simple use of the telephone for one-to-one interactions for a range of student issues and/or comments on study and assignments. Slightly more complex use of technology might include the use of audio-conferencing by telephone for more collaborative group work and the rising potential of voice-mail for providing a variety of announcements on the course or assignments. The higher end of the continuum would include complex audio-graphic systems that simultaneously allow for the sharing of voice and graphics/text on a screen. They also provide access for using audio on prepared web sites or through other linked sites on the Internet. Again, these technological uses provide opportunities for a range of interactions between teachers and their students and between groups of students.

Video-based systems

Video-based systems mirror (albeit more expensively) audio-based systems in term of the degrees of the complexity of the technology that may be involved. They range, again, from sending videocassettes – or even CD-ROMs and DVDs – through the post to the much more advanced use of video-conferencing systems for lecturing – including interactive forms of lecturing. They also include the use of video on web sites and related Internet sites for enhancing and providing wider resources and materials. Again, these technologies provide opportunities for multiple relationships and types of interaction between teacher and students. There are, however, debates as to how much the visual actually adds to learning and teaching situation, particularly with respect to the lecturer him or herself. Mason (1994) argues that video contributes to a more social and facilitative learning environment. Taylor and Swannell (1997), on the other hand, criticize the idea of video-conferencing that simply reproduces the lecture in its transmission mode as 'the tyranny of futility'. The debate, of course, raises the important issue of the human/social dimension in the use of new technology.

Multi-based systems

This category consists of those technologies that merge any or all of the above three systems. One global technology dominates it: the Web. The

Web weaves and unites the other three systems of media within one, and it does so comprehensively. While access to it through the Internet is still limited for significant parts of the population, particularly in the less developed parts of the world, every passing day sees more and more people connecting up to its broad services. It is also still somewhat limited in terms of the quality and magnitude of video and audio segments that it is easily able to deliver. Again, these are technical issues which are continuously being addressed and improved. The ability to download software programmes as well as material from the Internet will permit students access to whatever range of course materials in whatever format higher education institutions wish and are able to provide.

Synchronous and asynchronous learning

Most scholarship and research on the use of new technology in learning and teaching make a widespread distinction with respect to time. If new technology provides a more flexible approach to space in its ability to transcend distance within learning and teaching, it also provides a more flexible approach to time. The main distinction here revolves around synchronous interactions in teaching/learning and asynchronous interactions. In synchronous interactions, teacher and students are 'present' at the same time in the learning environment. The advantages of this kind of interaction are usually described in terms of social and human 'presence'. The fact that the situation is actually 'happening' in 'real time' focuses group energy, cohesion, feelings of community and decision-making. It permits more 'authentic' dialogue, including issues of tone, nuance and emotion, and allows for immediate comments and 'feedback'. It also provides support, discipline and motivation for students to keep up with the course and the group pace. Asynchronous interactions, on the other hand, are often seen in terms of the student's more personal learning. It provides students with flexibility as to when they access the course materials. It allows them opportunities for going back over and working on the materials both at their own pace and at their convenience. It also provides time for reflection on the material and for integrating it within their working and/or home environment.

The synchronous-asynchronous division is, of course, not unique to the use of new technology. It has always existed. Contrast, for example, the immediacy of lectures and seminars with the asynchronous reading and study which students have traditionally done outside the classroom. For all its advanced paraphernalia and wizardry, new technology does not extend the basic types of human and social interactions through which teachers and students have traditionally engaged (Table 9.1). It does, however, extend and enhance the potential of those interactions for addressing our 'learning matrix'.

Table 9.1 *Types of human and social interactions in teaching and learning*

Interactions	Traditional	New technology
Teacher–learner	Tutorials	E–mail, voicemail
Teacher–learners	Lecturers, seminars	Video–conferencing
Learner–learner	Projects/lab work	Audio–conferencing
Learner–material	Books, journals, etc.	Cassettes, CD–ROMs
Learner–others	Open/public lectures	Internet, intranet

Extending the matrix

In terms of the learning matrix, the development and use of new technology is most commonly characterized by an *independence* context of learning and teaching. It involves, as we mentioned earlier, the delegation of responsibility to learners and is highly reliant upon their ability to work autonomously and independently from teachers. While it provides opportunities for developing *interpersonal* contexts, it is probably least effective at present for students requiring highly *support*-oriented contexts. A significant number of students who take courses that are primarily self-paced and asynchronous end up contributing rarely, and quickly falling behind with exercises and tutorials. The optimum student profile for *independence*-structured courses employing large degrees of new technology will be those who are highly motivated independent learners, good at self-pacing, employment focused, computer literate and interested in technology-mediated environments (Mason, 1998). This should not exclude other students who do not match this profile from profiting from new technology. It does suggest that teachers designing courses offered to students who require more support will need to recognize the potential pitfalls when developing their designs. One of the chief challenges to the future expansion of the use of technology in learning and teaching will focus precisely on this issue – devising more clearly developed systems for supporting students online (see below).

Before we look at some of the issues involved in the design, it is worth looking at the role which new technology might play with respect to the four main dimensions of our learning matrix: intellectual, practical, personal and social. Table 9.2 summarizes some of the positive and negative attributes with respect to these dimensions.

Many of the negative effects associated in Table 9.2 with the use of new technology are concerned in some way with losses related to face-to-face human contact. Thus 'flaming', or expressions of rage and the use of inappropriate language, linked to feelings of anonymity, isolation, 'techno-stress' and information overload are less likely to occur in face-to-face situations. The 'human' aspect of communication needs to be emphasized. On the other hand, this technology offers positive learning expe-

Table 9.2   *Positive and negative effects of new technology on four learning dimensions*

	Positive	Negative
Intellectual	• Promotion of interactive learning • Increased written output • Access to wider range of material • Opportunity for reflection/revision before contributing • Access to multiple frameworks/ discourses/perspectives	• Slowness in decision-making • Less reading • Reduced feedback • Loss of impetus to reply
Practical	• Acquisition of computer skills • Opportunities for 'learning by doing' • Management of multiple perspectives • Language skills enhanced through activity in the new technical and disciplinary 'literacies'	• Over focus on computer and keyboard skills at the expense of others
Personal	• Removal of time and space constraints to learning • Opportunity to take control of one's learning • 'Empowerment' of learner • Opportunity to develop self-skills: self-discipline, self-motivation, self-confidence, self-disclosure	• Contextual deprivation • Information overload • Techno-stress • 'Dehumanization' of learning • 'Aloneness factor'
Social	• Opportunity for dialogue with wider groups • Increased collaboration between teachers and learners and between learners • Increased participation by minority groups • Opportunity to develop multiple 'voices' within rapidly changing discourses	• Need for a skilled moderator to facilitate (control?) dialogue • 'Flaming' • Lack of account-ability • Reinforcement of existing inequali-ties

Source: adapted from Peterson, 1997

riences for students along all four learning dimensions. It is also worth stressing the potential it offers students for developing capacities to engage with and manage rapidly changing multiple frameworks. This includes both different ways of thinking about a discipline or subject, or even multiple subjects, as well as developing diverse ways of handling the varied 'knowledge' and 'understanding' associated with these range of frameworks. The comprehensive access to a wide range of frameworks afforded by new technology (including its own developing discourses) provides a platform for teachers to challenge their students.

Designing 'flexible' courses

In designing a flexible course, it is critical to explore beforehand the extent of the role which new technology might play in delivering a course's overall aims and objectives including, where appropriate, the negotiation of those aims and objectives with the students. Which aspects of the learning matrix will it focus on and which aspects are better left to other forms of teaching? And how will this be integrated with the rest of the programme? Will the use of technology play a relatively minor role, providing, for example, social support – e.g. social chat-rooms for informal discussion between interested students – with a reduced role for delivering on intellectual and practical objectives? Or will it play a substantial role in delivering aims and objectives encouraging the intellectual, social and practical independence of students by integrating, for example, online seminar and project groups with video-conferencing, extended web-site materials, access to specially prepared CD-ROMs and so on? How elaborate such a programme should be will depend to a large degree on the institutional resources available. Moran and Myringer suggest that such programmes need to be initiated within 'comprehensive university-wide strategies . . . plus a set of organizational systems and networks to support them' (1999: 60). More specifically, the evidence available from experienced practitioners suggests that online courses need to observe a number of indispensable principles:

- staff and students are trained in the relevant technology;
- the course is clearly structured;
- the course provides access to collaborative activities;
- the course both caters to individual and group student needs.

Relevant skills training

While the first of these appears obvious, teachers and course designers often underestimate its importance. Basic skills are often assumed, as are skills in more than one technology. Students, themselves, are often not the best judges of their own abilities, frequently not realizing the complexity of either the technology or their own access to that technology. Many teachers and faculty members also mistakenly assume they have the requisite skills for a course to which they have agreed to contribute. Many courses recognize that not all students will have the whole range of technological skills at the outset of a course, including, crucially, the collaborative and teamworking skills associated with technology-mediated programmes. Therefore, many programmes now integrate training and development in the relevant educational technologies alongside the actual content of the course.

Course structure

Technology-mediated learning needs substantially more structure than was originally assumed. Mere access and arranged provision for discussion groups, for example, is not sufficient to develop a shared sense of 'community' or substantially to engage all students. While some may actively thrive, other students 'lurk', remaining in the background, observing without actively contributing. In addition, unstructured or understructured discussion groups without the 'presence' of the teacher often lack rigour, leading to a corresponding reduction in the quality of the learning.

Collaboration

Ways of providing structure centre primarily on the organization of online groups and might include:

- setting collaborative tasks for students in pairs or small groups;
- establishing discussion groups around specific topics, readings, activities;
- assigning a specified number of students to groups to prevent overloading;
- reviewing group composition and changing composition if necessary;
- providing opportunities for peer leadership and facilitation.

Balance

In designing group work, teachers will always need to strike a balance between the level of structuring involved and the flexibility it provides for the student. In this, Pincas (1999) suggests that the main factors to take into consideration are:

- there is a purpose and good reason for working as a group;
- the students understand a specified outcome at any stage;
- there is a facilitator (usually tutor but occasionally a student);
- there are options (as far as course regulations allow), e.g. the time in the week when they do their work, the length of required work, the number of contributions expected, the knowledge they bring, and so on.

Guidelines

Finally, as with traditional courses, it is important to give students clear information and guidelines about the programme or course, especially the relationship between online and non-online elements. What, for example, are the overall aims and objectives of the programme? What are the primary methods of delivery and the methods of assessment and evaluation? What is the credit rating of the programme? What provision is there for student support, advice and counselling? What access to technical support and help-lines will be available? Are there any hidden costs associated with provision? Two key areas unique to online provision which will need to be specifically spelled out concern:

1 guidelines for face-to-face contact that students might expect and/or be entitled to;
2 guidelines for encouraging students to consider fully, in light of a full programme description, how they will organize and adjust their study and approaches to study to the requirements of the course.

Are they fully prepared to engage with the course intellectually, practically, personally and socially, given its particular parameters?

Conclusions

Many commentators exploring developments in new technology to enhance learning and teaching in higher education have focused on three essential features it offers. These are its potential for developing learner-centred approaches to teaching, its capacity for promoting collaboration and teamwork, and its central role in encouraging autonomous, independent learners. These features are not unique to new technology but, rather, powerful outcomes of its imaginative and innovative use. Innovation, here, does not therefore simply rest in the new technology, nor does it arise through its educational application. It consists, rather, in the new and creative ways in which technology can be used to develop, support and extend student learning in the myriad ways described by the 'learning matrix' described in Chapter 4. It embraces a wide and diverse range of inventive and resourceful 'flexible' strategies for integrating traditional and new methods of educational delivery. It appreciates the intrinsically 'human' character of technology as being essentially concerned with the development of 'dialogue' and community. Finally, however, it recognizes that new technology is not another way of extending educational delivery, but is itself a defining cultural and social feature of our increasingly unpredictable, changeable and contestable world. Its very application is now a necessary part of higher education's role in preparing students for the culture of the future, as it rapidly becomes the present. In this way, innovation, itself, becomes 'content' in the higher education curriculum, its very use a model for students to critically and creatively reconstruct for themselves in their own learning.

Further reading

Brown, J.S. and Duguid, P. (2000) *The Social Life of Information*. Boston: Harvard Business School Press.

Campbell, D. and Campbell, M. (1995) *The Student's Guide to Doing Research on the Internet*. Reading, MA: Addison-Wesley.

Harry, K. (ed.) (1999) *Higher Education through Open and Distance Learning*. London: Routledge.

Mason, R. (1994) *Using Communications Media in Open and Flexible Learning*. London: Kogan Page.

Mason, R. (1998) *Globalising Education: Trends and Applications*. London: Routledge.

Moro, B. (1997) 'A pedagogy of the hypermedia', in A.-K. Korsvold and B. Ruschoff (eds), *New Technologies in Language Learning and Teaching*. (Education Committee: Council for Cultural Co-operation) Strasbourg: Council of Europe Publishing.

Noss, R. and Pachler, N. (1999) 'The challenge of new technologies: doing old things in a new way, or doing new things?' in P. Mortimore (ed.), *Understanding Pedagogy and its Impact on Learning*. London: Paul Chapman.

Pincas, A. (1999) 'Problems and principles in the use of computer networks for course delivery', *Certificate in Online Education and Training*. London: Institute of Education, University of London.

Talbott, S. (1995) *The Future Does Not Compute*. Sebastopol, CA: O'Reilly and Associates.

Taylor, J. and Swannell, P. (1997) 'From outback to internet: crackling radio to virtual campus', in *Proceedings of InterAct, International Telecommunications Union*. Geneva: ITU (CD-ROM).

10

Assessing: Student Assessment

If we wish to discover the truth about an educational system we must look into its assessment procedure. (Rowntree, 1987: 1)

Writing four questions on a three hour exam paper is a total contradiction of what you've been training yourself to do throughout the year. (Student, in Cox, 1985: 2191)

Introduction

Assessing students is perhaps the most emotionally sensitive part of our education but at the same time is intellectually demanding and can be socially disturbing and divisive for the students. It is easy for students to feel that it is not only their learning that is being assessed, but their developing identity as persons. Associations with right and wrong can trigger the more primitive associations with good and bad and create fear and loss of confidence especially in subjects, such as mathematics, where being wrong can be painfully obvious. Whether assessment, therefore, appears to be valid is not a trivial issue. Students need to feel that they have been given the best opportunity to express their ability in their discipline, but also to convey something of themselves on what the subject means to them. Without this it becomes more closely associated with a system of control. With younger students this can produce either conformity or alienation, while older students can see it as a rejection of what they have to offer as mature adults.

For these reasons it is particularly important to match the whole experience of assessment with what the programme is trying to achieve and the culture it is trying to create. This will require innovation and a wider variety of modes and methods than we currently employ. This chapter will not, however, simply review the wide range of new methods now being used but will discuss the most important in relation to the matrix of learning described in Chapter 4. The introduction will address a number of general concepts and issues pertaining to assessment. It will be followed by an exploration of assessment as it relates to the intellectual, personal, social and practical dimensions of learning. The approach adopted here is intended to be of more direct and specific help in integrating assessment and course design with key issues of student learning. It is supplemented by an exercise or guide (Appendix 1) – analyzing a wide range of different methods and systems of assessment – designed to aid in the development of a balanced assessment strategy for effectively measuring student achievement and enhancing learning.

Formative and summative assessment

These two general purposes of assessment – measuring student achievement and enhancing learning – are often referred to as 'summative' and 'formative' assessment respectively. Brown and Knight provide useful and succinct descriptions of these two concepts:

> Summative assessment includes end-of-course assessment and essentially means that this is assessment which produces a measure which sums up someone's achievement and which has no other real use except as a description of what has been achieved. Formative assessment is where the purpose is to get an estimate of achievement which is used to help in the learning process ... Formative assessment includes coursework where the student receives feedback which helps him/her to improve their next performance. (1994: 15)

Although different methods of assessment may tend towards fulfilling one or the other of these two purposes – e.g. exams/summative, draft essay/formative – almost all methods can be applied to either of these two purposes. Neither should the two purposes be regarded as mutually exclusive. 'Enhancing learning', as we saw in Chapter 4, could mean either deep-transforming ideas of learning or surface-reproducing ideas of learning. Similarly 'measuring achievement' could suggest a measurement of either deep or surface learning. 'What' we assess becomes more important that 'why' we are assessing.

This distinction is important, particularly if we agree with Rowntree (1987: 1) that 'to discover the truth about an education system we must look to its assessment procedures'. Working purely for marks or grades can be an indication of a cynical and purely strategic approach to assessment. Traditional finals, for example, have often elicited these approaches, primarily with respect to course content, frequently enabling students to evade some of the more serious deeper demands of their courses and still pass. If, however, assessment goes beyond basic information and techniques to include higher-level intellectual demands, and reflects a commitment and enthusiasm for education and the deeper values of the discipline, then 'high grades' will reflect the deeper issues that the course may really be about. In this respect 'high grades' might reflect an appreciation of alternative perspectives, a need to change, to reconceptualize and construct knowledge, and a capacity to cope with unexpected and new complexities. In addition, there will be other valuable experiences at college that should neither be incorporated into grades nor marginalized by them, experiences which are more appropriate to formative assessment.

Norm-referenced and criterion-referenced assessments

Marks and grades are, of course, essentially norms by which to judge the difference between students. This form of assessment is often referred to as 'norm-referenced' assessment. The ultimate aim of this kind of assessment is to enable effective and reliable discrimination amongst students. While students often seek information about these differences, this does not necessarily tell them much about the quality of their thinking, or what they are able to do. The issue is not so much about what they achieve but more what is their status in relation to other students. If too many students achieve the required outcome then the norm-referenced assessment has been a failure since it will not discriminate.

Assessments which grade against sets of predetermined criteria on the other hand are 'criterion-referenced' forms of assessment. With criterion-referenced assessment everyone is pleased if all students realize the levels established by the set criteria since the course will have achieved what it was trying to achieve. In this respect criterion-referenced achievement helps students to understand how far their thinking and their performance has progressed.

Issues arising from traditional assessment

Despite the intentions of faculty, and even students, traditional exams do not give an adequate picture of the many and varied abilities which are developed in higher education. Distortions are frequently encouraged by exaggerated and stereotyped perceptions that students have of traditional exams. They are sustained by the idea that exam results provide a grand verdict on a student's academic worth. This verdict, however, is rarely based on evidence accumulated from a variety of settings that resemble the sort of tasks and situations they will face in later life. Instead, under the traditional system, it is based on a situation, 20–30 hours of writing with very tight time constraints and a heavy memory load, that they will probably never face again. Criticisms of such traditional assessment will be familiar to many teachers in higher education and include:

- too much emphasis on memory;
- too much stress on factual knowledge;
- too great a reliance on speed of writing and thinking;
- too great an element of luck;

- too much pressure of a kind seldom found in later life;
- too little scope for originality and sustained writing;
- too little opportunity for constructive feedback.

A major difficulty with the traditional exam system is that it gives teachers so few leads on how to learn more about the process. A great deal can be done within departments once a start is made in trying to diversify our assessments so that different desired outcomes are evaluated separately. While the administrative functions of assessments may be simplified by overall one-dimensional grading, they are not necessarily efficient (even as predictions for graduate work). Overall assessments may differentiate students reasonably consistently, but the purpose of this particular way of categorizing students is too general. What is needed is a range of information about the very different abilities of students that can be used in different ways depending upon why that particular selection is being made.

Formative assessment is also not well served within the traditional system, primarily because of this lack of differentiation of abilities, but for other important reasons as well. The timing of traditional assessments is usually too late for early feedback; information is often regarded for some reason as confidential; but perhaps even more important are the attitudes of faculty and students. Few students regard their exam performance as an accurate indication of their ability, and faculty rarely encourage discussion with students who do not seem to want it. Traditional exams can be used to direct students' efforts to important areas of the course, but they are generally not good at directing students' efforts towards developing a higher level of intellectual abilities to be used in these areas. The general purpose of providing an incentive to work is often successful but extrinsic motivation is a unconvincing part of higher education. Indeed. it conflicts with the often stated aims of education which rank love of learning and intellectual development above all else. This distinction may not always be very clear but intrinsic motivation is generally considered more valuable. It can certainly make a greater contribution to the important question of student identity mentioned earlier.

This chapter focuses on students, how we assess them affects the way they learn and develop, but any system must be acceptable to faculty and not unduly increase their already excessive workload. As assessment becomes more closely integrated with learning and teaching, the time spent on it is not just concerned with grading but is an integral part of teaching. The acceptance, moreover, of peer- and self-assessment methods can save faculty time as well as contribute to students becoming more independent professionals. It can counter, for example, some of the unfortunate consequences of objective, machine-scored exams, which while saving time can encourage routine low-level learning and dependency. 'The excessive employment of selective examinations is gradually subverting all that is best in the education of our youth and a reaction is threatened which may bring the use of examinations altogether into discredit if remedies be not found for the worst abuses of the system' (Senate Committee on Examinations, University of Edinburgh, nineteenth century).

The intellectual dimension
Providing support

This section will focus on how we can support student learning through assessment. It provides a rationale for the way we assess students which will enable them to achieve a clearer understanding of the criteria and standards, give them more confidence in the reliability, validity and fairness of the system, and provide better feedback and reporting.

Students often derive more understanding of a course from the demands of its assessment system than from tutors and course handbooks. If we want students to be clearer about what their courses are meant to achieve, better descriptions and detailed objectives will not be enough. They need to understand the 'real' demands of the assessment system. And merely telling students, as Hounsell (1997) suggests, may have little effect. Students often approach their exams and assignments with assumptions and conceptions of the criteria used to judge their work that are very different from those of their tutors. They interpret the written criteria and feedback comments in a way that fits their assumptions rather than the tutor's intentions. Helping them develop a deeper understanding of the course by looking at the demands of the assessments is challenging and involves a gradual development of skills that require practice.

Marking exercises and criteria   One of the most important ways of improving students' understanding of the criteria and thereby enabling them to feel more confident about their understanding of the demands of the course is to engage them in marking exercises. This can take the form of giving them an essay or assignment but instead of writing the assignment, asking them to mark perhaps one of the previous students' attempts at answering it. As part of this, discussions about how this should be done and what sort of criteria should be used can be more helpful than simply giving them the official line on criteria and marking standards. They are likely to learn a great deal more about marking if they attempt to formulate the criteria themselves. When their marks are compared and discussed with the tutor they can begin to revise and develop their criteria in ways that might improve their own work. Gibbs (1991: 81) provides an interesting exercise where students mark two contrasting approaches to the same essay title that brings out interesting points related to the issues of deep and surface learning.

SOLO and standards Biggs (1999) gives an interesting taxonomy of levels of academic work – SOLO (Structure of the Observed Learning Outcomes) – which can also be useful in helping students (and teachers) understand some of the standards used in assessment. It involves five levels (see Table 10.1). These levels are not easy for students to understand. Considerable time and effort in discussing them may be necessary together with opportunities to apply them to a wide range of examples.

Table 10.1 *SOLO and assessment*

1 Pre-structural	Answer misses the point and/or is irrelevant
2 Uni-structural	Answer focuses on only one relevant conceptual issue in a complex case
3 Multi-structural	Answer focuses on more than one issue but they are a disorganized collection of items: reproduces a 'shopping list'
4 Relational	Answer shows understanding, applies or uses a concept(s) which integrates a collection of data, issues, etc.
5 Extended abstract	Answer goes beyond existing principles; higher-order principles are used to bring in a new broader set of issues

Source: adapted from Biggs, 1999: 47–8

Another way of increasing students' understanding and ability to operate with varied criteria is to give them a range of essays on a particular topic which have already been graded by faculty. Their task is to rank them, and their ranking is then compared with that of the faculty. Their performance on this task can be evaluated in terms of how far their ranking corresponds to the faculty ranking. This has two very practical advantages: it enables students to see and consider a range of alternative responses to a set question and it enables faculty to mark large numbers very quickly. This type of activity can be a useful preliminary to more serious attempts to develop self and peer assessment. It can enable students to move from a quantitative view of the value of their work, expressed in terms of more and more detailed information, to a more qualitative approach based on differences that reflect different levels of intellectual understanding.

Student views on assessment This is not to suggest that all students come with very naïve views about the nature of academic work. Early work on face (perceived) validity (Jones et al., 1973) suggested that students were very concerned about what was being assessed within traditional examinations. Two-thirds of students in a wide range of disciplines agreed with the statement that 'in planning my work I frequently found my real intellectual interest had to take second place in the need to get good marks'. A high proportion felt that the intellectual qualities that the lecturers valued were not tested in the examination. Later research has confirmed many of these findings. Despite claiming to know what lecturers wanted, almost two-thirds of students felt that they were not given a clear idea of the academic qualities faculty expected in their work.

In another study, Cox (1975) revealed that students often found their experience of assessment contradicted their own personal and educational aspirations. Table 10.2 gives a selection of the vivid reactions that draw attention to the life-stage of students where control, dependence and autonomy are influential in the development of personal and professional identity. Assessment, the dominating instrument of control in higher education, gets bound up with the struggle for independence. Conformist students may lose out in this battle and become passive learners whose view of education is dominated by memorizing. Other students can become rebellious and find their energies are dissipated in hostility or may withdraw in apathy from a system they disagree with. Only the more independent students can cope with the system and yet maintain a sense of integrity.

Table 10.2   *Student experiences of assessment*

'You despise yourself for wanting to do well in exams: it's a conflict inside yourself';
'Writing four questions in a three hour exam paper is a total contradiction of what you've been training yourself to do throughout the year';
'The more cold-blooded you can become the better, you have got to make yourself like a machine';
'I don't think without distorting my personality beyond recognition I could get a 2(1) in this place. I would have to conform to the right model';
'It's a great mistake to be over sophisticated in exams: it's part of the technique not to be: one has to limit oneself'.

Source: Cox, 1975

One way of supporting our students and enabling them to feel that the assessment system reflects the true nature of the subject and the abilities required, is to 'contextualize' assessment and make it more naturalistic. An important example of this is the development of problem-based learning (PBL). Courses are designed around real-life problems. The more abstract and, sometimes, less engaging aspects of the course are learned in relation to a close involvement with problems which are highly relevant to students' more concrete ideas of what the course is about and what competence would mean within it. This approach has been particularly influential in medical education where concerns about 'taxing the memory but not the intellect' (GMC, 1994: 5) have resulted in medical schools throughout the USA, UK, Canada and Australia taking up BPL approaches to learning and teaching.

Reliability   Lack of reliability or consistency of marking, both perceived and real, has contributed to students' lack of confidence in marking systems. As long ago as 1963, Pieron concluded that 'assessment by different examiners produces marks with considerable variability such that in the determination of these marks the part played by the examiner can be greater than that of the performance of the examinee' (1963: 140). Nevertheless, academics frequently discuss marks as if they were accurate and absolute. Although marking can sometimes be reasonably reliable, on average a particular percentage mark is only accurate to within a range of about 16 points in any particular case. To be accurate refers to the hypothetical mark that might be obtained if marks given by a large number of markers were averaged. Again, this does not mean that there is an absolute, true and accurate mark but rather that the mean of one large group of examiners will tend to agree with the mean of another large group of examiners.

Much more important than averages, perhaps, are the wide discrepancies that can occur in individual cases. While it is recognized that examiners can disagree on the value of particular answers in the arts and social sciences, students can present examiners with very difficult problems in more scientific subjects. Hill (1975), for example, reports research on the marking of ten candidates on an actual fluid mechanics exam, where there was a formal marking scheme and six problems to be answered in three hours. The eight markers were all experienced in fluid mechanics and two were the official markers of that examination. For some candidates the range of marks was close, for others wide but tolerable. Two candidates, however, presented serious problems; one received marks ranging between failure and near distinction and the another between clear failure and very creditable.

Reliability can be improved through marking schemes but also by engaging teachers in more discussion about their approaches and interpretations of marking. Double marking – conducted in a blind fashion with the second examiner not seeing the first mark and the two marks simply pooled and averaged – might, for example, contribute a partial solution to the above problem. However, the real use of double marking is to encourage the discussion of issues that the discrepancies throw up, to encourage a clarification of the criteria and their interpretation. Real improvement will only occur when these issues are resolved through the development of a genuine community of assessors with a shared culture of standards. While such approaches to marking are undermined by increasing modularization of courses and pressures on time, examiners' meetings need to focus on developing shared contexts and criteria for marking as well as determining the actual marks.

Objective testing Where factual information is an important aspect of the course to be assessed objective testing – such as those employing true–false and multiple-choice questions – can make an important contribution to the overall assessment of student learning. They are a particularly significant feature of any assessment system in the physical and medical sciences and can now be drawn and developed from elaborate computerized item banks. In one sense, they can also be very reliable, answers are right or wrong and frequently machine graded. In another sense, however, the choice of right answer and the nearness of the 'distracters' to this right answer can create areas of ambiguity and uncertainty that diminish this 'objectivity'. In addition, such assessment methods frequently appear artificial and detached from any meaningful context. Indeed, it is now becoming common to insert factual questions within a narrative – often within a computerized format – where the questions are linked to a specific, concrete context, argument or diagnosis.

With faculty time becoming such a crucial issue there is a danger of overusing objective tests. It can lead to faculty finding in the final years of an undergraduate course, that they are having to encourage students to unlearn study practices – such as memorization and rote-learning – developed from too much emphasis being put on objective tests. There is a need to compensate for their defects by including them alongside other forms of assessment that do not require the reproduction of excessive factual information. The more important challenges of assessment are essentially holistic, demanding the demonstration of understanding and the construction of meaning. Such abilities are difficult to assess within objective format, although more objective kinds of questions can be successfully integrated into complex texts that require a more holistic approach from the student (Brown *et al*, 1997).

Feedback to students Frequent feedback to students can be particularly supportive especially for those who are rather anxious. It is important for students to have a sense of their own progression through the course and how they are coping with it. Feedback from summative assessments in the form of grades or marks alone might provide them with a general sense of where they stand in the course and amongst their peers, but might not contribute much to their sense of intellectual growth. These, of course, can be supplemented with constructive comments where appropriate and possible. Criterion-referenced assessments at least provide the student the opportunity to reflect upon and understand how far their thinking and their performance has progressed. Summative feedback from norm-referenced assessments provide little more than a sense of peer positioning which might, depending on that position, develop or undermine student confidence in their progress. Support for students through formative assessment is generally criterion-referenced, helping the student to achieve the learning outcomes of the course in accordance with its established criteria and standards.

The dangers of feedback, however, are that students can become over dependent on this support. The ultimate aim in students becoming professionals is of course that they are no longer highly dependent on others for judgements about the quality of their work. As Bruner comments 'the tutor must correct a learner in a fashion that eventually makes it possible for the learner to take over the correcting function himself, otherwise the result of instruction is to create a form of mastery that is contingent on the perpetual presence of the teacher' (1966: 53). This is where the self- and peer-assessment techniques (see below) and the necessary training for doing this can play a useful role. It can aid students in developing the skills to reflect upon and assess their own work and progress.

Encouraging independence

If, as suggested above, we are too supportive, students may become dependent and avoid the more challenging demands that would enable them to become independent learners and professionals. In this section we shall be looking at what methods of assessment might be most appropriate in encouraging intellectual independence and helping students achieve higher-level objectives – creativity, choice and self-evaluation.

To encourage independent thinking, however, it is necessary to make it clear to students that their work needs to reflect those deeper higher-level processes. These will include processes of analysis, synthesis and evaluation described, for example, by Bloom (1956) in his classic *Taxonomy of Educational Objectives* and the higher-level outcomes expressed in the SOLO taxonomy mentioned above. Operating at these levels is not easy and a major obstacle to doing so is lack of time. Overloaded courses are notorious in encouraging surface-level approaches to learning and assignments. Examinations with high time constraints can give little opportunity for reflection, considering alternatives, appreciating different contexts and integration. The tasks set on many courses, especially on foundation modules, are very often short term, to be completed in a few minutes or perhaps an hour. Work which requires extended concentration over weeks or months is usually restricted to the final year of a programme but the quality of the thinking which is generated out of long-term commitment can be very important for encouraging independence.

Projects Projects have long been recognized as perhaps the most important area for self-expression and commitment (Cox, 1975). For many students, the first two years may be memorizing other people's work and only in final years are they able to begin to seriously engage with the discipline and subject matter. Table 10.3 provides a list of the educational advantages suggested by Brown et al. (1997), augmented by comments from students on project work from research by Cox.

Table 10.3   *Student experiences of projects*

Advantages	Student Experiences
1 Enable the student to explore deeply a field or topic	'It's the only time you do your own work'
2 Develop initiative and resourcefulness	'It's not just an exercise, it's good that you have to do it all on your own and fit it into a theoretical framework'
3 Enhance time and project management skills	'The best opportunity we had, other work is other people's thoughts'
4 Provide personal ownership of learning	'Very much me, my biases and beliefs' 'It's something you can get your teeth into, something you choose yourself'
5 Foster independence and creative problem solving	'Some original thinking is required, essays are more regurgitatory of other people's opinions'

Source: adapted from Brown et al., 1997; Cox, 1975

Project work also provides a good opportunity for students to engage in divergent – as opposed to convergent thinking (Rowntree, 1987). Although this will vary among students and disciplines, the undergraduate in particular is frequently not provided with substantial opportunity to engage with coursework which permits them to diverge across a range of possible answers, concepts, meanings, solutions, approaches, and so on. Yet, this is an essential feature of any creative work or in depth inquiry or research. Many if not most of our methods of assessments encourage convergent thinking, asking students to converge upon a right or best answer. While project work like any coursework can be derivative, poorly planned, badly referenced, tedious, etc., it does also offer students opportunities for choice, creativity and divergent thinking – indeed it can be written into the criteria for project assessment.

The disadvantages of project work include concerns that it is time-consuming to set up, monitor and provide feedback on, and difficult to fairly assess failure. Wide variations in the help sought by students and the fear of plagiarism – the latter perhaps enhanced by access to the Internet – are also obstacles to consider. None of these disadvantages is, however, insurmountable and Brown et al. (1997) regard problems in assessing projects as no more than those involved in assessing course work, essays or written papers.

Portfolios   Portfolios are another form of assessment that focuses upon enabling students to have a wider range of choice than more traditional methods. Students may be asked to provide a portfolio of evidence of achievement in terms both of outcomes specified by the course and also a wider range of abilities and achievements which are more personal to the individual students and their particular interests. Research on the personal development and motivation of students often stresses the importance of them having a sense of control over their own environment. This is typically expressed in terms of how many choices they are able to make in terms of what they learn and how they learn (Cox, 1996). They can show a respect for individual differences and the varied contexts in which people work. Portfolios are now becoming a widespread way of assessing professional and continuing development – including now the accreditation of teaching in higher education. Nevertheless, their use is usually accompanied by guidelines as to what should be included and how they should be structured. They have similarities with records of achievement and are quite often used for assessing prior learning and prior experiential learning.

Open-book exams   Most assessment that is concerned with encouraging independence is much more open than traditional assessments. Allowing textbooks into examination rooms may encourage a certain amount of independence but is not necessarily going to achieve this. It may assess an ability to locate information quickly rather than the ability to use it in more independent, creative ways. Open-book exams usually specify the texts and resources that may be consulted but with the expansion of coursework as opposed to examinations, it becomes more difficult to justify making these types of assessment within an examination hall.

Prior-notice exams   A more useful method of assessing the ability to produce work under time pressures and in a more secure environment, are examinations where the topics or the actual questions are given out in advance. Students can carry out research and develop their understanding in libraries beforehand. Cox (1975) found that sociology students reacted differently to the change in constraints. While prior-notice exams relieved the constraint on memory, many students feared that the standards expected would be correspondingly higher. However, they provided the more independent students with the opportunity to explore issues in depth and to take risks and express what they themselves thought about issues rather than reproducing textbook answers. They had the chance to justify their ideas in a way in which they felt they never had in traditional exams. For some dependent students this form of assessment provoked anxiety and they found it difficult to stop preparing for it. The majority, however, found it quite liberating.

Problem-based learning   As suggested earlier, the development of PBL is an important development for encouraging independence in students. Although PBL courses use examinations, they are generally less important than in courses that are more traditional. The actual solving and understanding of the problems is the most prevalent form of assessment. This more contextualized and naturalistic assessment enables students to feel that assessment is not a control mechanism but is a natural feature of learning.

Self-assessment   The development and increasing use of methods of self-assessment is, perhaps, the most important innovation in assessment for the development of intellectual independence. In contrast to the vast majority of assessment methods, it directly addresses the paradox of a highly dependent education leading to the independent responsible status of a professional person.

> Unilateral control and assessment of students by staff mean that the process of education is at odds with the objective of that process. I believe that the objective of the process is the emergence of an educated person; that is a person who is self-determining – who can set his own learning objectives – devise a rational program to attain them – set criteria of excellence by which to assess the work he produces and assess his own work in the light of these criteria – indeed all that we attribute and hope from the ideal academic himself. (Heron, 1981: 57)

Boud (1995) develops these themes, noting, however, that there are many pitfalls in introducing it. It may be particularly difficult in those academic cultures that are not used to innovation, and/or those in which students are unduly competitive. It requires a culture of mutual trust between students and between students and faculty. Teachers have also frequently resisted the development of self-assessment methods, suggesting that students can be over generous in their marking. In fact, there is evidence to suggest the opposite. Generally, student reactions are very positive. Five times as many students found it a worthwhile experience as those who did not, and a similar ratio found the exercise helped them to pinpoint their strengths and weaknesses (Boud, 1995: 87).

A critical issue in the development of self-assessment concerns strategies for generating criteria against which the student will assess his or her work. It is important that teachers do not simply issue criteria from above but rather provide students with a role in formulating and refining them together with teaching faculty. Exercises in peer marking can be helpful in this respect. Although learning from mistakes has its benefits, there can be serious problems in introducing self-assessment into an unprepared environment. Early bad experiences can easily make it extremely difficult to try to introduce it later. It is important to establish clear rationales for involving students in developing the criteria. In the process they will also learn to make qualitative judgements, including justifications for the assessments they make. Boud (1995) also stresses that self-assessment practices should permeate the total course. They should make an identifiable contribution to formal decision-making and be part of a profiling process in which students are actively involved.

> Self-assessment can be viewed, not as a distinct element of teaching and learning, but in relation to reflection, critical reflection and meta-cognitive practices. It is part of that set of activities which encourage students to take responsibility for their own learning, monitor their learning plans and activities, process their studying and assess their effectiveness. Self-assessment then would become something which is embedded in courses designed from the very start to assist students with their learning. (Boud, 1995: 215)

Developing the interpersonal

Historically higher education has been primarily focused on the individual, encouraging the student to 'think for himself (*sic*) and work on his own' (Hale, 1964: iii). Collaboration with respect to assessment was highly suspect. The development of interpersonal skills, co-operation and abilities to work in teams is, however, increasingly valued. In this section, we shall briefly look at widening the scope of our assessment systems to engage with interpersonal skills.

Peer assessment   The discussion of self-assessment inevitably raises questions of peer assessment since the ability to become an effective self-assessor is often enhanced by assessing peers and being assessed by them. It is an important issue in assessment generally to be able to appreciate different perspectives and points of view. Attempting to assess a range of different student assignments can be extremely interesting for students, enabling them to see a wider range of perspectives and solutions. Of course, in seminars, students will be exposed to different views but this is a very different experience to critically assessing and analysing them for their different strengths and weaknesses. These skills are also critical in a multicultural society that expects people to understand and tolerate multiple views and perspectives, which values the intellectual virtues of parallel thinking (De Bono, 1994) rather than patterns of critical thinking which encourage the rejection and substitution of intellectual positions. Employers value interpersonal skills and communication in a way they have never done before. Modern companies are less hierarchical and their employees are more likely to work collaboratively on projects rather than simply follow instructions. Issues of co-operation and competition permeate all levels and activities in society. We think less in terms of single-dimensional intelligence (IQ) and more in terms of 'multiple intelligences' (Gardner, 1993) which include the interpersonal which can be enhanced by peer assessment as well as the intrapersonal intelligence which can be enhanced by self-assessment.

One of the most valuable aspects of British higher education has been the opportunity for detailed discussion with tutors on assignments. Written comments on assignments followed by discussion can be one of the most effective learning activities in academic life. It is still an essential aspect of PhD supervision but with the larger staff–student ratios is becoming harder in undergraduate courses. Peer assessment can provide students with new perspectives in a way tutor assessment is now seldom able to. As with self-assessment, peer assessment is not something that can be effectively introduced without considerable practice and reflection. This development, however, may be done in larger groups and the investment of considerable time in extending the skills of giving and taking criticism can be an extremely valuable learning activity. It is important to see this as a skill that is developed over the whole range of teaching and learning in higher education. Traditional student-led seminars, for example, are often painful experiences, either in the sense that criticism is badly given and/or badly taken, or in the sense that serious discussion and criticism is difficult to initiate and sustain. Process-oriented time in seminars – conducted in an atmosphere of mutual trust – can be a useful occasion for developing the interpersonal skills that are essential in peer assessment. Equally, what is learnt in peer assessment may enable group work to function in a more constructive and helpful way.

Consultants and assessors exercise   An interesting way of combining group work with peer assessment is the simulation exercise of consultants and assessors. This very useful teaching exercise consists of setting up consultant teams to address a specific problem in the particular subject area. (See Chapter 6 for a full description.) Briefly, the class is divided into consultant teams of about four to six members. Each team prepares a report on the problem for a group of assessors drawn from each team. The assessors' group formulates criteria by which to judge the several consultant team presentations. The exercise can take anything from an hour and a half to several days and may involve purely thinking and discussing in the groups or consulting various resources. Questioning by the assessors can draw out many issues in assessment, as can the judgements themselves. As important, however, is a debriefing session when the consultants assess the assessors on the criteria they devised and applied. The way in which they are applied can come under very active scrutiny by both the student consultants and the tutor. The debriefing can also be a further time for co-operation both in terms of the intellectual task set and understanding the process.

Group projects Group projects provide a further opportunity for intellectual and interpersonal development with respect to assessment. Their increasing use in higher education parallels the growth of project-orientation approaches developed in industry. The traditional focus on assessing the individual is one reason why group projects have not been used as often as they might. How do you 'fairly' allocate marks? Do you give all members of the group the same grade despite the fact you may know that some have actually played very little part in it? Many teachers feel that competition for marks within the group may not facilitate effective problem-solving, co-operation and learning. Answers to this question are very much dependent on the nature of the projects and the aims which they are designed to achieve. There are at least three different approaches.

In the first, the tasks are divided into sections that are completed by individuals and marked separately. The introduction and the conclusions would need to be considered by the whole group as well as a general sharing of views about the individual sections. In this context, two marks might be given to each individual: one which is common to all members for the quality of the project as a whole and the second for the separate sections which will vary for each individual contributor. This can be an effective approach where the project can be divided into equally challenging sections for all members to undertake.

A second approach – when dividing the project into separate sections is difficult or too artificial – consists of giving the same mark to all members of the group or team. Each, however, may be asked to write a reflective commentary on the process and their contribution that is marked separately and recognizes the different levels of commitment and understanding within the group. Encouraging and rewarding reflective practice through the assessment is an added advantage.

A rather different approach involves aspects of peer assessment. This approach asks the group to allocate a proportion of the total mark to each of the participants. Conducted badly such an approach can be a recipe for antagonism within the group. As with other forms of peer assessment, it needs to be carefully discussed and planned with the students before they actually begin to work on the project. Students will need to reach agreement on how the decisions are going to be made and what the criteria for dividing the joint mark will be.

In any group work, of course, the issues are not purely intellectual. There will be many personal issues raised and the social composition and practical functioning of the group will be crucially important and will materially affect the outcome.

The personal dimension
Providing support

In this section, we stress the importance of assessment in providing support for personal development and suggest some ways of doing this by encouraging choice, learning contracts or agreements and reflective commentaries.

Encouraging choice   We have suggested in earlier chapters that higher education is not just about transmitting information and developing particular competencies and skills. It is a time for self-understanding and personal development, both in the sense of coming to know ourselves better and also coming to know what sort of professionals we may be. In professional courses, the match between the student's understanding of what it means to be an engineer or a doctor and what the course seems to be providing can be crucial both for motivation and for intellectual development. Higher education is often less about learning specific topics and more about developing constructive ways of approaching them. Our own identities are very much an expression of the successive choices we make in life. This is extremely important for students beginning to know themselves. If there is little choice in the courses and the assessments they have to cope with, then they can easily feel they are being shaped and moulded by others. In extreme cases, students, very good students, will rebel against what they perceive and experience as external control and the lack of choice, even to the extent of failing. Indeed, failing in such cases – where narrowly constructed parental and academic expectations are experienced as oppressive – is often seen as the only way for some students to exert choice and develop themselves personally. 'Success' simply acknowledges the pressure to succeed and conforming to it. Choice and opportunities for self-direction might alleviate this desire to frustrate the aims of others by failing.

Learning contracts or agreements   Providing students with the opportunity for informed choice and time to take that seriously is an important part of the teacher's role. As noted above, project work provides one way to do this, but many other assignments can also offer choice amongst alternatives. The development of both informal and formal learning contracts – where teacher and student agree procedures and areas of inquiry – can also encourage students to feel they have a more personal role in their education. These can also provide an important platform for personal reflection. In arts subjects and, to some extent, social sciences the expression of personal perspectives has always been valued but in the sciences and medical sciences this has been be difficult. With the decline of positivism and a willingness to take more open positions in many areas, the possibility of developing personal views is increasing.

Reflective commentaries Supporting students to reflect on their choices and judgements is also an important way of enabling them to feel they are developing personally while in higher education. In some disciplines, it may appear difficult to find areas of personal expression. Even in very technical projects, however, asking students to write a section in reports on their personal response to the experience can be a useful way of encouraging them to understand and extend their own responses and experiences of learning.

Encouraging independence

Many of the issues discussed under personal support are designed to enable students to have a more secure sense of personal identity. This is also, of course, an essential aspect of developing independence. Changes in the nature of higher education in the past three or four decades have, however, emphasized 'independence' aspects of a student's identity more acutely than it once had. In the earlier more homogeneous and restricted 'elite' system of higher education, students could expect to develop their identity through 'identification' – stressing an apprentice role. In the 'radical' changes in the 1960s and 1970s and the development of 'mass' higher education (Trow, 1981), the focus of student 'identity' shifted towards exploration, gaining self-knowledge and intellectual autonomy. The traditional examination system corresponds to the 'apprentice' role and the more modern, open and diverse forms of assessment corresponded to the 'exploration' route (Cox, 1973). This distinction matched the parallel changes in society in relation to conceptions of the structure of knowledge, occupational structure, teaching, participation, adolescent development and cultural and social life. The 'traditional' cultural life involved fewer boundaries and expectations, identity was more prescribed, there was more consensus of values and duties, and clearer artistic styles and conventions. The more 'modern' social life – with its blurred boundaries and expectations, lack of prescriptions about identity, lack of consensus upon values and duties and lack of conventions in artistic expression – is even more prevalent in today's 'supercomplex' world.

Ironically, academic pressures – lack of resources and rising staff–student ratios – threaten to return academics and students to some of the more formal, traditional approaches to assessment of the past and fears for the student experience (see Table 10.2). We still find within some of the more formal subjects, fears that under the pressure of overloaded curricula there is no scope for individuality and creativity, only for learning the right answers and reproducing them. On the other hand, PhD guidelines (Sloboda and Newstead, 1995) are recommending reflective commentaries on the experience of writing a PhD and conclusions about what they have learnt from doing it. Even the personal pronoun 'I' is not automatically rejected, and contextualizing writing in terms of particular personal responses is seen as more academically respectable. Encouraging this generally within assignments might weaken the tendencies towards bureaucratization and commodification of higher education and assessment.

Developing the interpersonal

Encouraging the interpersonal within the personal dimension is very close to considering the interpersonal within the social dimension. An important distinction to recognize is the aspects of self-knowledge – crucial to working within groups – which group work and assessments/reports on group work can emphasize. We learn a great deal from reflecting on our own behaviour; this is particularly the case when we reflect on it in terms of the responses, reactions and interactions of other people. While it is still somewhat unusual for courses to emphasize self-knowledge and interpersonal skills in their assessments, recent interest in transferable skills has, as we noted above, raised their profile in this respect. At present, this might be more in theory than in practice but assessment, even formative assessment, may help to make it a more important aspect of education. Accurate and reliable assessment in this area is still problematic. Nevertheless, the development of reflective commentaries which, for example, ask students to look at how far they have changed in response to a course and what they have learned about their own participation and reactions to various events and activities during the course can be invaluable. Careful programmes in peer-tutoring and peer-mentoring might also provide a valuable interpersonal role in assessing self-knowledge. Encouraging students to look at their own strengths and weaknesses and their own ways of benefiting from a range of different relationships can contribute to their overall formative assessment.

The social dimension

Providing support

Traditionally, there has long been an emphasis upon the value of college life at university and the importance of participating actively in the social life and student societies. Seminars and group work, however, do not have a reputation as valuable social experiences. More recently, however, there has been more emphasis upon syndicate learning, peer-managed groups and group projects. The development of more reflective study has often focused upon peer support but, generally, there has been little emphasis on the assessment of the social dimension of learning. Assessment has always generated emotional problems for students and even with less emphasis placed on finals, considerable anxiety is still felt by many students undertaking and completing assignments. Isolation can be a serious problem for foreign students and for those who feel less able and may be liable to fail. Very often this is simply not true but it is usually difficult for teachers to convince them of this. The opportunity to discuss drafts and problems and the way they are approaching their work with fellow students, however, can be very useful in allaying the anxieties that can make their pessimistic predictions self-fulfilling.

Many students provide each other with support in informal 'learning communities', usually without assistance from staff. Unfortunately, the students who most need such support often cannot do this. The formalization of such 'learning communities', while not simply focused on assessment, can play an important role in supporting and fostering student approaches to assessment. Innovative approaches with new technology, for example – particularly through the use of online chat rooms and discussion groups – have been valuable in helping courses become more robust learning communities rather than merely a collection of individuals. Such groups, for example, might engage in the kinds of formal marking exercises and/or activities setting up criteria for self and peer assessment, discussed above. The social dimension of coming together, however, extends broader its pragmatic and utilitarian reasons. The enjoyment of social interaction can often provide an important context enabling students to discuss their problems and worries.

Developing the interpersonal

Encouraging independence within a social dimension seems rather paradoxical. Nevertheless, developing students' interpersonal skills might merge the somewhat incongruous aims of encouraging independence and providing students with emotional and intellectual support. Working in teams or groups – attempting to solve problems, develop knowledge or design new objects and processes – requires mutual group support and encouragement within a strong emotional and intellectual climate. At the same time students also need to make independent contributions and not simply reflect the prevailing opinions and ways of working. They need to learn to preserve their sense of individual identity while, at the same time, working in harmony with the group. Contributing to the working climate of the group demands accepting support and making contributions which others cannot or are less able to make. Assessment can be an important aspect in achieving this. Higgins et al. (1989) report on an initiative in a department of chemical engineering to encourage problem-solving skills. They developed a two-week programme for the first weeks of the first term as an introduction to university life with respect to both the problem solving and the social perspectives. Teams of about six worked on general problems and then problems in chemical engineering. At the end of the programme they presented two kinds of written and oral reports, the first concerned with solving the problem and the other on how the group functioned as a group. From the beginning, assessment was used to indicate the value of the social dimension of learning and students encouraged to reflect upon the nature of their interpersonal contribution to the group and its ways of interacting to solve problems.

Students' commentaries on their group participation need not be formally assessed. In some universities, while it is a condition of assessment, the commentary is not itself assessed. Group work, of course, is generally designed to encourage openness and risk-taking, and assessment can be an inhibiting factor to such social interaction, especially if the criteria are left vague. Nevertheless, assessing a student's actual contributions to a group can be managed effectively although it is very different from encouraging students to write about their experience and simply assessing their writing. If, for example, reflective commentaries are an integral part of the learning on the course, the task can be less threatening and criteria can be developed which are more attuned to individual variations within the group and the context in which they work.

The practical dimension

Providing support

There have been many changes in practical assessment over the past few years and there are many disciplinary differences. We shall begin each section, therefore, with some general characteristics. Essential aspects of giving support in practical work include providing:

- clear detailed instructions/briefs/checklists;
- close tutor/technician supervision;
- clear support documents/materials/equipment supplied and specified;
- clear criteria for correct methods and solutions;
- tutor assessment for both process and product.

Objective structured clinical examinations   Hounsell et al. (1996) note that while practical examinations are rare in the traditional form now, they have often been replaced by variants of the objective structured clinical examinations (OSCE) common in the health disciplines. They consist of about 20 short clearly defined practical tasks that represent the key objectives of the course. Students move from one problem/task to another at specific 'assessment stations' every five minutes. They might require taking the history of a patient and diagnosing a problem, interpreting test results, interpreting radiographs or slides of tissues. They might involve setting up or using equipment, making dissections or putting in stitches in simulated wounds. Each task can be assessed in a variety of ways and might involve simulated patients and/or the completion of short answer questions. Generally a trained observer or a trained interviewer conducts the assessment. Although setting up the tasks can be time-consuming, the system can be very efficient – in two hours 20 students can be assessed on 20 different tasks. Careful attention will need to be paid to security issues – particularly for summative assessment – although the tasks can be varied for subsequent groups of students.

Objective structured clinical examinations are only really effective in assessing specific goals of practical work. They can improve individual technical skills and even develop problem-solving skills, but how far they can improve understanding of scientific enquiry, reinforce good practice and/or nurture professional attitudes is more problematic. As part of a practical assessment, however, they can play an important and practical role and have now spread to non-clinical areas (Harden and Cairncross, 1980).

Performance evaluation guidelines   Another way of introducing highly structured and supportive practical assessment is to document activities with comprehensive report sheets. Brown et al. (1997) describe details of performance evaluation guides and a self-assessment manual of standards developed for practical work in dentistry. Levels of practical competence are defined very closely for failing, passing and excellent grades. A failure, for example, is defined as: 'unacceptable outcomes as a result of treatment or lack of treatment which has already caused irreversible damage to the patient's aural environment, or will cause severe damage in the future' (ibid.: 107). Further criteria employed in the assessment include both the 'aesthetics' and the 'structural and biological integrity' of the task. Such comprehensive reports can be made for observing groups of students who are doing such things as setting up apparatus with such headings as reads instructions, checks layout of apparatus, checks instructions in relation to apparatus, seeks advice from the demonstrator. Each can be given an estimate of the proportion of time spent on each activity.

Reports on laboratory work, of course, are common forms of assessment now. While they may be concerned with more open forms of assessment, they can be very closely structured according to rigorous guidelines. Such detailed and rigorous guidelines and criteria are often obligatory – particularly with respect to health and safety procedures – and have the added benefit of improving the overall reliability of the assessment. There are disadvantages however. While such guidelines need not restrict independent activity, in general the more detailed and prescriptive, the less scope there is for individual and independent response and expression. Students can end up reproducing practical techniques without understanding the principles behind them. Detailed criteria and guidelines may not be sensible if used to the exclusion of more open forms of assessment.

Encouraging independence

As in the other dimensions, encouraging practical independence involves a higher degree of student involvement in the assessment process. Generally it will include:

- a wide choice of practical tasks or problems;
- student involvement in planning and decision-making;
- student responsibility for finding and providing support materials;
- student involvement in criteria for success;
- student self-assessment;
- time for development;
- risk-taking and creative responses.

All these characteristics take time but they should be seen as contributing not only to the assessment and development of practical work, but also to the general development of students. Such characteristics can apply to many different forms of practical work as well as straightforward work in laboratories.

The development and use of portfolios (see above) can be a useful way of enabling students to work independently, permitting them to assemble evidence of their practical achievements and skills – including their laboratory work. Broad practical outcomes can be negotiated and established with students regarding both what would be included and what criteria would be used for assessing them. The types of problems and tasks considered appropriate are important in widening the scope for independent work. Brown and Knight (1994) report a range of alternative possibilities for practical work including production or generation of: artefacts and products, designs, drawings and plans, design and build, games and simulations and IT-based work. Wherever design and production are involved there is also considerable scope for creativity or at least for significant differences between the various student 'products' which highlight possibilities for more independent and engaging practical work. Broadening the scope of this work can also contribute to overcoming some of the dull routine that can characterize work in laboratories and other practical settings.

Developing the interpersonal

Developing interpersonal skills through conduct and assessment of practical work requires, again, a substantial focus on students as operating in 'learning communities' or, at least, within active groups. General aims here would be to:

- establish a reasonable proportion of group practical work and projects;
- focus on group process and development as well as group tasks;
- emphasize group negotiation in executing and completing tasks;

- include the group in setting of assessment criteria;
- involve the group in actual assessment.

These aims or characteristics are similar to those we have discussed for other areas of assessment but they take on an added significance in practical work, particularly when it involves a more emotional engagement. The actual concrete experiences of practical work can engage people as whole people rather than simply intellects. Experiential learning (as we saw in Chapter 4) involves observing, feeling and acting as well as thinking; areas in which the development of interpersonal skills can be particularly powerful. Of course, these skills can be developed through reading, discussing and watching videotapes, but the more realistic the setting, the greater the possibility for deeper learning. Real life settings can be the most effective but can often be difficult to arrange. Partial versions of actual experience, however, can be effectively developed. Brown and Knight give an interesting example of a practical assessment using real people in real situations: 'Surveying students are assessed on how they undertake negotiations between a client and a housing association for the lease of premises. Local professionals are involved in the setting of the assignment, using actual local properties and, when possible, role-play themselves, before contributing to the student's assessment' (1994: 85). Such activities are not restricted by discipline and provide a useful and valuable compromise between students actually operating in the 'real' world – as in practice placements and fieldwork – and in the more formal environment of the seminar room.

Interpersonal issues can easily be lost in such activities unless care is taken to ensure particular concern that students do reflect upon the nature of the interactions and begin to develop more sophisticated understanding and responses. As with seminar work in general, the topic or task can completely take over from the development of interpersonal understanding and the ability to respond to the demands of the process.

Conclusions

The approach we have taken towards the issue of assessment in this chapter has been to offer information and arguments from which readers will draw their own conclusions and make their own professional judgements. There are no ultimate prescriptions or rules for the practice of assessing students in higher education. It is, rather, a developing 'genre' of the language of learning and teaching. It needs, as we have indicated, to be reconsidered and reflectively practised within the context of both our changing understanding of higher education generally and of learning in particular. In this respect, it is a multifaceted and multidimensional phenomenon positioned at the heart of teaching and its scope for innovation and the improvement of student learning should not be underestimated.

We mentioned earlier an exercise or guide (Appendix 1) for helping lecturers design assessment systems in relation to both the methods they are using and methods they would like to use and how these might function both in practice and in an ideal situation. This guide can draw attention to a wider range of issues than normally considered when designing assessment and can involve the teacher in many of the issues raised in this chapter, including reducing the anxiety and competitive aspects of assessment. The characteristics set out in the guide are not described in detail but we hope the chapter has enabled those who are able to review their assessment to use it constructively. Using the guide to reflect on and review assessment design – especially in the company of a colleague or even small teams – may be a valuable tool for further developing an understanding of how assessment systems work and why they sometimes fail.

For intellectual and academic reasons there is a need for assessment to carefully and accurately balance and emphasize the key elements of a course. For the student personally, and for the development of his or her sense of identity, the control and certification functions of assessment need to match the intellectual, personal, social and practical demands of a course. In this assessment needs to be less a rite of passage and more a significant and relevant personal achievement. This relevance needs to be apparent not just in terms of today's needs, reinforcing a status quo, but in terms of the demands of tomorrow's 'supercomplex' challenges. Graduation must promise a stake in the future, not just the past; its rituals need to take students beyond traditional culture to a world of change and uncertainty. A forward looking quote from the past might be a useful way of ending: 'Only when the students become competent evaluators of their own goals, experiences and accomplishments do they become truly educated (liberally educated, one might say) and capable of engaging in the individual fundamental processes essential in a democratic society' (Dressel, 1976: x).

Further reading

Biggs, J. (1999) *Teaching for Quality Learning at University*. Buckingham: Open University Press.

Boud, D. (1995) *Enhancing Learning Through Self-Assessment*. London: Kogan Page.

Brown, G., Bull, J. and Pendlebury, M. (1997) *Assessing Student Learning in Higher Education*. London: Routledge.

Brown, S. and Knight, P. (1994) *Assessing Learners in Higher Education*. London: Kogan Page.

Dressel, P. (1976) *Improving Degree Programmes*. London: Jossey-Bass.

Gibbs, G., Habeshaw, S. and Habeshaw, T. (1986) *53 Interesting Ways to Assess your Students*. Bristol: Technical and Educational Services.

Gronlund, N.E. (1982) *Constructing Achievement Tests*. Englewood Cliffs, NJ:

Prentice Hall.

Harden, R. and Cairncross, R. (1980) 'Assessment of practical skills: the objective structured practical examination', *Studies in Higher Education*, 5 (2): 187–96.

Heron, J. (1981) 'Philosophical basis for a new paradigm', in P. Reason and J. Rowan (eds), *Human Inquiry: A Source Book of New Paradigm Research.* Chichester: John Wiley.

Hewton, E. (1982) *Rethinking Educational Change: A Case for Diplomacy.* Guildford: SRHE.

Heywood, J. (1989) *Assessment in Higher Education.* Chichester: John Wiley.

Hounsell, D. (1997) 'Contrasting conceptions of essay writing' in F. Marton, D. Hounsell and N. Entwistle (eds), *The Experience of Learning.* Edinburgh: Scottish Academic Press.

Knight, P. (ed.) (1995) *Assessment for Learning in Higher Education.* London: Kogan Page.

Rowntree, D. (1987) *Assessing Students: How Shall We Know Them?* London: Harper & Row.

Trow, M. (1981) 'Comparative perspectives on access', in O. Fulton (ed.) *Access to Higher Education.* Leverhulme Studies 2. Guildford: SRHE.

11

Evaluating: Teaching and Course Evaluation

Happy are they that hear their detractions and can put them to mending. (Benedict in Shakespeare's *Much Ado About Nothing* Act 2, Scene 3)

Introduction

Assessment can make all of us feel anxious and defensive whether it is through examination, appraisals, reviews, observations, rating form results or even friendly critics. As academics, we can even feel anxious when only we ourselves are judging what we have done. But as Benedict found, anxiety can change to pleasure provided we can put our detractions to mending. This suggests that, as with comments on student work (Chapter 10) we should link the critical process with a constructive one. To do this, evaluation needs to be well balanced. It will need to be derived from many complementary sources since none are adequate by themselves.

Good evaluation then will be time-consuming and require good reasons for doing it. Of course there are external incentives. In the UK the Quality Assurance Agency evaluates programmes through subject review where observation of teaching is a common feature as, too, is the emphasis on monitoring and evaluation of core skills. The professionalization of teaching in higher education is also beginning to require reflective commentaries and portfolios for achieving accredited teacher status. But are these incentives and the traditional need to improve our courses enough?

In Chapter 1 we stressed that there have been two important developments in higher education, the emphasis upon generic skills, especially learning to learn, and the change of focus from teaching to learning. What has been seriously underestimated is the role of evaluation activities in enabling students to understand more about the way they learn from the different styles of teaching and the different environments and learning

195

resources they encounter. This can help them to become more effective lifelong learners when the constraints and supports of formal courses are behind them and they take full control of their own learning. Hurried completions of brief institutional questionnaires may contribute little by themselves, but many of the 14 evaluation methods we shall discuss in this chapter have much to offer in helping students to understand themselves and their responses to different ways of learning. Reflective exercises in evaluation can become important features of courses rather than conformity to institutional demands, but, like the development of study skills and writing skills, they need to be regularly integrated activities.

As in the previous chapters we shall be considering this particular 'genre' of teaching in higher education with respect to the matrix of learning described in Chapter 4. Evaluation needs to reflect all aspects of a course and at the same time draws on the distinctive contributions of a very wide range of methods and approaches. While some evaluation methods may be more appropriate to certain contexts or dimensions of this matrix, many will address several of its aspects and will be highlighted in the text. We shall draw upon them in discussing the ways of achieving a well-balanced structure to an evaluation.

We are not attempting a comprehensive review of all the issues and possible methods of evaluating teaching. This discussion will primarily draw on those categories of evaluation which are concerned with the effectiveness of teaching including, perhaps, doing small-scale studies of the courses or teaching with which the reader is chiefly concerned. In reviewing and developing their evaluation strategies, readers may find it helpful to look at the evaluation guide which provides an overview to the chapter (Appendix 2). It is also presented as an exercise that some readers may find useful to go through in full, drawing upon the discussion of methods presented here. Before we consider the particular methods, however, a brief overview of some of the key dimensions of evaluation research might be helpful.

Dimensions of evaluation

Figure 11.1 gives an idea of the complexity of issues and dimensions of evaluation that would need to be considered in any major research study and suggests some which are important in more local evaluation reports. The arrows are meant to indicate the variety and range of factors that influence and/or shape the sort of approaches that might be taken towards evaluation research.

Especially important amongst these dimensions is the educational 'ideology' or values associated with different approaches. The technology of evaluation has often been described as ideology in disguise and it is worth considering whether the recent emphasis on the traditional styles of behavioural or 'payoff' research are in fact based upon vocational and utilitarian ideologies rather than any of the others. This rather market-

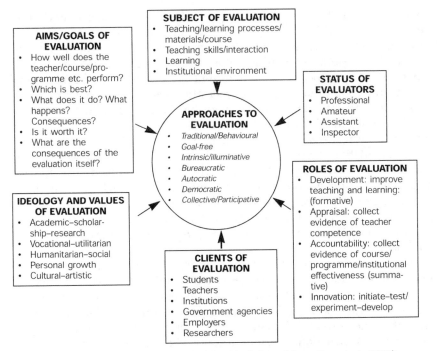

Figure 11.1   Styles and dimensions of evaluation (adapted from Cox et al., 1981)

driven approach is at odds with the major developments in social research which have tended to moved away from a more positivist 'agricultural–botany' paradigm towards a more qualitative 'anthropological' paradigm. Parlett and Hamilton who pioneered these approaches refer to it as 'illuminative evaluation': it being primarily concerned:

> with description and interpretation rather than measurement and prediction. It stands unambiguously within the alternative anthropological paradigm. The aims of illuminative evaluation are to study the innovatory programme: how it operates; how it is influenced by the various situations in which it is applied; what do those directly concerned regard as its advantages and disadvantages; and how students' intellectual tasks and academic experiences are most affected. (1977: 13)

Although quantitative research is still highly valued, qualitative enquiry, which gives a deeper impression of the experience of an educational programme, has enabled us to appreciate the more complex context of education and understand more about the unintended outcomes as well as the achievement of specific objectives. We have become more aware of the importance of perceptions and of motivational effects of programmes. Courses that might appear to be very efficient in one way may be very inefficient in another and liable to generate alienation and distortion of deeper, more holistic learning. If, for example, we look at the 'pay off' of problem-based learning, purely through the perspective of formal test examination results we may feel that it is not worth the effort. On the other hand, if we focus on the nature of the discipline and professional values and commitment we may feel otherwise. This is not to suggest that measurement should not be made in these more diffuse areas but the difficulties involved may dissuade researchers from trying to give an intellectually respectable account of it. Much educational research now gives 'qualitative' accounts of the experience of learning and teaching, using the actual words of the staff and students involved. This has led to a deeper appreciation of the different ways in which students learn and value their different experiences. We are less inclined to talk about students in general and more aware that average ratings may conceal differences which are important in developing better courses and teaching methods.

The emphasis with 'illuminative' approaches to evaluation is very much on the educational processes, what it is like to actually participate as a teacher or a student. It is not simply employing a different set of methods or methodology. The starting point is different. We now appreciate that the formalized plans or descriptions of the courses or programme or 'instructional system' are not taken as seriously by modern evaluators since what actually happens in practice is now often regarded as being different from what is specified. A central preoccupation is the 'learning milieu'. This represents 'a network or nexus of cultural, social, institutional and psychological variables. These interact in complicated ways to produce within each class or course a unique pattern of circumstances, pressures, customs, opinions and work styles, which suffuse the teaching and learning that occurs there' (Parlett and Hamilton, 1977: 14).

Since measures of accountability will affect the financing of programmes as well as issues such as promotion (and tenure), it is important that we do not allow simplistic scores and ratings to dominate our understanding of what we are doing. We shall need to show evaluations of our teaching – not only with respect to programme review and, in the UK, subject review by the QAA, but also possibly for the formal accreditation of our teaching. Hopefully, such bureaucratic pressure will not drive us to take the line of least resistance, providing the simplest data that we can manage. The following section of this chapter will explore a range of other methods that might be taken. In emphasizing the need for multiple perspectives of evaluation, we hope it will contribute to providing a richer account of the value of what we are doing, not only to those to whom we are directly accountable but also to ourselves.

Teaching and courses: methods of evaluation

Interactive teaching

We all learn a great deal from our experience of teaching but some learn more than others and some use ways of teaching which can offer more in terms of understanding student responses than others. Even with traditional, non-interactive 'transmission' lectures, we can observe certain features in our students that tell us whether or not learning is occurring. We may see signs of attention and non-attention, for example, although the actual quality of learning may be difficult to discern from the expressions of faces or the activities of pens. Reflecting on our lecturing, even keeping reflective diaries – an activity encouraged by many accreditation programmes – can make us more aware of our own activities and be useful for many lecturers, but it may not tell us very much about learning.

One of the best ways for learning about learning is through 'interactive' teaching or lecturing. As a method of teaching it improves learning by enabling students to consolidate their thinking and relate it to their own experience and their knowledge of the field (see Chapter 6). It can also function as a good method of evaluation, helping lecturers see whether the way they are teaching is appropriate to the level and interest of the students. While focusing upon the learning of specific content of the session, it can also enable a lecturer to understand where the students are coming from and the sorts of expectations, assumptions, and even hang-ups they might have about the topic of the session. Beginning a lecture with a quick exploration of what the students already know will not only enable them to feel the lecturer cares about and values their experience, it can also be a valuable method of 'evaluation-in-action', indicating whether the lecture is appropriate for their current development. We all make assumptions about what our students already know but rarely do we test out those assumptions.

Sometimes, rather than open questions to the group, a quick 'brainstorm' may be appropriate, eliciting and outlining some of the students' major concerns and preoccupations regarding the course. It can contribute to creating a shared agenda that can be an excellent basis for understanding whether our teaching is producing effective learning. During the session short buzz groups, with or without setting specific tasks or problems, can also provide a concrete basis for evaluating how much and what sort of learning is occurring. Open tasks such as asking them to 'discuss what we have talked about so far and raise any problems or other issues you would like to' are also useful at getting at more unexpected problems. And specific tasks calling for the application or interpretation of some of the content can be useful for checking on what sort of learning is occurring and how far students are changing. This kind of evaluation is excellent for adding to our understanding without contributing to our workload. Teachers and students may, however, feel they are covering less content if used too frequently. On the other hand evaluation feedback from this source may indicate that the course is going too slowly.

This type of evaluation is mainly concerned with issues of 'intellectual support', helping to clarify problems and explore misconceptions. Engaging students with their responses can, for example, lead to a clarification of what is expected and the criteria for making progress. A study of engineering students (Cox, 1987) found that a major problem of comprehension was not the difficulty of the material but the speed of lectures. They did not allow students to consolidate their learning. The opportunity to reflect when you feel you understand is not widely appreciated in the rush to cover the ground. Rushing on can create a sense of 'retroactive inhibition' blurring earlier learning by passing on before the 'ink has dried', so to speak. Asking the group as a whole to explain or discuss a diagram or graph or perhaps even a quotation again, might enable the lecturer to understand where the students are coming from and some of the conceptual problems they might be having. It provides the lecturer time out from their 'monologue' as well, valuable time to evaluate-in-action.

'Intellectual independence' can be emphasized in a similar way, but we might ask for more creative responses and applications. Students often talk of taking down notes which they do not understand and which often undermine their confidence. Providing students with time and opportunity to explore and express their own ideas and ways of understanding can help them to become more independent learners. It also enables teachers to understand how far they are assisting their students to become more independent as opposed to conformist learners.

Within the *personal dimension*, if the questions and the problems are not too difficult or posed too aggressively, such exploration can enable students to feel a closer personal relationship with the staff. It helps develop a sense of security and even enjoyment. Interactive teaching generally encourages students to behave and feel more as engaged people and not simply passive recipients. In addition their sense of 'personal independence' may be strengthened by a sense of participation in exploring their own relationship to the subject. Interactive teaching can contribute to deeper learning by encouraging students to relate a topic to their own experience and interests.

Interactive teaching can also address the 'social dimension' of learning, helping to generate an atmosphere in which staff and students work together. Teaching is not that of a remote teacher doing their own thing with a group of unrelated others, but rather a mutual exploration which facilitates participation. It can assist in reducing the impersonality of higher education which many students experience. Where periods of group work are interspersed with more formal teaching, this can also help to develop 'interpersonal' skills. Students often learn from each other things that it is difficult for the lecturer to help them learn. As one student said 'when another student speaks you prick up your ears, it's something different'.

General questionnaires

Questionnaires have long been used to evaluate teaching and are highly developed in the United States. In Britain and other countries, they are increasingly used as part of the general move towards accountability. Many myths have grown up which are still often heard despite research that shows most of them to be unfounded. Ratings are, for example, thought to be unreliable but generally reliability is quite high (coefficients of .7 to .9) although it can be lower in the humanities. Neither do they differ substantially from colleague ratings. The assumption that if you give students good grades they will reward you with good ratings, again, is not generally borne out by research. Neither is the view that popular faculty experience a 'halo' effect resulting in good ratings for teaching as well. Nor do gender differences appear to be relevant. There is also very little difference in ratings dependent on the difficulty of the course, although compulsory subjects are generally rated lower than chosen courses. Class size does make a difference, with groups of less than 15 being rated more highly. Ratings for groups of between 36 and 100, however, are less than those for more than 100. As might be expected the student's personality is also relevant to what type of teaching they like. Some students dislike digressions and ambiguities, and value ideas in terms of immediate utility. They will give the highest ratings to different lecturers from those who are more artistic and have diverse interests.

Some of the biggest disparities in ratings, however, are found between different disciplines. Ramsden (1992) reports research – using a course experience questionnaire (CEQ) – which indicates that the visual and performing arts are the most highly rated subjects, with the health sciences and engineering rated the worst. Social sciences come in the middle, rated higher than the natural sciences but below the humanities.

Unfortunately, questionnaires and scales constructed in accordance with normal psychometric processes are very rare. All too often, questionnaires are a simply collection of isolated ad hoc items that can be reported in terms of particular questions or as overall scores, both of which are dubious if we are trying to diagnose problems and 'put them to mending'. Questionnaires can be constructed in terms of scales or major themes and tested to see whether these themes are a reality. Computer programmes are available which enable analyses to be simply run and they can give a good indication of whether or not the suspected or proposed themes are reflected in the actual way in which students respond.

The design of questionnaires is, as Oppenheim writes 'an intellectual exercise in the course of which we are continuously trying to clear our own minds about our goals' (1992: 7). He provides thorough and useful chapters on constructing questionnaires, as do Cohen et al. (2000). And the latter focus primarily on educational methods. In general questionnaires vary a great deal in how much background information is collected. It is often important to know whether high ratings are restricted to certain types of student: for instance, women, older students and those doing very well academically. Or overseas students rating the courses badly, might entail addressing issues of background qualifications or the language abilities of such students. How can these be remedied? Some courses may have cultural biases, again this might affect the ratings given by different students.

An aid to diagnosis of problems might be to offer students a range of course objectives and ask them to say whether they feel the particular course reflects these objectives. This works best when they do not assume the teachers want all the objectives rated highly. The matching of the staff ratings and the student ratings on these can be particularly interesting. Students and teachers often have different perceptions, and where discrepancies are seen it is useful to clarify them early in the course. Other questionnaires have asked students to compare one course or one lecturer with another and comparisons are often more useful than attempts at absolute measures. Other useful variants can include asking students how important they think certain characteristics of the course are, again perhaps comparing them with staff views. Assuming that all the characteristics are equally important can often make interpretation very suspect.

Questionnaires for particular sessions

Observation of teaching sessions is now becoming quite general both within institutions in peer evaluation and during visits from the Quality Assessment Agency. In general, such questionnaires concentrate rather too much on how far the lecturer is being supportive to the students and far less, if at all, on how far the teaching is challenging and encouraging more independent learning. This can be a serious issue if we are wanting to encourage deeper learning and a move away from a more reproducing orientation. Questionnaires for particular sessions can be very helpful in checking:

- student understanding of difficult sections of the course;
- whether the course is being taught at the right intellectual level;
- whether there is an overload of material;
- whether the lecturer is going too fast or slow;
- whether more general student perceptions are related to particular sessions rather than averaged over a course.

The widely reported concept of the 'one-minute test' can also be very helpful in evaluating particular sessions. This is where students are asked to answer just two questions at the end of the session:

1 What is the most important thing you learned during the session?
2 What is uppermost now in your mind at the end of the session?

Apparently an American physics professor developed this approach, claiming that he learned a great deal about his students' thinking, concerns and problems from reading these or a sample of them. Although it was not done at every session he noticed a gradual improvement in the sophistication with which students were responding to his lectures.

Questionnaires can be helpful in exploring some of the problems of group work as well although often the most important source of feedback is time out on discussing some of the problems. Jaques (2000) gives a number of examples of questionnaires about group work which can also be particularly helpful as a basis for helping the group to reflect upon its own processes.

With both group work and lecture sessions the ratings quite reasonably focus upon judgements about quality of teaching but it can be helpful to ask more descriptive questions about structures and purposes of the session. If, for example, the teacher is intending to focus a session around a particular problem – clarifying the problem, presenting particular forms of analysis and evaluating different solutions – it is essential to know whether students perceive the session as such. Often it simply appears to them as an ordered presentation of data or information. Similarly, if a lecturer is focusing on a comparison of different interpretations or approaches or theories, it would be important to know whether the session was being interpreted in this way. A mismatch between student perceptions of a session and the teacher's intentions is an essential issue which questionnaires can disclose. (For an example of such a questionnaire and guidelines to its use, see Appendix 3.)

Questionnaires for courses, parts of courses or projects

A serious criticism of many questionnaires is that they tend to concentrate on the 'intellectual support' aspect of the learning matrix. Teachers interested in doing more – in encouraging students to think critically or relating the course to other problems in the field or students' own experience or questioning assumptions or conceptions or generally wishing the students to participate actively giving their own views and ideas – may suffer if the questionnaire has no way of evaluating whether these aims are being achieved.

Table 11.1 gives an overview of the CEQ (Ramsden, 1992) mentioned above which provides an opportunity to look at some of the issues which individual teachers may wish to address in their own questionnaires.

Table 11.1 *Categories and examples of questions in the course experience questionnaire*

Category	Example of question
1 Good teaching	Teaching staff here normally give helpful feedback on how you are going.
2 Clear goals	You usually have a clear idea of where you are going and what's expected of you in this course.
3 Appropriate workload	The sheer volume of work to be got through in this course means that you can't comprehend it all thoroughly (negatively scored).
4 Appropriate assessment	Staff here seem more interested in testing what we have memorized than what we have understood (negatively scored).
5 Emphasis on independence	Students here are given a lot of choice in the work they have to do.

Source: Ramsden, 1992: 104

Of the five main categories the first three – as in many questionnaires – are mainly concerned with providing support. Scoring well on these three scales suggests staff are both aware of student concerns and generally supportive to their students. The fourth category, however, begins to address wider issues of understanding – although not exclusively – and the fifth category addresses the issue of encouraging independence. As a general questionnaire designed for widespread use, it does not, however, address the range of learning issues particular to individual learning and teaching situations. In this respect, teachers should feel free to extend the design of their questionnaires to an even wider range of learning issues focused on what is appropriate for the students on their particular courses or parts of a course.

In relation to 'intellectual support', for example, they might want to know more about student experiences of the resources available through the course or the intellectual level of the work or, indeed, the extent to which students are able to gain a sense of achievement. In relation to 'intellectual independence' teachers might wish to augment CEQ-type questions with those about whether there is an opportunity to identify medium and long-term tasks, or become involved in creative work or design and/or how far students have been able to increase their confidence.

Similarly in the 'personal dimension' of learning, if we are trying to evaluate how far our courses are being 'supportive', a questionnaire might look at how far students have a sense of security, to what extent they enjoy the work and how close their relationships are with faculty.

The CEQ category about emphasizing independence might also be extended to exploring the more personal aspects of choice. This might be emphasized by asking more about the scope for responsibility, how far students are trusted and how far they perceive themselves as having the kind of independent status they never had at school. The engineering students mentioned earlier, for example, felt that their personal identity was undermined by having to conform to more surface ways of learning not because they were told to but simply because of the overload in the curriculum. They were not able to work in a way which they felt was contributing to their sense of developing personal identity or even occupational identity. These are not terms which tend to come into questionnaires even though they are clearly important for motivation and for enabling students to become independent professionals in their later life.

In considering 'social dimension', questionnaires might address the development of peer learning communities and the general academic and departmental culture they are learning within. To what extent are there opportunities for supportive peer working groups and those that run independently of the staff? Course teachers, with some reason, often feel they are not responsible for the students' social life or their accommodation and yet these can be vital to student learning. Many students, moreover, are clearly concerned about the social relevance of their courses but this again is usually not considered.

In relation to 'interpersonal', peer assessment activities, learning from alternative perspectives and peer teaching sessions which focus on understanding, self-knowledge or communication skills can all be important aspects of student life which evaluation questionnaires might help us to understand. Group projects or peer-managed learning or problem-based learning often focus upon interpersonal skills and processes. These are much more valued than they used to be but they seldom appear in evaluation questionnaires. Such issues might, as we shall see, be better addressed through different forms of evaluation but quite often the 'hard' data of questionnaires carries more weight than that from less formal methods.

Group discussion

Very often questionnaires raise more problems than they solve, especially in relation to divisions between those who rate the course highly and those who rate it poorly. Background questions can sometimes help solve this problem but they can also become too cumbersome or numerous to manage efficiently. In these areas group discussions can be an effective form of evaluation. They not only help focus on the background data but also on why there are certain likes and dislikes. They can be very formal with pre-specified agendas and topics or can arise more informally. Less formal open questions, for example, can explore more fully the issues behind good and poor ratings and the disparity between students. The responses are frequently very enlightening but, unfortunately, they are also often ignored. Although spontaneous meetings are helpful, it is useful to prepare students with an idea of what you would like to hear from them. Questionnaire responses provide a basis for discussion but may also be too restrictive. Discussion that is cursory or unreflective may repeat some of the 'off-the-cuff' likes and dislikes often obtained from questionnaires.

The methods guide/exercise (Appendix 2) sets out a number of the advantages of group discussion, particularly where flexibility and the development of a genuine dialogue are essential. In such situations teachers can encourage deeper criticism and work through the nature and implications of these criticisms. It also provides an opportunity to focus on the essential themes and to be more responsive to student perceptions and perspectives. Discussions, however, can be over-influenced by a few dominant personalities. The initial tone of the discussion can make it difficult to explore diverse points of view and more subtle differences. For some, the lack of anonymity is also inhibiting often making it difficult to assess the distribution of opinions.

Reflective triads – groups of three students reflecting together on their learning at the end of a session (see Chapter 5) – are a useful way of stimulating evaluation through discussion. They not only remind students what has happened, they also encourage deeper thinking about the nature of the session and their own learning. If there are a large number of students in the group, reflective triads enable students to think through their ideas and what they wish to say without too much interference (unless, of course, they happen to be with the one or two dominant personalities in the group). It is often helpful to begin the discussion with a review of the course. It is important that the discussion is not seen as just a collection of views and opinions, but rather puts those opinions to test. Ideally it should provide time to work through criticisms and help students to understand intellectually what the course is doing and what it is not doing.

The timing of evaluative discussions is also very important vis-à-vis student learning. Discussing aims and objectives after the experience of a course is very different from discussing them at the beginning or during the course. Provided some discussions are held halfway through the course or at other times before the end, discussion can be very 'supportive' for students who may have concerns, anxieties or misconceptions about what the course is doing. 'Independence' can be encouraged by not treating students as passive 'consumers' for whom evaluation is conducted simply to improve the quality of the 'product'. Students need to feel like and be active participants in the evaluation and its role in course development. As such they will be expected to respond intelligently to the positive features of the course as well as its faults and problems. As in the example of the general medical practitioners (see Chapter 5), responsive discussion after a poor start can be extremely useful in encouraging a strong sense of commitment to making the course develop in a way that both the students and teachers feel is useful. More formal courses may not have the opportunity to substantially restructure but there is always some flexibility. Students should not feel the only point of them being engaged in evaluation is to improve future courses.

In the 'personal dimension', discussion can be very supportive in providing students with a sense that staff value their views and priorities and encourage them to express these. Appreciating the alternative perspectives within the group will also contribute to developing student independence. Without the opportunity to hear about these, students often feel their own opinions are what everyone else thinks. Discussion should be an opportunity for them to learn more about their own responses to the constraints and opportunities of the course. Finally, as in any group process, if the discussion goes well it can be experienced as an enjoyable social event contributing to the interpersonal context of learning. It can help generate a genuine dialogue among students and teachers in which each learns to share and appreciate other points of view and learning.

Individual discussion

As with group evaluation through discussion, individual discussion may range between formal approaches such as interviews and informal discussion as the opportunity arises. Such discussion helps to explore both particular issues and the significance of the course as a whole at a more individual and personal level. It can also be a good chance to get to know students rather better as some can be very inhibited within groups. On the other hand, personal impressions might bias evaluation if generalized to the course as a whole. Teachers cannot expect to have long discussions about the course with all students so the sample and the lessons learned need to be carefully judged.

Individual discussions are also useful for exploring and understanding differences in individual perceptions and responses to the course. Substantial differences in preconceptions of what a course consists or should consist of can make the role of evaluation extremely problematic if not more clearly understood by the teacher. Table 11.2 gives two contrasting responses to a workshop/session on supervision reflecting the extreme contrasts many teachers often experience.

Despite the description of the course as a 'workshop', participant A came to it with quite fixed ideas about what courses should be about, expecting 'transmission of information' to be the main mode of teaching. The quantity of information learned in the time available was the key criterion for success. Participant B, on the other hand, came with an open mind and was keen to make it as useful and enjoyable as possible. If the first participant were a student on a longer course it would be important to recognize and address such substantial differences early on, whatever

Table 11.2   *Contrasting responses to a supervision course*

Question	Participant A	Participant B
What were the most successful parts of the workshop?	'The two rather formal lectures.'	'I enjoyed all of the workshop. I found the whole course helpful.'
What were least successful?	'Working in small groups and reflective triads.'	'None, it ran very smoothly, the frequent changes in teaching, learning style maintained interest. I have learned a lot.'
What was most surprising?	'How much time was wasted, just as much if not more can be got by reading the book.'	'That supervision at so many different levels can have so many similarities.'
What changes would you suggest?	'Replace the 'games' with solid, sound lectures and whole group discussion.'	'None! I expected more guidelines in the beginning but accepted my role in deciding my responsibilities and negotiating other people's.'
What is your overall impression of the workshop?	'Not a fruitful use of two whole days, uninspired and uninspiring.'	'Excellent. I will recommend it to colleagues. I now feel much more confident about supervision and supporting colleagues.'

they may be. Students from different cultures and countries may be particularly prone to experiencing such disparities. Students, of course, may be less forthright than this lecturer. Individual discussion can assist both in identifying such mismatches between expectation and what is happening on a course, as well as helping students to adjust their expectations appropriately. Alternatively it may enable them to choose to courses which more closely match their expectations.

Observation by a peer, colleague or adviser

Observers drawn from peers and colleagues provide a very valuable alternative perspective to those obtained from students. They will likely have the benefits of:

- having relevant subject expertise;
- having personal experience of teaching;
- experiencing the course over a longer time perspective;
- having knowledge of related courses;
- understanding the constraints under which the course is operating.

While aspects of such 'peer observation' will typically elicit additional anxieties and concerns about one's teaching abilities, in some respects the process can also be less inhibited, particularly if the arrangement is handled sensitively and is reciprocal, each person learning from being a critic as well as receiving criticism. There are, of course, other problems that may need to be addressed. The process might be especially intimidating if there is a power and/or status difference between observer and observed. Observers with their own 'agenda' and/or a different conception of teaching to that of the observed could seriously undermine the observed teacher's development. They might also de-emphasize the student perspective leading to mutual support for undesirable or restrictive views of teaching. Ideally, issues such as these should be discussed prior to the observation. (See Appendix 3 for an example of peer observation guidelines.)

The activity of observation, including prior and post observation discussion and/or reports, should be supportive and challenging. It should – especially if participants are able to share some of their fears and inhibitions – also encourage independence in the teacher's learning about their teaching. 'Co-counselling' is another valuable way of enabling teachers to work through some of their teaching concerns and problems, although it entails the development of skills that have wider application than evaluation. Under the impact of programme and quality reviews, observers are increasingly coming in to directly assess the quality of individual departments. Observations are becoming a much more common feature of these reviews, but the 'accountability' purpose behind them is likely to restrict significant mutual learning. Peer observation has the added benefit of preparing colleagues for these visits.

Evaluation from assessment

Ironically, teacher evaluations of students' work through assessment offers valuable opportunities for teacher evaluation. Assessment provides a mutual 'object' for engaging students about problems or issues in their learning and from which teachers may gain valuable insights about their course. Examination results do not typically provide good opportunities for extended insights but will often indicate gaps in course content or difficulties with understanding specific concepts. Reports, essays and projects will generally provide more in depth opportunities: the feedback given to students – whether written or oral – should alert teachers to student problems which may need to be dealt with more comprehensively. This feedback also frequently provides the basis for discussion through which teachers might understand their students' problems on the course more fully.

This method allows closer integration of student work with evaluation and can provide an opportunity to explore areas of high concern. There is often a tendency, however, for students to want to be told what to do to improve their assignments. If teachers do this in a rather prescriptive way, then as Hounsell (1997) suggests the student may not understand – as they bring different assumptions about learning – and it may make very little difference. If, however, the teacher explores alternatives with the students, getting them to suggest possibilities, then they may enable students to take more responsibility for the improvement. It is a process that can enable teachers to better understand student problems and why they have them. Simply telling them what to do to improve may add little to the teacher's understanding of student learning. Although such discussions usually fall within the 'intellectual' dimension, they are also an opportunity for addressing 'personal' issues; for developing a better understanding of why students fail and how personal motivation and/or 'social' issues might be more responsible than pure intellectual failings.

Portfolios and reflective commentaries

There are a number of less traditional forms of student assessment that deserve a separate mention with respect to evaluation. They display many of the benefits described above but, in addition, provide scope for evaluation over a longer period of time, comparing, for example, recent written feedback with earlier feedback. They also enable the development of a much broader perspective of student learning on a course.

One of the most useful assessment methods which teachers might use for evaluation purposes is the reflective commentary which frequently draws upon material collected in private reflective diaries as well as from the course itself. Students are increasingly submitting such commentaries either as assessment or as part of assessment, often as part of extended portfolios (see Chapter 10). They usually comment on a wider set of issues of student experience and learning than simply course content. At different times they may focus upon all the aspects of the matrix but perhaps are most useful in enabling students to develop towards more independent reflective practitioners. They involve many personal choices and are designed to encourage independent reflection on responses. Their very breadth and depth mean they can be extremely valuable documents for teachers wishing to learn more about the impact of their courses and teaching on their students.

Diaries and session reports

The use of diaries and session reports can be related to and even provide the basis for much of what is written in more public reflective commentaries and portfolios. They are, however, not methods of assessment so much as group and class learning activities providing extensive scope for evaluation. Students might, for example, be encouraged to keep reflective diaries over the period of a course, describing their learning experiences – including concerns, delights, responses to particular sessions – across all four intellectual, personal, social and practical dimensions. Despite good intentions, such diaries are rarely put into practice. Linking them with specific activities and responsibilities on the course helps maintain a commitment to them. Providing time for diaries in class and even – as was done very effectively on the course for general practitioners mentioned above – asking for individual students in pairs to report back to the class in turn on previous sessions has wide ranging benefits. It extends and consolidates learning, generates interest among the students in the different ways in which different students experience and learn on the course and provides the teacher with substantial evaluative data.

The rich information that diaries contain and the reports generated from them will frequently become part of further diary sessions. Time permitting, these reports and diary reflections can be developed as part of group projects on which groups can be asked to report back both halfway through a course or at the end of it. Reports may be written or oral or both, and can be integrated with more elaborate student presentations. It is worth emphasizing, however, that the quality of the material generated – both for individual learning purposes and for course evaluation purposes – is dependent on students being given the choice to retain those reflections they wish to remain as private and/or to anonymously report material to the course.

Audio- and video-recording, playback and discussion

Recording and especially video-recording has long been a very important part of educational development workshops designed to improve skills in lecturing and small group work. Telling teachers what is wrong with their teaching is not, as we have seen, always the best way of achieving significant change. It is particularly true where there is a strong emotional element in what we are doing, and certainly teaching styles are quite closely bound up with a sense of personal identity. This is not to say that comments from others cannot be extremely helpful but they are likely to raise far fewer defensive responses when the teacher can plainly see what the observer is talking about. Even viewing a recording by yourself can enable you to take a more objective stance and a greater sense of responsibility for what is happening and how you might improve. The tape can be stopped and time given to thinking why mistakes were being made and how they could be avoided in future. Simple reflection after a teaching event can of course be very helpful but it is easy to forget the more worrying parts.

There is more likelihood for change if this activity is seen in a positive light. It is useful to have agreement on the kinds of areas of teaching performance and their relationship to learning that will be looked at. It is also usually better to begin reviewing a performance from the point of view of what was successful about it. If the recording is watched in the company of students, peers or educational developers a positive attitude may, indeed, be reinforced by their comments if the positive side is explored before suggestions are made for what can be changed. In approaching the areas needing improvement, it is often better to begin with critical comments from the observed teacher rather than from the observers. We are far more likely to actually change our behaviour or attitudes in response to criticisms we have made of ourselves than we are from those of others. Nevertheless, we all have our blind spots and, given the right atmosphere, critical comments can be taken on board and acted upon, especially within the context of a revealing tape and discussion within a supportive atmosphere.

There is considerable scope within such reviews, particularly if students are involved, to explore the 'performance' with respect to the various dimensions and contexts of the learning matrix which the recorded session is addressing. What aspects of learning are being addressed? What are the teacher's intentions in this respect? Are they appropriate? Are they shared with the students? It is worth mentioning that the matrix also informs the teacher's learning in such situations. Intellectual support and challenge is essential when working with students, but perhaps the most important area is development within the 'personal dimension'. Achieving the right support–independence–interpersonal balance in an atmosphere of mutual respect and shared responsibility is a necessary ingredient of good (and enjoyable) professional development.

Student-generated statements combined with group discussion

This method usefully combines some of the characteristics of questionnaires with that of group discussions. In this case the questionnaire elements are statements generated by students that may concern various elements of the design, content, methods and environment. Individual students are asked to write four to six statements and three recommendations related to some or all of these areas on separate slips of paper. Pairs of students then look at each other's statements, discuss them and select the four or six most interesting statements and three most appropriate recommendations. These pairs then join another pair and do the same selection in a group of four. Teachers can also introduce and test out their own concerns in statements that are then rated by the class in conjunction with the student statements. Asking the group to rate the statements and recommendations as to how far they agree with them can also produce useful numerical data. If there is time, rated collections can be circulated to the total group for more general discussion. Especially important themes or issues for the course can also be taken up in subsequent sessions, pursued in small groups and/or integrated with student presentations.

Students are not only introduced to the variety of each other's alternative perceptions but they have to engage with this in making decisions as to which they should select for the next move. In our experience they frequently enjoy the process and find it provides the basis for moving beyond 'off-the-cuff' comments and perfunctory general discussion. It enables them to think more deeply than they do when filling in questionnaires and is often very effective in generating engaged discussion about learning across the intellectual, personal, social and practical dimensions in a very interactive way. It also produces a wide range of interesting issues that may not have been reflected in teacher-designed questionnaires.

Time can be a consideration here but, as with some of the other methods mentioned in this chapter, it can also be an effective learning and teaching activity (in contrast to a bureaucratic task) and is worth spending the occasional half an hour pursuing. The details of this process can be varied to suit the particular situation, discipline, institution as is appropriate.

Nominal group process

This process has many similarities with the previous one and typically is more responsive to participants' viewpoints than most other methods. The students, without staff present but with their own chairperson, each in turn, suggest one aspect of the course which is so good it should not be changed and one aspect so poor that it should be changed. At this stage approval or disapproval from the rest of the group/class is not permitted. When the round is completed the group/class votes to identify a group perspective on these positive and negative aspects. Students in small groups may then discuss and propose how the most commonly agreed good aspects may be extended and the most commonly agreed poor aspects might be remedied.

The method has the advantage of not having an agenda set by either the teacher or by one or two influential or dominant students. It can also provide teachers with a wealth of information without taking up too much teacher time. It will need some planning and explaining. It is also a good way of identifying the group's priorities and with appropriate follow-up can be a useful stimulus to change and provide students with opportunity to participate in change. In addition it can provide an opportunity for both personal expression and group interaction, enhancing a sense of social participation and enjoyment. It may even provide an opportunity for students to let off steam. On the downside, the teacher's interest in the learning and teaching encounter may not be well represented and the activity may not provide any in-depth account of why these opinions and priorities exist.

Less conventional methods

There is clearly a wide range of other ways of learning about the effectiveness of our teaching – even if using 53 of them is asking a lot of teachers! (see Gibbs et al., 1989) Teachers should feel free to explore (with colleagues and students) other, less conventional approaches to evaluation that may address specific issues important to their course or enhance learning in an innovative way. Indeed, they may regard it as part of their professional role.

One example of such an unconventional method might be using role-plays of various kinds. In this category of method the student and/or teacher steps outside their normal roles and assume other roles, and even 'persona', to examine complex issues of the course, or even to instigate development of it. Participants in role-play are permitted to express things which are very difficult to express when they are constrained within their normal roles. Students (and/or teachers) may take on the role of, for example, a 'traditionalist' or 'radical' teacher (and/or student), interpreting that in ways which can be instructive to developing a shared understanding of what the course is about and the different ways it is being perceived. As with most role-play, debriefing about the experience afterwards is particularly important, not only to look at the reality behind the roles but also to reconcile and come to terms with some of the things expressed, some of which may have been more emotional than expected.

The widespread use of communication and information technology also provides opportunities to engage in more unusual approaches to evaluation. Establishing a course 'chat room' or discussion room for students to exchange their views on the course can be a useful way of eliciting information on a course. This may be left entirely up to the students to operate with the teacher simply 'eavesdropping' in on the conversation, or it may be one in which the teacher plays an active role in the discussion. Similarly it may be very open to 'whatever happens' or it might be set up more formally with guidelines and specific themes preset by the teacher and/or negotiated with the students. It needs to be handled with care and the limitations of IT-based systems taken into consideration (see Chapter 9), but can be an instructive and rich supplement to more traditional methods. Collecting concrete critical incidents of good and bad experiences is another less conventional method which can make evaluation more interesting and help to reveal the unexpected. Such methods generally may meet with traditional resistance to change and there can be difficulties in interpretation as well as finding the time to actually make them happen. On the other hand, developed and used creatively, they can be very useful for addressing issues that are unseen and/or ignored by more customary forms of evaluation.

Evaluation of academic outcomes and change

Ultimately the success or failure of a course depends on whether or not students change in the way desired by them or their teachers. Of course, the relationship between this type of change and the quality of teaching is highly problematic. Notoriously, large- and small-scale studies of teaching methods and teaching resources often fail to show the relationship to academic performance as measured by traditional means. This is likely mainly due to a restricted nature of the assessment systems, but compensation for inadequate teaching must be another important factor – the course succeeds in spite of the teaching rather than because of it.

An added difficulty in most normal teaching situations is that there is very little pre-testing so that assumptions have to be made in order to credit students with actual gains in academic achievement. In general, it would seem that pass rates and academic standards are relevant to teaching evaluation but the relationship is a difficult one to interpret. At present they are mainly useful as warning signals when there are large fluctuations over time or between similar courses. An important limitation on their use that deserves more attention is the infrequency of follow-up assessment of past students. When it is done it is usually very restricted. Ideally, it should address:

- how what was learned on the course was or is being used;
- how efficiently it is being used;
- whether it was relevant and effective.

While such an approach is not essential for all types of courses, it would be a strange course that did not expect to have some positive intellectual, personal, social or practical impact on the future life of the student.

We suggested earlier that problem-based learning, for example, may not lead to a greater improvement in the student's actual knowledge or competence in specific skills and techniques than traditional courses, but it does seem to have a significant effect upon their attitudes and their desire to go on learning. Despite a long history in psychology of attitude measurement, it is still not common within academic courses, despite the fact that employers are increasingly interested in many of the attitudes towards learning and lifelong learning which students will bring to their future work. In the long run, these may be more important than knowledge and the development of specific skills. While maintaining a degree of scepticism about the accuracy of our attempts to measure these attitudes, the actual attempt to do so may, nevertheless, be a useful way to more fully understand the sort of attitudes we are attempting to encourage.

It is important not to regard the assessment of attitude change as completely separate from academic assessment. Less highly formalized methods of student assessment – such as diaries and portfolios (see Chapter 10) – can reveal a great deal about the more emotional and personal changes in students' attitudes brought about by their educational experience. They have an important role to play in enabling students to become more aware of the relationship between their education and their developing sense of identity, and enabling teachers to become clearer about the way in which teaching relates to the personal and social concerns of their students.

Conclusions

Despite social pressures transforming accountability into a system of 'accounting' that favours quantitative evaluation methods over qualitative ones, there is a clear need for a wide variety of complementary methods. No single method is likely to have the necessary range or depth for evaluating the complex processes and outcomes of university teaching. The emphasis on institutional and subject review plus the explosion of 'league tables' has raised the profile of evaluation in recent years, but it is also an essential feature in the appointment and promotion of individual staff. It is essential that its processes and methods live up to high standards of academic work expected elsewhere in the academy and that they contribute to the maintenance of the academic values which place learning and knowledge at the centre of higher education. Critically reviewing our evaluation methods with respect to the extensive and complex wealth of that learning is at the heart of both future educational development and the practices of the reflective professional.

An essential part of that review, however, will take the reflective professional beyond simply an examination of which methods most comprehensively address which aspects of student learning. It will (as much of the above discussion suggests) transform the conception of evaluation (found in most of the literature) from its focus on assessing teachers and teaching quality in terms of student learning to an engaged process which itself facilitates student learning. The most significant developments in the evaluation of teaching will come not from teachers thinking about their own courses as delivering quality or from students as consumers expressing their judgements about the quality of the courses provided for them, but by an integration of evaluation into the learning process. In this conception, evaluation is, itself, an important part of a student's learning and self-knowledge, helping them to explore the strengths, weaknesses, inhibitions and styles of their thinking, and working in relation to the constraints and opportunities of the course. Just as the assessment of students' academic attainment has become increasingly integrated into actual learning activities, so the evaluation of teaching may develop away from retrospective and external judgements towards the constant reflection upon the significance of the educational experience and the transition to becoming genuine reflective professionals.

Dressel's (1976) comment at the conclusion of the previous chapter that 'only when the students become competent evaluators of their own goals, experiences and accomplishments do they become truly educated', is equally applicable to teachers. Indeed the two are mutually interdependent.

Further reading

Ashcroft, K. and Palacio, D. (1996) *Researching into Assessment and Evaluation.* London: Kogan Page.

Brown, S. and Race, P. (1995) *Assess Your Own Teaching Quality.* London: Kogan Page.

Entwistle, N. and Tate, H. (1990) 'Approaches to learning, evaluations of teaching and preferences for contrasting academic environments', *Higher Education*, 19 (2): 169–94.

Gibbs, G., Habeshaw, S. and Habeshaw, T. (1989) *53 Interesting Ways to Appraise Your Teaching.* Bristol: Technical and Educational Services.

Hamilton, D., Jenkins, D., King, C., MacDonald, B. and Parlett, M. (1977) *Beyond the Numbers Game.* New York: Macmillan Education.

Hounsell, D., Tait, H. and Day, K. (1997) *Feedback on Courses and Programmes of Study: A Handbook.* Edinburgh: Centre for Teaching, Learning and Assessment, University of Edinburgh.

Kerlinger, F. and Lee, H. (1999) *Foundations of Behavioural Research.* New York: Harcourt.

Kogan, M. (1989) *Evaluating Higher Education.* London: JKP.

Oppenheim, A.N. (1992) *Questionnaire Design, Interviewing and Attitude Measurement.* London: Pinter.

Owen, J.M. and Rogers, P. (1999) *Program Evaluation: Forms and Approaches.* London: Sage.

Ramsden, P. (1992) *Learning to Teach in Higher Education.* London: Routledge.

Tessmer, M. (1993) *Planning and Conducting Formative Evaluations.* London: Kogan Page.

PART 3: PERFORMANCE STRATEGY

12

Realizing the Reflective Professional

Introduction: developing a strategy

In this chapter, we shall address the third component of the 'language' of the reflective professional that we introduced at the beginning of this book. We shall draw upon the foregoing discussion to propose and describe a general strategy of 'professional realization'. It is a strategy for engaging with and mastering the 'language' of reflective practice. Despite its crucial role in the achievement of the reflective professional, the realization of such a professional 'language' has generally been overlooked or addressed in a rather perfunctory fashion in higher education. There are a number of reasons for this.

In the first instance, academic practice, which has prized and rewarded research and scholarship above all else, has either failed to recognize its relevance and importance or tended to dismiss it as irrelevant and unimportant. Second, many individual academics who recognize the development of teaching as an essential part of their own learning are often left to their own devices. Working in a 'paradigm 1' situation (see Chapter 1), they are primarily relying on a combination of their own experiences as a student and/or on what they observe as good practice from their colleagues. They cobble together an impoverished 'language', used more or less skilfully as personal and situational factors permit. Finally, academics working in an institutional paradigm ('paradigm 2') have tended to perceive the development of teaching in terms of the accretion of 'handy' performance, communication and associated technical skills. The realization of practice is essentially additive, mechanical and decontextualized, and resides within a rather limited 'language of skills'.

The aim of this chapter is to move a stage further, to describe a 'paradigm 3' strategy for the realization of the reflective professional. It integrates a reflective and critical use of practical skills with the appropriate professional knowledge, an understanding of relevant conceptual frameworks, and a command of the central 'genres' of practice. It locates the development of learning and teaching within the concrete teaching situation of one's discipline, department, students and institution. The intention of this strategy is neither to be restrictive nor to be prescriptive but, rather, open and flexible. It offers a critical approach for the development of documentary evidence and reflective articulation vital to realizing and improving professional practice.

Three descriptive dimensions frame the general structure of this strategy, which we hope we may be forgiven for expressing as *space, time* and *matter* (Figure 12.1). The first dimension describes the concrete spatial location of the realization. It is not a neutral space – as suggested by many predominantly generic skill-based programmes – but rather is situated within the discipline, department and institution in which the teacher is teaching. Ideally, it describes a space in which dialogue between and engagement with students, colleagues and the disciplinary material (knowledge) are critical to a full and complete realization of the language. The second dimension reflects the idea that the overall strategy is not simply a one-off programme set within bounded temporal limits but, rather, draws on past experience and looks forward to continuous and ongoing experience and development. The third descriptive dimension focuses on the nature and character of the 'matter' within these two dimensions of space and time and will constitute the focus of our discussions. It encompasses the wide range of material, experience, practices, situations, relationships and values with which the academic engages. It suggests that teachers be informed in their relationships with that 'matter' by the conceptual framework of engaged-dialogical 'learning', and guided by the critical learning matrix, which have been the central themes of this book. It emphasizes 'learning' as the underlying concept integrating the worlds of teacher, researcher and student (Chapter 3). Research and teaching were characterized as the same practice, providing exemplars and models of learning for one another and, notably, for the student. The third dimension of our strategy, then, describes an active, research-focused, evidence-based, theory-informed approach to realizing the professional 'language' of practice within the space–time dimensions described above.

This strategy is entirely consistent with the 'spirit of enquiry' which defines academic life and practice. In this, it is not new. It is new in helping to bring about a 'rapprochement' between the methods of enquiry which faculty engage in while doing research/scholarship and those methods of enquiry which they are developing with their students. It

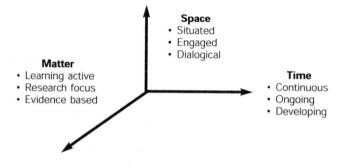

Figure 12.1 Professional realization: three descriptive dimensions

does so by transforming the process of teaching into such a 'process of enquiry', into the 'scholarship of teaching' (Boyer, 1990). The spirit of enquiry envisaged in this scholarship elucidates a further feature of the professional 'language' to be realized, a feature recalling the idea of language from Chapter 2: it is 'active' – 'language is part of an activity' (Wittgenstein, 1968: 11).

This book has, so far, drawn upon and been informed by a wide range of valuable educational research and theory. Active research with colleagues into learning and teaching is, however, Zuber-Skerritt reminds us, 'likely to have a more powerful effect on the improvement of learning, teaching and staff development than research (solely) produced by educational theorists' (1992: 115). This chapter will look at how to initiate and implement such an approach. In the first instance, it will explore a sequence of four critical ways to understand and actively develop the relationship between research and practice within professional development programmes. This sequence will culminate in a detailed examination of the fourth way – 'activity' or 'action research' – that draws upon and incorporates the first three. This form of 'action research' offers 'ways of investigating professional experience which link practice and the analysis of practice into a single developing sequence and link researchers and research participants into a single community of interested colleagues' (Winter, 1996: 14). It provides us with the principal model and method for realizing the professional 'language of practice'. The rest of the chapter will flesh out the essential aspects of this approach to 'professional realization'.

Integrating practice and research

In Chapter 3, we saw how the relationship between subject-based research and the practice of teaching in higher education is characterized by a problematic, often deeply uncomfortable relationship. Both research and teaching have traditionally focused on the distinctive nature of the particular subject or discipline, rather than their mutual aspirations in learning and their shared aims in the construction and extension of knowledge. The focus on the common goal of learning and the advancing of knowledge highlights the critical significance of this research–teaching relationship within disciplinary practice.

The following discussion employs the term 'research' in a broad sense – including both quantitative and qualitative approaches, and incorporating a wide range of empirical, scholarly and creative perspectives drawn from across the range of disciplinary cultures. It also regards 'research' as intrinsically fused with theory in so far as it informs theory, modifies theory, subverts theory, embodies theory and/or generates new theory. We can broadly group the research and theory regarding the practice of teaching explored in this book into four categories. The first concerns research looking at the practice of teaching. See, for example, the research looking at conceptions of teaching in higher education described in Chapter 3. The second category draws together the vast reservoir of research on adult and student learning (Chapter 4). The third focuses on research of more specific relevance to the individual 'genres' of practice (addressed in Chapters 5–11). The fourth category draws upon research concerned with the professional issues facing learning and teaching in higher education (Chapters 1, 2 and 3). It addresses the social and epistemological issues and values of the professional role of teaching within academic practice, higher education institutions and society in general. It challenges academics to reflect upon and think about their teaching in the changing wider social, political and economic contexts in which it is situated.

These categories offer a wide range of research that can be drawn upon in the development of the practice of learning and teaching. They do not describe a practical framework for understanding the different relationships between research and practice in the realization of professional practice. In the following, we offer a schema for considering and managing these relationships. Again, it is not intended as an authoritative or prescriptive programme, but rather as a conceptual tool for reflecting upon, developing and improving practice. Figure 12.2 illustrates four ways in which research and practice may be conceptualized in the realization of the professional practice: *practice defined by research; practice versus research; practice informed by research and practice as research.*

These four ways of conceiving research and practice are four phases or movements in the realization of the reflective professional. They do not describe a necessary sequential order. Realization will always be a recursive process in which teachers will individually and collectively

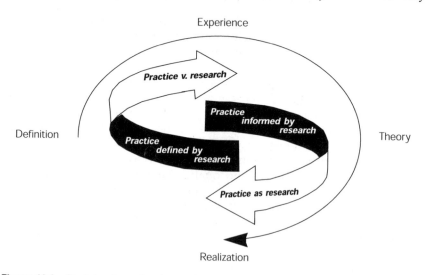

Figure 12.2   Realizing the reflective professional

reflect upon and rethink their practice in light of their various academic and personal experiences. Our discussion, here, will comment briefly on the first three phases. Other chapters in the book have considered the essential issues of these phases in some depth. In the following section, we shall address the fourth phase in some depth.

Practice defined by research

The initial movement which may be referred to as the 'definitional phase' challenges practitioners to critically reflect upon their own implicit, often unspoken, definition or conception of teaching practice in respect of research and theory. In the first instance, this reflection will most likely consist of the relation of teaching to issues of learning and knowledge. Watkins and Mortimore, for example, define pedagogy or teaching as 'any conscious activity by one person to enhance learning in another' (1999: 3). But making the link between teaching and learning is not, of itself, sufficient. It does not take a huge critical leap to recognize such a relationship. What does demand a more critical approach is our personal examination of the nature of that relationship. We shall not rehearse this in depth here as we have already explored the essential issues in Chapter 3. It is worth reiterating, however, that this phase challenges us to 'de-centre' teaching and to 're-centre' learning within our personal definitions of practice. Traditional perceptions of teaching tend to understand its relationship to learning as essentially linear, one in which teaching 'causes' or 'produces' learning. The definitional phase looks for a reversal of this perception in favour of one which views teaching as an 'outcome' of learning, or as defined by learning. Teaching 'is authenticated only by the authenticity of the student's thinking (learning)' (Freire, 1972: 50). If there is learning – if there is a 'genuine' engagement with 'knowledge', with ideas, concepts, facts, theoretical perspectives, and so on – the teacher can be said to be teaching. If, on the other hand, learning is not 'genuinely' occurring, then irrespective of the teacher's efforts, one may legitimately question their right to the use of the term 'teaching'.

Such a redefinition, of course, has implications, particularly with respect to our understanding of the nature and character of learning and knowing. This leads us to the next two phases or movements of the schema, which respectively address the practitioners' experiential and conceptual/theoretical understandings of learning.

Practice versus research

The juxtaposition of the second and third phases is not, as suggested above, a straightforward sequential matter. They do not occur separately or consecutively but are significantly interlocked in both development and ongoing improvement. The point of their separation here is to emphasize the often overlooked commonality of learning (see Chapter 3) at the heart of all our academic practices. Teachers in higher education bring their own deep and rich experiences of learning to the learning and teaching situation. Through their own academic research and scholarship, they can also bring to the encounter with their students a shared experience of the struggle and exhilaration of learning. This includes considered and proficient exemplars or models of its achievement in an academic environment.

Unfortunately – even given the recognition of learning as central to practice – all too often we leave the potential and richness of this common experience of research and teaching untapped and unexplored. More ominously within academic practice generally, teaching and research are frequently, even habitually, regarded as rivals: time and status pitting the 'learning' of one against the 'learning' of the other. This phase or movement in realizing practice, then, is characterized by the challenge to examine critically this rivalry of *'learning versus learning'* and the associated fragmentation of 'learning' more generally which it causes. The issue is not the academic role of researcher versus that of teacher but rather of developing practice beyond this partition and establishing an inclusive culture of learning – 'culture of inquiry' (Clark, 1997) – which encourages active engagement in learning by all.

This idea of rivalry extends beyond the traditional opposition of research 'versus' teaching to encompass that gap or 'displacement' between educational research and practice. The pre-eminent Cambridge writer and thinker Raymond Williams posed the 'paradox' between 600 years of English literature versus only two centuries of English literacy (1983: 3). He was of course referring to the widespread development of English literacy, but the irony is, nonetheless, poignant. A similar irony might reasonably be ascribed to the gap within the academic sector between the centuries of educational research/scholarship on practice versus the few decades, if that, of a more prevalent 'literacy' of practice. This poses a challenge to faculty. A challenge to become professionally 'literate', to become, if not 'educationalists', at least 'educators'. This challenge takes us to the next phase or movement in our sequence.

Practice informed by research

This phase of integrating research and practice has recently become the most prevalent or conspicuous. There has been a huge surge in research in student and adult learning (Chapter 4) and widespread employment of this research in both the design and content of training and development programmes for teaching staff in higher education. The development of individual and collective practice is not limited to any one or two categories of research and theory. It will draw upon all four of the main categories mentioned above (those we have been primarily concerned with in this book). It will also inquire about and explore others, particularly those from other disciplines, other practices and other professions that are of special significance and relevance to the individual practitioner.

Teaching informed by relevant research, by theory, by specialized knowledge, by expert and critical ways of understanding is a vital ingredient of reflective and professional practice. It provides the knowledge and the conceptual frameworks for reflecting upon and 'critiquing' one's knowledge, practice and common experience as a learner. In this, it describes a movement or phase of educational and professional 'literacy'. Such a 'literacy', as we have attempted to show throughout this book, embodies the development and practice of a common and comprehensive 'language' of learning and teaching. Characterized and informed by research, theory and scholarship, such a language offers opportunities for:

- sharing a common understanding with colleagues and students;
- moving beyond the mere acquisition of a series of communication and performance skills, tips or specialized teaching competencies;
- re-positioning practice within a deeper and more critical understanding of professional life, practical engagement, reflective skill development, 'genre' refinement and continuing professional development, etc.;
- conducting personal micro-research – or even larger-scale collective research – as part of professional and academic development;
- reconciling academic practice, both through common experiences of learning and through a shared academic discourse of theory, evidence, argument and notions of rigour;
- managing uncertainty and change;
- improving personal scholarship on practice.

Practice as research

The phase or movement of understanding 'practice as research' is not an end result so much as the bringing together of the phases into a process/method of practical realization. It articulates a strategy for professional realization that incorporates and integrates the other three. In this, it describes a process of becoming critically engaged in practice through action research. It aims at 'professional realization' by transforming 'academic practice' – habitual or customary action – into '*academic praxis*' (Zuber-Skerrit, 1992a: 113) – informed, critical and committed action. This is accomplished through 'critical and self-critical reflection which help practitioners to emancipate themselves from the often unseen constraints of habit, custom, precedent, coercion and ideology' (ibid.: 113).

Action research differs from more traditional forms of educational research in the degree to which it involves issues such as critical practice, improvement, participation, and the actual environment or situation of practice. The main aims and benefits of action research are 'the improvement of practice, the improvement of the understanding of practice by its practitioners and the improvement of the situation in which the practice takes place' (ibid.: 110). Carr and Kemmis (1983) describe three kinds of action research which address these issues, albeit at different levels of practitioner engagement. They are differentiated by the relationship between the educational researcher and the practitioners: by the degree to which the practitioners are or become the principal researcher. In the first, *technical action research*, the researcher who facilitates the process establishes and judges the standards for improving the effectiveness of educational practice. The practitioner is mainly engaged in the process at a technical level. The second, *practical action research*, also aims to improve the effectiveness of practice but encourages the practitioner to engage more fully and self-reflectively in the research process to develop their practical understanding and professional development. The third type, *emancipatory action research*, encourages the full participation of practitioner-as-researcher to explore critically the effectiveness of practice and its practical understanding within the social and organizational constraints that enclose practice. Improvement, here, encompasses 'organizational enlightenment'. It is characterized by a more complete 'engagement' and critical 'dialogue', essential to the full realization of practice.

According to Carr and Kemmis only *emancipatory action research* meets the three minimal requirements for action research: 'having strategic action as its subject matter; proceeding through the spiral of planning, acting, observing and reflecting; and involving participation and collaboration in all phases of the research activity' (1983: 177). Action research in this more inclusive guise is characterized by strategic action in its design, methods and realization. It consciously and deliberately sets out to improve, enhance and realize practice through actions informed, but not constrained, by research and theory. It is flexible, open to change necessitated by experience and circumstance, and it is subject to the practitioner's critical and rational practical judgements. Kemmis and McTaggart describe the implementation of this strategic action as a continuous cycle of four moments:

- a plan of action to improve what is already happening;
- action to implement the plan;
- observation of the effects of action in the context in which it occurs;
- reflection on these effects as a basis for further planning, subsequent action and so on, through a succession of cycles. (1988: 7)

Zuber-Skerritt (1992a: 114–15) has explored and described many of the reasons for employing action research for the improvement of teaching and learning practice in higher education in what she refers to as the CRASP model. It emphasizes the power of action research to encourage the *critical attitude* we wish to foster in our students but also in ourselves

– personally and as exemplars for students. It incorporates the integration of educational theory with personal *research into teaching*. It provides a rigorous research basis from which to understand and contribute to the debate concerning academic *accountability* to society, giving academic staff a professionally grounded voice with respect to academic policies, future curriculum decisions and so on. It offers practitioners a robust and critical method of *self-evaluation* for ongoing development. Finally, it sustains the capacity to contribute to the development of *professionalism* in higher education. In the next section, we examine a practical way of reconstructing the ideas and methods of action research in professional realization.

The reflective professional through action research

The following discussion presents a 'tripartite' framework for thinking about and engaging in action research with the aim of realizing professional practice. As a method of professional development, one of its essential 'outcomes' is the degree to which it integrates the issues of learning apparent in research and scholarship with those of learning and teaching. It views professional development as moving beyond learning and teaching practice to embrace all academic practice (Chapter 3) – one of the key aspects of our third paradigm of learning and teaching (Chapter 1). It is not a one-off event but rather an ongoing progression arising out of the unfolding developments in one's practice. It is possible to use the general approach within a formal programme of training or to engage with it more informally. Categories of programmes might include:

- institutional – programme provided by an institution;
- disciplinary – programme provided by discipline associations;
- peer – programme established within parameters agreed with peers;
- individual – programme individually constructed.

As the basis for action research, however, programmes require a systematic and strategically planned approach. Figure 12.3 illustrates three broad areas that such an approach would embrace: situated practice, educational resource and research documentation. We shall look at these features individually below, but it is worth briefly expanding on them here. Practice does not exist in a vacuum. It is *situated practice* and, in so far as the practitioner/researcher is researching their own practice within their particular department and institution, both the research project and the associated research documentation will also be concretely situated and grounded in their own academic discipline(s). Development programmes and projects are not, therefore, focused on helping practitioners to compile evidence of generic skills and competencies *in vacuo*. They are aimed at helping them to identify, critically examine and develop expertise and skills in relevant practices embedded within their own discipline, depart-

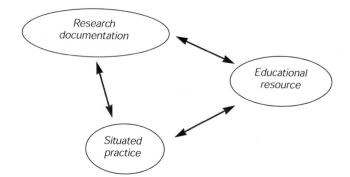

Figure 12.3 Professional realization: a research framework

ment and institution. They shall do so, of course with respect to a broad range of *educational resource.* While these are often associated and drawn from generic or cross disciplinary aspects of a programme, they are not regarded here as 'answers' to teaching and learning problems, so much as tools for critically reflecting on 'situated' practice.

Finally, the realization of practice will need to proceed towards the production of *research documentation,* for provision of evidence of professional realization, for sharing with colleagues in the best tradition of peer review and for informing and developing ongoing development. The documentation most commonly associated with programmes for the development of learning and teaching practice has mainly consisted of the development of a portfolio of evidence related to a number of carefully selected outcomes. In the UK, the Staff Education Development Association (SEDA) pioneered and widely promoted this practice. More recently, the professional Institute for Learning and Teaching (ILT) in higher education has encouraged the practice further. Neither organization, however, regards the portfolio explicitly as a research document so much as a professional record of achievement. The approach taken here reinterprets the professional parameters of the 'portfolio' – its outcomes, evidence, professional requirements, etc. – in research terms. In this way, the portfolio may be conceived as a research document or research report informed by situated practice and educational resource. It provides critical, practical evidence and theoretically informed analysis of those areas of teaching and learning relevant to the teacher's practice.

Situated practice

The disciplinary situation of practice is at the heart of professional realization through action-research approaches. It provides the vital context of the practitioner's investigations and explorations. It is, ultimately, the space in which the 'research' is embedded – where the plans are designed, interventions constructed, methods identified and developed. Within the situation, the multiplicity of the designs, interventions and methods available need to be understood in terms of the overall 'realization' objectives of the research. These will be dependent on the general parameters of the research (e.g. national professional requirements, institutional criteria, programme objectives) as well as the initial questions and the outcomes (e.g. improving learning, teaching development and improvement, evaluation of learning and teaching).

Action-research of this sort is not aiming at wide-scale generalization or application but rather at individual development. Essentially it employs case study methodology in which the case is the researcher's own practice within their own concrete academic situation. Closely associated with participative methods (Cohen and Manion, 1989: 127), the case study provides an overarching methodological perspective for researching situated practice. Case studies are 'strong in reality'; 'attend to subtle and complex relations'; 'recognise the embeddedness of social truth'; 'admit subsequent re-interpretation' and most importantly 'begin in a world of action and contribute to it' (Adelman et al., 1983: 148). Case-situated action-research will work with and draw from concrete categories of experience, evidence and activities including:

- Learning and teaching practices and resources, etc.;
- Programme, course, module and session materials and documentation;
- Relevant departmental and institutional documents;
- Disciplinary and syllabus subject matter – texts, readings, techniques, etc.;
- Disciplinary research and scholarship;
- Students, colleagues, mentors/advisers.

While not exhaustive categories, each offers significant research potential employing a broad range of methods and techniques of data collection and analysis. It is not possible to elaborate on the character and scope of these methods and techniques in any detail, but it is worth noting examples that might be effectively used (see also Chapter 11). These will include, for example, *document or textual analysis*: not only of the kind of institutional and programme/course documentation listed above but also, crucially, of student essays, papers, online discussion, project and lab reports (including drafts), etc. It may also include systematic collection and analysis of both formative and summative written comments given to students. Practitioners may also employ techniques and methods of *observation*, particularly with respect to classroom practice. This might include formal peer observation conducted with colleagues on your and/or on your colleagues' teaching practice. It could also include planned observation of student interactions: between the students, with the teacher and so on.

Interviews with students also offer an invaluable source of data for analysis, reflection and further development. These might be structured and/or semi-structured. They might aim, for example, at coming to a better understanding of student experiences and/or conceptions of learning within the practitioner's particular teaching and learning situation. They might focus on a particular aspect of learning or be used across the learning matrix. Strategic *surveys* of students, including but also extending beyond standard course evaluation and/or rating instruments, might also be effectively used. The use of interviews and surveys could also extend to other members of appropriate and relevant faculty and staff members. In addition, practitioners might wish to ask students – and colleagues for that matter – to participate in exercises utilizing a range of *focus-group* techniques. Depending on permission, time and resources, practitioners might also find methods of cognitive *experimentation* valuable. The point here, however, is not to fully elaborate the diversity of methods, techniques or instruments that can be employed, but to suggest the scope of the 'research' that can be strategically and creatively employed for the improvement of practice.

Educational resource

Realizing professional practice through action research and the development of research documentation will normally need to be grounded in the learning and teaching situation of the teacher's discipline, but also drawing upon material and resources from other disciplines concerned with understanding higher education. The tension between these two is often uneven and uncomfortable, and successfully managing it becomes an indispensable ingredient to realization. It is best managed if one accepts that professional realization is not generic but disciplinary. While it draws upon a range of different sorts of educational resources – which we shall look at in a moment – it takes place for the most part in the practitioners' discipline(s). The research is 'disciplinary' research – albeit drawing as much disciplinary research does on research 'tools' from other disciplines as well those of its own.

We shall not describe in detail the nature of the education resources available to practitioners in conducting action research. This book itself is intended as an essential resource. It is worth noting, however, the extent of the resources available for use. Three factors organize educational resource here: location, resource and activity (Table 12.1). They do not describe an exhaustive list of potential resource but, rather, constructive and useful dimensions for the design of development/improvement programmes and personal initiatives/projects undertaken within such programmes.

While ideally located in the concrete learning and teaching situation – characterized by discipline, research, scholarship, and so on – the professional realization of practice, nevertheless, increasingly draws upon the enabling structures and motivational impetus of generic programmes of staff development. Such programmes mainly occur at institutional level, but normally expect participants to draw upon learning and teaching resources from actual teaching, requiring, for example, portfolios of

Table 12.1 *Educational resources*

Location	Resource	Activity
International	Development programmes	Workshops/seminars
National	Sessions and workshops	Peer consultancy
Institutional	Educational literature	Mentoring
Departmental	Tutors/consultants	Appraisal
Course	Fellow participants	Support groups
Personal	Students	

evidence of such teaching. While the 'course-institution' is the main 'location' link, and at the heart of action-research approaches to development, educational resource from other locations can effectively supplement it. The expansion of national and international organizations for the support of learning and teaching can provide a wealth of information, materials and assistance. The ILT, for example, oversees 24 subject centres within the UK, which provide materials for practitioners focused on issues that are more discipline specific. In addition, there are a growing number of national courses, workshops and programmes focused on particular disciplines or on specific issues and/or 'genres' of learning and teaching. They will normally provide access to the kind of educational literature and materials covered in this book as well as sessions and workshops for exploring this literature with respect to individual 'genres', 'sub-genres' and/or combinations of 'genres'. Such literature and materials will be available from a range of sources including: books, teaching materials, video, the World Wide Web, academic and professional journals, conference papers, etc.

The provision of sessions – workshops, conferences and seminars – is not the preserve of integrated development programmes. An increasing number of organizations – regional, national and international – are providing valuable and specialized sessions outside institutional programmes. These are provided both in face-to-face modes and increasingly through distance and online education technologies. These sessions do not simply provide access to the expertise of the tutors and consultants facilitating them, they provide invaluable access to the experience, knowledge and skills of the other participants. The shared experience of fellow participants provides personal and social support as well as invaluable intellectual and practical help. They permit both the scrutiny of one's knowledge and understanding of practical issues in a shared discipline and intellectual culture as well as the exploration of new possibilities across disciplines and other academic cultures. Students will also be a rich resource. Many will bring articulate and critically constructive accounts of their learning within and across disciplines. Practitioners will also have their own personal resources to tap, not the least of which may be their own encounters with education through children, community groups, volunteer and charity work, etc.

We have noted some of the activities – workshops, seminars, lunchtime sessions, etc. – through which resources become available but the very processes of these activities are themselves often a significant resource. Other useful activities – many of which are becoming more widespread in university staff and management processes – include mentoring activities with senior and/or experienced colleagues with regard to learning and teaching within the discipline and department. This can be extremely useful in contextualizing teaching as well as helping to develop effective communities of shared and constructive practice. In the same vein, peer mentoring and consultancy activities with colleagues exploring at a range of learning and teaching 'genres' can provide useful resource for both personal and collective action research aimed at improvement. Peer observation has, for example, become a more widespread tool for examining practice – mainly focused on classroom performance but can be extended to considerations of activities central to other 'genres' such as supervision, assessment, evaluation, curriculum design.

Many institutions also provide appraisal schemes for faculty, which offer another potentially rich source of evidence and data for reflection and critical analysis. Informal support groups with colleagues sharing similar concerns and issues are also a promising resource upon which to draw. While many of these activities may be institutional or departmental, others have a much wider remit. Finally, it should be re-stated that the staff development perspective emphasized here does not view these resources as ends in themselves but rather as means by which professional practice might be realized through strategically planned and implemented 'research' initiatives.

Research documentation: portfolio of practice

Brockbank and McGill describe a portfolio of evidence of teaching practice in higher education as 'a compilation of learning intentions, accounts of learning activities, learning outcomes, records of reflective dialogues. It includes evidence from a variety of sources including your private learning journal/diary/log, and, most important of all, a reflective document detailing your learning process' (1998: 103).

As suggested above, the portfolio as 'research document' goes beyond such a 'reflective reportage' of evidence to embody the idea of critical and strategic action. It will need to incorporate in its design a strategic plan related to and embedded in the situation in which the investigation(s) will be taking place and the educational resources on which it will be drawing. In the case of professional accreditation programmes – such as those nationally accredited in the UK by the ILT – portfolio design will need to strategically consider and incorporate requirements to show a command of a range of 'genres of practice' (Chapters 5–11). These will need to be informed by the relevant educational literature (Chapter 4) and by 'academic values and principles' (Chapter 3). In addition, portfolios may need to meet institutional requirements such as those for appointment and promotion. This does not preclude – indeed may entail – a critique of the parameters and criteria of such programmes.

The portfolio is, nevertheless, a 'research document' providing evidence of the process and results of personal 'scholarship' and 'empirical' research into teaching and learning practice. In this respect, it requires identification of relevant research 'questions and methods', the appropriate discovery, development and generation of a variety of evidence of personal practice and the critical analysis, assessment and presentation of this evidence within a substantive theoretical context. It calls for the practical development of reflective skills of self-assessment and self-evaluation. It will, ideally, be characterized by a form of the action research cycle of 'plan–action–observe–reflect' described above. Such a cycle might include the kinds of activities as given in Table 12.2.

The presentation of portfolios will require a scholarly format, including appropriate table of contents, referencing, bibliography, relevant appendices, accuracy of presentation, etc. Indeed, the overlap of research and teaching practices might extend here to academic publication. The results of the 'action research' supporting professional development may also be written up for publication in appropriate academic and professional journals. As well as contributing to the research and scholarship of teaching, it may have the added benefit of furthering professional careers. The general publication of personal or collective 'action research' on issues of learning and teaching in one's discipline(s) as a commonplace activity for faculty would go some distance towards integrating academic practices. On the other hand, we must sound a note of caution. Publication confining itself to the research results can distort the professional developmental nature of the research. As Donald Kennedy, the past president of Stanford suggests, writing 'in a portfolio devoted to forms of scholarship related to teaching [is] ... scholarship beyond that reported in peer reviewed journals.' (1997: 65).

Conclusion

It is important to recall at this point the critical concept and idea that has been driving this book forward: a 'professional language of practice'. The realization of this 'language' is keenly interrelated with the other essential components that we have been examining throughout: the 'critical conceptual framework' and the appropriate 'genres'. It integrates a reflective and critical use of practical skills with the appropriate professional knowledge, an understanding of relevant conceptual frameworks and a command of the key 'genres' of practice. It 'realizes' a critical and reflective capability for sharing, communicating, engaging and practising.

Table 12.2 *Action research cycle: illustrative activities*

Illustrative Activities	Diverse Examples
Plan	
• Determine relevant research question(s).	Do my teaching methods achieve the optimum balance of learning activities?
• Identify 'genres' of learning and teaching for research.	Lecturing, facilitating, innovating, assessing.
• Design a teaching innovation.	Construct a method of peer assessment.
• Explore and establish research methods.	Interviews with staff and students, follow-up questionnaires, etc.
Action	
• Employ strategies and methods of evaluation.	Conduct interviews with students; focus groups with past students, etc.
• Engage and/or test educational resources.	Attend a conference or workshop on methods for assessing students' practical skills.
• Introduce changes, innovations.	Introduce 'group activities' into a lecture situation.
Observe	
• Collect/interpret empirical evidence/data.	Observe student classroom responses and interpret survey of attitudes to using online materials in class.
• Examine and interpret educational resources.	Conduct a statistical analysis on student questionnaires concerning their motivation in a particular course.
• Map evidence to relevant areas of practice.	Map research evidence on course design to a particular course in a subject discipline.
Reflect	
• Critically analyse outcomes.	Critically analyse grade and exam data on the impact of using problem-based curriculum design in a single course.
• Draw conclusions.	Draw conclusions and evaluate the implications of the survey data looking at the provision of feedback on student assignments online.
• Develop new plans/strategies.	Modify and extend a new design for the evaluation of the impact of one's lecturing on learning to other courses.

In many ways, however, the themes and content of this chapter must remain incomplete. This is partly due to the space limitations and the sheer possibility that the development of practice embraces. It is also due, in great part, to the critical 'openness' that must inevitably characterize 'realization'. Realization must sustain this 'openness' with respect to its creative potential but also with respect to the diversity, multiplicity, complexity and uncertainty of the students, the university and the future with which it must continually and fully engage.

Further reading

Boud, D. and Walker, D. (1998) 'Promoting reflection in professional courses: the challenge of context', *Studies in Higher Education*, 23 (2): 191–206.

Boyer, E.L. (1990) *Scholarship reconsidered: Priorities of the Professoriate*. San Francisco: Carnegie Foundation for the Advancement of Teaching/Jossey-Bass.

Brew, A. (1999) 'Research and teaching: changing relationship in a changing context', *Studies in Higher Education*, 24 (3): 291–301.

Carr, W. and Kemmis, S. (1983) *Becoming Critical: Knowing Through Action Research*. Victoria: Deakin University Press.

Carr, W. and Kemmis, S. (1986) *Becoming Critical: Education, Knowledge and Action Research*. London: Falmer Press.

Cohen, L., Manion, L. and Morrison, K. (2000) *Research Methods in Education*. London: Falmer Press.

Gibbs, G. (1995) 'Changing conceptions of teaching and learning through action research', in A. Brew (ed.), *New Directions in Staff Development*, Buckingham: SRHE/Open University Press.

Prosser, M. and Trigwell, K. (1999) *Understanding Learning and Teaching: The Experience in Higher Education*. London: SRHE/Open University Press.

Winter, R. (1996) 'Some principles and procedures for the conduct of action research', in O. Zuber-Skerrit (ed.) *New Directions in Action Research*. London: Falmer Press.

Zuber-Skerrit, O. (1992a) *Professional Development in Higher Education: A Theoretical Framework for Action Research*. London: Kogan Page.

Zuber-Skerrit, O. (1992b) *Action Research in Higher Education: Examples and Reflections*. London: Kogan Page.

Zuber-Skerrit, O. (1996) *New Directions in Action Research*. London: Falmer Press.

Appendix 1: Checklists

CHARACTERISTICS OF PARTICULAR METHODS OF STUDENT ASSESSMENT

Checklist A is designed to summarise the characteristics of the dominant methods of assessment used on a course unit or in a department or institution. Up to 6 methods should be written in on the right and each one rated for its present use and how it may be ideally used in terms of the characteristics on the left. Use a cross in each column.

The column headers (repeated for methods 1–6) are:
a) present use
b) ideal use

A. General Characteristics

Objectives

No.	Characteristic	1 a) present use	1 b) ideal use	2 a) present use	2 b) ideal use	3 a) present use	3 b) ideal use	4 a) present use	4 b) ideal use	5 a) present use	5 b) ideal use	6 a) present use	6 b) ideal use
1.	Is primarily concerned with assessing a *narrow* range of objectives												
	Is primarily concerned with assessing a *broad* range of objectives												
2.	Is concerned with assessing the acquisition of information and basic comprehension — *High / Medium/indeterminate / Low*												
3.	Standard application of principles or theory, or models in simple problem-solving — *High / Medium/indeterminate / Low*												
4.	Critical/analytical ability or the use or development of argument — *High / Medium/indeterminate / Low*												
5.	Ability to present information clearly in a well organised way — *High / Medium/indeterminate / Low*												
6.	Creative or imaginative ability or high level problem-solving or experimental design — *High / Medium/indeterminate / Low*												
7.	Attitudes and Values — *High / Medium/indeterminate / Low*												
8.	Social Skills — *High / Medium/indeterminate / Low*												
9.	Physical motor skills — *High / Medium/indeterminate / Low*												

Predictability

10.	Questions or tasks *are known in advance* or highly predictable												
	Questions or tasks *are unknown in advance* and difficult to predict												

Timing

11.	Time allowed for individual tasks or questions is very short - *less than 15 min*												
	Time allowed for individual tasks *is restricted to ½-1½ hours*												
	Time allowed for individual tasks *is restricted to 1½-3 hours*												
	Time allowed for individual tasks is open within a period of *about 1-4 weeks*												
	Time allowed for individual tasks is open within *about 1-12 months*												

Weighting

No.	Characteristic												
12.	The method as a contribution to the qualification or total grading for the year *is heavily weighted (½ or more)*												
	The method has a *medium weighting (1/5 - ½)*												
	The method has a *low weighting (less than 1/5)*												

Pervasiveness

13.	The method *is pervasive* - occupies students regularly throughout most of the year												
	The method *is not pervasive* - occupies students for short periods only												

			1......a) present use / b) ideal use	2......a) present use / b) ideal use	3......a) present use / b) ideal use	4......a) present use / b) ideal use	5......a) present use / b) ideal use	6......a) present use / b) ideal use
Access to information								
14.	Access to information	- is free						
		- is not allowed						
		- is restricted						
Reliability								
15.	Marking is *completely objective*							
	Marking reliability *average*							
	Marking reliability *low*							
Sampling								
16.	Representativeness of students' work in area to be assessed	*high*						
		average						
		low						
Contamination								
17.	Potential contamination of students' work by irrelevant factors	*high*						
		average						
		low						
Administration								
18.	Administrative convenience	*high*						
		low						
19.	Staff acceptability	*high*						
		average						
		low						
Correlation with other methods								
20.	Correlation with other methods	*high*						
		average						
		low						

B. Characteristics Related to Learning

			1	2	3	4	5	6
21.	General attitudes of students	*positive*						
		neutral						
		negative						
22.	Usefulness as feedback to students	*high*						
		low						
23.	Degree of stress felt by students	*high*						
		average						
		low						
24.	Encouragement for students to seek information and ideas from a wide range of sources	*high*						
		low						
25.	Effect on staff-student relations	*beneficial*						
		neutral						
		detrimental						
26.	Encourages *competitiveness*							
	Encourages *co-operation*							
27.	Simulation of 'real life' activity	*high*						
		low						
28.	Independence	*is encouraged*						
		not affected						
		is discouraged						
29.	Opportunity for students to participate in determining the nature and/or use of the method	*high*						
		low						

B. Characteristics Related to Learning *cont.*		1........a) present use	b) ideal use	2........a) present use	b) ideal use	3........a) present use	b) ideal use	4........a) present use	b) ideal use	5........a) present use	b) ideal use	6........a) present use	b) ideal use
30. Opportunity for self assessment	*high*												
	low												
31. Opportunity for peer assessment	*high*												
	low												

CHECKLIST B

CHARACTERISTICS OF A TOTAL SYSTEM OF STUDENT ASSESSMENT

Checklist B is designed to characterise the total system of assessment used on a course unit or in a department or institution. Put a cross in each column on the right to indicate your judgement about the characteristics on the left as they apply to the present system and to an ideal system in your field.		Present System	Ideal System
1.	*Complexity of the system high* i.e. many methods used and operation complex *high* Complexity *average* *average* Complexity low i.e. very few methods, simple operation *low*		
2.	*Saliency* i.e. most assessments count for qualification *high* or models in simple problem-solving *low*		
3.	*Pervasiveness* i.e. frequency of assessments of any kind *high* *average* *low*		
4.	*Similarity of assessments* used for qualification *high* (summative) to those used for learning *average* (formative) *low*		
5.	*Administrative convenience* *high* *average* *low*		
6.	*Staff acceptability* *high* *average* *low*		
7.	*Opportunity for student choice* *high* *average* *low*		
8.	*Opportunity for student participation* *high* in design and operation of the system *low*		
9.	*Degree of stress* imposed by the system *high* *average* *low*		
10.	*Content validity of summative assessments* in relation to *high* knowledge, i.e. sampling of *knowledge* objectives - facts, *average* concepts and theories *low*		
11.	*Content validity in relation to skills and abilities* *high* *average* *low*		
12.	*Content validity in relation to attitudes* *high* *average* *low*		
13.	*Predictive validity* i.e. in relation to future study or work *high* *average* *low*		
14.	*Construct validity* i.e. how far overall grade is related to psychological constructs underlying ability in the subject - *high* this might be an estimate of how far your conception of ability in the subject is related to the grade - are students *average* with high grade invariably those you consider to be the best, say. mathematicians, sociologists or physicists *low*		

Appendix 2: Exercise on Methods of Evaluating Teaching

Here are some ways of learning about your teaching which have been used successfully but which are not without their difficulties.

Could you go through the list and

1. see how far you agree with the suggested advantages and disadvantages deleting or amending any you feel are inappropriate and adding any you feel have been omitted (the methods have not been defined in any detail and in practice much will depend on the context and the ways they are introduced and used, but some broad generalizations about a wide range of possible methods can be a good starting point for planning an integrated approach to evaluation);

2. imagine you and a colleague are in charge of a one-year interdisciplinary course unit for a degree and select the methods you would like to use to form the basis for the evaluation of the course and the teaching, assuming it is a fairly new course and you are willing to put considerable effort into it despite the lack of assistance available.

At this stage you are not being asked to plan a detailed strategy but merely to select methods which may be appropriate.

Examples of 'pros' and 'cons' for different methods

1. Interactive Teaching

- General discussion during lecture/class
- Buzz groups – (splitting into small groups for discussion)
- Testing with feedback during session

a) *Advantages – usefulness*

1. Integration of teaching and evaluation
2. Frequent – immediate link with remedial action
3. Specific learning problems identified – linked to specific teaching
4. Not explicit teaching evaluation so less inhibition
5. Students learn about own learning in concrete situation
6. Students share problems
7. More enjoyable
8.

b) *Disadvantages – problems*

1. Students feel over-controlled
2. Exclusively concerned with teacher's learning objectives
3. Too specific – not linked with general review
4. Tendency to avoid teaching process
5.
6.

2. Questionnaires for Particular Sessions

- completed by participants   ) Lecturing
- completed by observers   ) Small groups
) Laboratory work

a) *Advantages – usefulness*

1 Broad coverage of opinion
2 Quantifiable for comparison
3 Easy to administer
4 Close link to particular teaching – immediate
5 Easily anonymous
6 Systematic coverage of themes
7
8

b) *Disadvantages – problems*

1 Students can be alienated especially if frequent
2 Oversimplifying or too long and complex
3 Ambiguity difficult to eliminate
4 Encourages 'off-the-cuff' responses rather than serious reflection
5 Can encourage complacency
6 Time perspective limited
7 Even with open questions teacher perspective dominant
8 Skill in questionnaire design and analysis needed
9
10

3. Questionnaires for Courses, Parts of Courses or Projects

a) *Advantages – usefulness*

1 1, 2, 3, 5 and 6 from previous method (2.)
2 Longer time perspective
3 Opportunity to explore links between different aspects of course
4 Can link responses to teaching to questions about students' background – academic, interests, orientations, motivations, perceptions of objectives, etc.

5
6

b) *Disadvantages – problems*

1 1 to 5 and 7 and 8 from previous method (2.)
2 More skill needed to answer some questions
3 Time perspective on quality of course often ignored – difficult to achieve
4
5

**4. Group Discussion   – Formal – timetables with agenda or topics
                                  – Informal**

a) *Advantages – usefulness*

1 Flexible – explore issues as they arise
2 Can set tone to encourage criticism
3 Can work through nature and implications of criticism
4 More time and encouragement to think – less 'off-the-cuff' responses
5 More responsive to students' perceptions and perspective
6 Can focus on really important themes
7 Can discuss staff views more easily – develop a dialogue
8 Check on information from other sources
9 Enjoyable
10
11

b) *Disadvantages – problems*

1 Dominant personalities can be over influential
2 Initial tone of discussion can make it difficult to change to a different point of view
3 Coverage of issues may be limited by time available
4 Difficult to assess distribution of opinion
5 Lack of anonymity may be inhibiting
6
7
8 Skill in group discussion needed

5. Individual Discussion – Formal Interviews
– Informal

a) *Advantages – usefulness*

1 Explore particular issues at a personal level
2 Explore significance of the course as a whole for individual students
3 Get to know students better
4 Help students to understand their own response to the course
5 Check on data from other sources
6
7

b) *Disadvantages – problems*

1 Can be biased by personal impact
2 Coverage of students poor or very time-consuming – biased sample unless careful
3 Skill in interviewing needed
4
5

6. **General Observation by Colleague or Evaluator – followed by a Report and/or Discussion**

a) *Advantages – usefulness*

1 Staff perspective different from students' but complementary – wider time perspective. More subject expertise (?), more experience of teaching, more knowledge of related courses, constraints, etc.
2 May be less inhibited in certain respects
3 Can be reciprocal arrangement, each learning from being critic as well as receiving criticism
4 General opportunity for sharing ideas about teaching
5 Enjoyable (?)
6
7

b) *Disadvantages – problems*

1 May be intimidating especially if status difference
2 May lead to underemphasis of student view point
3 May be mutual support for undesirable or restricted view of teaching
4
5
6

7. **Work Assignment Feedback (Reports, essays, projects, etc)**

  – Discussion about tutor comments
  – Student written commentaries on learning and writing problems

a) *Advantages – usefulness*

1 Close integration of work with evaluation
2 Link with areas of high concern
3 Enables students to learn self-evaluation
4 Enables students to be better critics of their own learning
5 Enables students to explore own interests and motivation
6
7

b) *Disadvantages – problems*

1 Can encourage too much introspection
2 Emphasizes work as learning exercise rather than 'real-life production'
3
4

8. **Diaries and More Specific Self-Reports**

a) *Advantages – usefulness*

1 1 to 5 of previous method (7.)
2 More developmental – comments linked with previous comments
3 More scope for interesting diversions
4 Broader perspective
5 Can be enjoyable
6
7

b) *Disadvantages – problems*

1 Needs more commitment – staff encouragement
2 More private therefore many need some way of dividing so staff see only less private sections
3 Can be time-consuming for staff to read
4 Little sharing – unless anonymous extracts are given out
5
6

9. **Student Oral Reports**

  – On particular sessions – i.e. one or two students report briefly on the content and processes of the previous session
  – On the course so far or as a whole (generally better as a group project)

a) *Advantages – usefulness*

1 Most of advantages of method (8.)
2 More sharing and learning from other students' presentations and discussion
3 Enjoyable, sociable
4
5

b) *Disadvantages – problems*

1 Public performance may be inhibiting
2 Time
3 More dominant students may be more influential
4
5

10. **Video/Audio-Recording Playback and Discussion**

- As feedback to the teacher, i.e. of lectures or small groups with or without colleagues or students present
- As feedback to students, with or without staff present

a) *Advantages – usefulness*

1 See ourselves as others see us
2 Opportunity for self-criticism – less resistance to what you see yourself than to what others tell you
3 Emotional changes more possible not purely intellectual discussion – can explore feelings and thoughts present at the time
4 Share feelings and ideas with others
5 Students can learn that they contribute to success or failure of the session
6 Can look at specific instance slowly and at leisure
7 Can compare sessions and be encouraged by progress
8
9

b) *Disadvantages – problems*

1 Can be disconcerting
2 Time
3 May overemphasize own reactions rather than others
4 *Could* confirm own prejudices or misperceptions
5
6

11. **Generating Statements and Recommendations about the Course or Session by Staff and Students Organizing them under Themes in Groups and Rating**

(Individuals write statements on cards and put them on the walls under headings, or groups may organize them into a manageable number which are then rated by all and discussed.)

a) *Advantages – usefulness*

1 Dimensions generated by individual participants and staff
2 Useful discussion (?) about themes in small groups
3 Numerical data from all students
4 Discussion about learning and implications
5 Enjoyable, sociable
6
7

b) *Disadvantages – problems*

1 Time
2 Staff interests may be underemphasized in final ratings
3
4

12. **Nominal Group Process**

A class of students with their own chairperson: each in turn nominates one aspect so good it should not be changed and one aspect so poor that it should be changed. Approval or disapproval from the rest of the class is not permitted. The class votes to identify the group (numerical) view on these positive and negative aspects respectively.

(Students in small groups propose how the most commonly agreed poor aspects may be rectified.)

a) *Advantages – usefulness*

1 Students identify aspects of personal interest
2 Individuals feel they can contribute without being influenced (silent majority has its say)
3 Letting off steam, without raising emotional temperature
4 Provides teachers with wealth of information with minimal expenditure of time, effort
5 Identifies the group's priorities
6 With appropriate following can be used as a progression of practical experiences towards ability to adapt to change and to participate in change
7
8

b) *Disadvantages – problems*

1 Aspects of interest to teachers may be omitted
2 May not provide causative information
3 More time-consuming for students
4
5

13. **Other Methods**

– Role-play (students or staff may play traditionalist or radical critics, for example)
– Critical incidents (collect specific examples of incidents illustrating particularly successful and unsuccessful teaching, etc.)

a) *General Advantages*

1 Can make evaluation more interesting
2 New methods may reveal the unexpected

b) *General Disadvantages*

1 Difficult to interpret
2 General resistance to change
3 Time

Appendix 3: Teaching Observation Guidelines

Points to Consider When Observing Teaching
There are no hard rules to be observed when observing teaching since individual differences on both sides are extremely important. The following points, however, may be worth considering when planning how to make the process an interesting and useful experience for both.

1. Aims and Structure of the Observation
- Are both clear and agreed about the purpose of the observation?
- Might there be any perceptions of a hidden agenda?
- How will the observer be introduced to the students?
- What role will the observer have during the session? Completely silent? Participant observer?
- Will the observer want to talk to the students about the session beforehand, during a break or after?

2. Aims of the Teaching Session
- A prior discussion about what the teacher is trying to achieve can be very helpful focusing on why the particular approach or format was chosen and what type of learning is to be encouraged; assimilating ideas/information; challenging assumptions; clarifying difficult ideas/theories; developing ways of thinking; inspiring students to go on learning! etc.
- Do observers help the teacher to clarify these?
- Do they discuss them and make suggestions?
- Is this part of the helping role?
- How is the session planned or structured?

3. Context
- Who are the students?
- What expectations/attitudes and assumptions do they bring?
- What level of attainment can be expected?
- What problems might arise and how might they be overcome?

4. Use of Rating Forms by Observer

- Should they be specially designed for observers rather than feedback from students?
- Should they draw attention to less traditional aspects of teaching?
- Are the QAA Quality Assessment forms useful?

5. Observer–Teacher Discussion

- When? Immediately after or when both have had time to think more deeply?
- Where? The teacher's room? Less formally in the common room?
- Style – formal? Serious? Relaxed? Challenging? Emphasizing being helpful, developmental rather than judgemental? (excellent/satisfactory/unsatisfactory!?)
- Format – should there be a definite structure to the discussion?
  A possible format might be
    Observer says briefly what he or she liked
    Rehearsal of what actually happened, observer's and teacher's perceptions of this
    Return to what went well, teacher then observer
    What was difficult? Teacher
    What were some of the less successful aspects? Teacher then Observer
    At this point the form may be referred to. If it is used initially it *may* set a rather negative tone and set up resistances.
    What might be changed?
    How might the changes be brought about?
    Possible practice – future observations or staff development activities.

Given the opportunity – and video recordings can help this enormously – teachers *can* be very perceptive and are more likely to actually change in response to suggestions if these are their own. But plainly we all have our blind spots even if we see ourselves on videos and in most cases gentle prompting can broaden our perceptions.

Teaching Observation Form

TEACHER:

COURSE: SESSION:

Programme   Topic

Module   Session Length

OBSERVER:

PART 1
Specific Learning Objectives Planned for the Session
(e.g. knowledge and understanding; key skills; cognitive skills;
subject specific – including practical/professional – skills)

PART 2: Description of Session Structure or Purpose	Primarily	To some extent	Very little
An ordered presentation of data or information	1	2	3
An example of problem definition, analysis, solution	1	2	3
A comparison of different interpretations/ approaches/theories	1	2	3
An analysis of a development/sequence	1	2	3
A presentation of an argument/thesis/point of view	1	2	3
A presentation of a case study analysis	1	2	3
A presentation of a network of related concepts/ideas	1	2	3
Other (*please specify*)	1	2	3

Teaching Observation Form

PART 3: Teaching Skills	SA	A	D	SD	N/A
A Maintains interest to the end of the session COMMENTS					
B Interprets the material clearly COMMENTS					
C Makes clear what is expected from the class COMMENTS					
D Encourages student to think critically during the class COMMENTS					
E Encourages the student to relate what s/he has heard/seen to their own experience and/or problems in the field COMMENTS					
F Encourages the student to offer their own knowledge and/or opinions COMMENTS					

PART 3: Teaching Skills	SA	A	D	SD	N/A
G Communicates effectively					
COMMENTS					
H Chooses and organizes the material well					
COMMENTS					
I Leaves the student feeling stimulated to think and learn more about the subject					
COMMENTS					
J Other *Please specify*					
Supporting Student A + B + G + H = **Encouraging Independence: C + D + E + F + I =**					

SA: **Strongly Agree**
A: **Agree**
D: **Disagree**
SD: **Strongly Disagree**
N/A: **Not Applicable**

Overall

Guidance Notes To The Teaching Observation Form

Introduction

This form is designed to help focus the teacher and the observer on:

(i)   The learning objectives of the teaching session.
(ii) The relationship of different kinds of structures available for teaching to those learning objectives.
(iii) The relationship of teaching to the student experience of the session. (To a certain extent, therefore, the observer will be placing themselves in the student role.)

Note: 'session' here is defined very widely and refers to any teaching session up to 3 hours.

PART 1: Learning Objectives

This part of the form requires a summary of the main learning objectives of the session and is, perhaps, best filled out by the teacher and observer during a pre-session. It includes:

knowledge and understanding;
key skills;
cognitive skills;
subject specific – including practical/professional – skills.

A discussion of these issues between teacher and observer in a pre-meeting can provide an excellent way for both to begin to share the context.

PART 2: Description of Session Structure or Purpose

This part of the form is intended to provide both the teacher and observer with a way of looking at the overall structure of the session and the relationship to its learning objectives. The observer is asked to complete this part during/after the session. The 'primarily' rating should apply to only one (possibly two) categories. The purpose, again, is to inform the post session discussion with the teacher not only about what structures predominated but also what other structure might have been available and how (if at all) they might have been effectively employed.

PART 3: Teaching Skills

This part of the form is intended to provide both the teacher and observer with a way of looking at the teacher's general teaching practice in the session; particularly with respect to the session's learning objectives and the students' potential experience. The observer is encouraged to make comments within each area.

The assessment for the general skills is on a four point scale.

1. (SA) suggests the skill has been very effectively integrated into practice.
2. (A) suggests the skill has been acceptably developed but it can be taken further in practice.
3. (D) suggests there are signs that the skill has been developed but it can be taken much further in practice.
4. (SD) suggests that the skill has neither been integrated into practice nor has it shown substantial signs of being developed.

N/A means not appropriate to the session.

Again, this part of the form has been designed to provide an accessible structure for informing the post-session discussion with the teacher about specific areas of their teaching practice. These 'scores' are mainly intended:

> to provide the observer with a useful way of quickly developing an overall sense of the session
> to aid the teacher and observer in their in post-session discussions
> to provide the teacher with an additional method from which to reflect and consider their practice further
> to help identify areas where improvement and further development may be appropriate.

Overall 'score(s)' may be calculated by assigning a number from 1 to 4 to the level of agreement with the respective 'teaching skills' statements: 1 for Strongly Agree through 4 for Strongly Disagree – lower scores suggesting more ability in the particular teaching skill. The distinction between 'support' and encouraging 'independence', here, is important and the different 'scores' are intended to help in the identification of issues concerning the balance between the two areas. (*Note*: to compare 'support' and 'independence' scores an average should be used.) Some criteria may, however, be less appropriate to some forms of session and this needs to be considered if scores are aggregated.

Descriptions of the Teaching Skills Areas

A Maintains student interest to the end of the session

This item focuses on the teacher's concern and ability for engaging the student's curiosity and interest throughout the session. It includes such things as:

setting the scene for the session
capturing their interest at the beginning
varying styles and modes of presentation
linking the session to the overall course, to wider contexts, to student's personal interests, etc.
ending the session in a stimulating and interesting way.

B Interprets the material clearly

This item focuses on the teacher's concern and ability for interpreting the material/content of the session in a way which allows students personal access to it. It includes such things as:

making the purpose of the session clear
being clear and understandable in his/her explanations
making good use of examples, illustrations and quotations
using visual aids effectively to interpret material
periodically taking stock
stressing important material
giving alternative explanations/descriptions of difficult concepts /ideas/issues.

C Makes clear what is expected from the class

This item focuses on the teacher's concern and ability for acknowledging and clarifying the student's role during the session. It includes such things as:

clarifying the role/value of note taking during the session
clarifying the student's role with respect to their participation
obtaining feedback on the student's understanding of the material
clarifying what work might be expected from the student after the session.

D Encourages student to think critically during the class

This item focuses on the teacher's concern and ability for encouraging the student to think critically during class. It includes such things as:

  providing time for reflection on problems, concepts, ideas
  providing time for students to test positions, ideas, concepts with respect to material and presented (in groups or with a fellow student or in the class as a whole)
  encouraging consideration of alternative views
  challenging assumptions.

E Encourages the student to relate what he/she has heard/seen to their own experience and/or specific problems in the field

This item focuses on the teacher's concern and ability for encouraging the student to relate their own experiences to the session. It includes such things as:

  providing time for reflection on their experience
  providing time for sharing experience in groups or with a fellow student
  encouraging active participation within the class as a whole
  ensuring access for a wide range of student experience.

F Encourages the students to offer their own knowledge and/or opinions

This item focuses on the teacher's concern and ability for encouraging the student to offer their own ideas, knowledge, opinions within the session. It includes such things as:

  providing opportunities and a 'safe' environment to contribute
  recognizing and managing a wide range of ways of articulating one's ideas, knowledge, opinions
  providing opportunities for student presentations
  providing opportunities for teamwork, leadership, group communication.

G Communicates effectively

This item focuses on the teacher's concern and ability for communicating and engaging with the students on a personal level. It includes such things as:

  using voice effectively through speaking to (not at) the student
  using gesture and body movement effectively
  making regular eye contact with the students
  using the space (accommodation) and resources (OHP, flip charts,

multimedia, etc.) effectively
being lively and stimulating
pacing the session appropriately
developing a good rapport: engaging the student.

H Chooses and organizes the material well

This item focuses on the teacher's concern and ability for choosing and organizing appropriate material to meet student needs and interest. It includes such things as:

choosing material relevant to the subject matter and objectives of the course and the session
organizing material in a form appropriate to the students' ability and level
presenting material which will stimulate and animate student interest and curiosity to explore it further
providing the right amount of material for the time allowed.

I Leaves the student feeling stimulated to think and learn more about the subject

This item focuses on the teacher's concern and ability to stimulate the student to think and learn more about the subject on their own. It includes such things as:

selecting interesting material
encouraging the students to enjoy the session
encouraging students to do further reading/research
encouraging students to review the session and to follow up their own ideas and lines of thinking
being positive with respect to student contributions and interactions
encouraging students to see the session as part of an ongoing open process of change and development.

J Other

This item covers any other issue which the observer feels is particularly relevant to the observation and is not covered above.

Bibliography

Abercrombie, M.L.J. (1966) 'Small group' in B. Foss (ed.), *New Horizons in Psychology*. Hammondsworth: Penguin Books.

Adelman, C., Jenkins, D. and Kemmis, S. (1983) 'Rethinking case study: notes from the second Cambridge conference' in L. Bartlett, S. Kemmis and G. Gillard (eds), *Case Study Methods 1: An Overview*. Victoria: Deakin, University Press.

Anderson, N. and King, N. (1995) *Innovation and Change in Organization*. London: International Thomson Business Press.

Argyris, C. and Schon, D. (1974) *Theory in Practice: Increasing Professional Effectiveness*. San Francisco: Jossey-Bass.

Argyris, C. and Schon, D. (1978) *Organisational Learning: A Theory of Action Perspective*. Reading, MA: Addison-Wesley.

Ashcroft, K. and Palacio, D. (1996) *Researching into Assessment and Evaluation*. London: Kogan Page.

Bakhtar, M. and Brown, G. (1988) 'Styles of lecturing: a study and its implications', *Research Papers in Education*, 3 (2): 131–53.

Bakhtin, M. (1986) *Speech Genres and Other Late Essays*. Austin: University of Texas Press.

Bales, R.F. (1970) *Personality and Interpersonal Behaviour*. New York: Holt, Rhinehart & Winston.

Barnett, R. (1994) *The Limits of Competence: Knowledge, Higher Education and Society*. London: Open University Press.

Barnett, R. (1997a) 'Beyond Competence' in F. Coffield and B. Williamson (eds), *Repositioning Higher Education*. London: SRHE/Open University Press.

Barnett, R. (1997b) *Higher Education: A Critical Business*. London: SRHE/Open University Press.

Barnett, R. (2000) *Realising the University*. Buckingham: SRHE/Open University Press.

Barnett, R. and Hallam, S. (1999) 'Teaching for supercomplexity: a pedagogy for higher education', in P. Mortimore (ed.), *Understanding Pedagogy and its Impact on Learning*. London: Paul Chapman.

Becher, T., Henkel, M. and Kogan, M. (1994) *Graduate Education in Britain*. London: Jessica Kingsley.

Becker, H. (1986) *Writing for Social Scientists*. London: University of Chicago Press.

Bennett, J.B. (1998) *Collegial Professionalism: The Academy, Individualism, and the*

Common Good. Phoenix, AZ: Oryx Press

Berg, B. and Ostergren, B. (1977) 'Modes for description and analysis of innovation processes', *Innovation and Innovation Processes in Higher Education.* Stockholm: Board of Universities and Colleges.

Biggs, J.B. (1999) *Teaching for Quality Learning at University.* London: Open University Press.

Biggs, J.B. and Collis, K. (1982) *Evaluating the Quality of Learning: The SOLO Taxonomy.* New York: Academic Press.

Bligh, D. (1998) *What's the Use of Lectures?* Exeter: Intellect Press.

Bligh, D. (2000) *What's the Point in Discussion?* Exeter: Intellect Press.

Bloom, B.S. (1956) *Taxonomy of Educational Objectives.* 2 vols. New York: Longmans Green.

Boud, D. (1989) 'Some competing traditions in experiential learning' in S. Weil and I. McGill (eds), *Making Sense of Experiential Learning: Diversity in Theory and Practice.* Buckingham: SRHE/Open University Press.

Boud, D. (1995) *Enhancing Learning Through Self-Assessment.* London: Kogan Page.

Boud, D. and Feletti, G. (1997) *The Challenge of Problem Based Learning.* London: Kogan Page.

Boud, D. and Walker, D. (1998) 'Promoting reflection in professional courses: the challenge of context', *Studies in Higher Education,* 23 (2):191–206.

Boud, D., Keogh, R. and Walker, D. (eds) (1985) *Reflection: Turning Experience into Learning.* London: Kogan Page.

Boyer, E.L. (1990) *Scholarship Reconsidered: Priorities of the Professoriate.* San Francisco: Carnegie Foundation for the Advancement of Teaching/Jossey-Bass.

Boyer, E.L. (1998) *Reinventing Undergraduate Education: A Blueprint for America's Research Universities: The Boyer Commission on Educating Under-graduates.* Washington, DC: Carnegie Foundation for the Advancement of Teaching.

Bramley, W. (1979) *Group Tutoring.* London: Kogan Page.

Bramley, W. (1997) *Personal Tutoring in Higher Education.* Guildford: University of Surrey: Society for Research into Higher Education.

Brew, A. (1999) 'Research and teaching: changing relationship in a changing context', *Studies in Higher Education,* 24 (3): 291–301.

Brew, A. and Boud, D. (1995) 'Teaching and research: establishing the vital link with learning', *Higher Education,* 29 (3): 261–73.

Brockbank, A. and McGill, I. (1998) *Facilitating Reflective Learning in Higher Education.* Buckingham: SRHE/Open University Press.

Brookfield, S. (1986) *Understanding and Facilitating Adult Learning.* San Francisco: Jossey-Bass.

Brown, G., Bull, J. and Pendlebury, M. (1997) *Assessing Student Learning in Higher Education.* London: Routledge.

Brown, G. and Atkins, M. (1988) *Effective Teaching in Higher Education.* London: Metheuen.

Brown, J.S. and Duguid, P. (2000) *The Social Life of Information.* Boston: Harvard Business School Press.

Brown, S. and Knight, P. (1994) *Assessing Learners in Higher Education*. London: Kogan Page.

Brown, S. and Race, P. (1995) *Assess Your own Teaching Quality*. London: Kogan Page.

Bruner, J. (1966) *Towards a Theory of Instruction*. London: Oxford University Press.

Bruner, J. (1986) *Actual Minds, Possible Worlds*. London: Harvard University Press.

Bruner, J. (1996) *The Culture of Education*. London: Harvard University Press.

Burgess, A. (1984) 'Diverse melodies: a first-year class in secondary school' in J. Miller (ed.), *Eccentric Propositions: Essays on Literature and the Curriculum*. London: Routledge & Kegan Paul,

Campbell, D. and Campbell, M. (1995) *The Student's Guide to Doing Research on the Internet*. Reading, MA: Addison-Wesley.

Carbonne, E. (1998) *Teaching Large Classes: Tools and Strategies*. London, Sage.

Carr, W. and Kemmis, S. (1983) *Becoming Critical: Knowing Through Action Research*. Victoria: Deakin University Press.

Carr, W. and Kemmis, S. (1986) *Becoming Critical: Education, Knowledge and Action Research*. London: Falmer Press.

Chomsky, N. (1968) *Language and Mind*. New York: Harcourt, Brace & World.

Chomsky, N. (1998) 'Chomsky Warns of Corporate Secrecy Threat', *Times Higher Education Supplement*, 20 November: 60.

Chopra, A.J. (1999) *Managing the People Side of Innovation: 8 Rules for Engaging Minds and Hearts*. West Hartford, CT: Kumerian Press.

Clark, B.R. (1997) 'The modern integration of research activities with teaching and learning', *Journal of Higher Education*, 21 (1): 31–42.

Coffield, F. and Williamson, B. (eds) (1997) *Repositioning Higher Education*. London: SRHE/Open University Press.

Cohen, L. and Manion, L. (1989) *Research Methods in Education*. London: Routledge.

Cohen, L., Manion, L. and Morrison, K. (2000) *Research Methods in Education*. London: Falmer Press.

Collier, K.G. (1983) *The Management of Peer Group Learning: Syndicate Methods in Higher Education*. Guildford: Society for Research into Higher Education.

Cox, R. (1973) 'Traditional examinations in a changing society', *Universities Quarterly*, 27: 200–16.

Cox, R. (1975) 'Students and student assessment: a study of different perceptions and patterns of response to varied forms of assessment in the University of Essex'. Unpublished PhD thesis, Colchester, Essex.

Cox, R. (1985) 'Higher Education: Assessment of Students' in T. Husen and T. Postlethwaite (eds) *International Encyclopedia of Education*. Oxford: Pergamon.

Cox, R. (1987) *Study of Students' Responses to the First Year of an Engineering Course*. London: Centre for Higher Education Studies (Institute of Education, University of London).

Cox, R. (1992) 'Learning theory and professional life', *Media and Technology for Human Development*, 4 (4): 217–32.

Cox, R. (1996) *Teaching, Learning and Assessment in Higher Education, An Anthropology in Action*. Vol 3: 2.

Cox, R., Kontianien, S., Rea, N. and Robinson, S. (1981) *Learning Teaching: An Evaluation of a Course for Teachers in General Practice*. London: UTMU Institute of Education.

Cryer, P. (1996) *The Research Student's Guide to Success*. Buckingham: Open University Press.

Cryer, P. and Elton, E. (1992) *Active Learning in Large Classes and with Increasing Student Numbers*. Sheffield: CVCP Staff Development and Training Unit.

Dahlgren, L.-O. (1997) 'Learning conceptions and outcomes', in F. Marton, D. Hounsell and N. Entwistle (eds), *The Experience of Learning*. Edinburgh: Scottish Academic Press.

De Bono, E. (1994) *Parallel Thinking*. London: Penguin Books.

Delamont, S., Atkinson, P. and Parry, O. (2000) *The Doctoral Experience: Success and Failure in Graduate School*. London: Falmer Press.

Dewey, J. (1938) *Experience and Education*. New York: Collier Books.

Douglas, T. (1991) *Common Groupwork Problems*. London: Routledge.

Dressel, P. (1976) *Improving Degree Programmes*. London: Jossey-Bass.

Duke, C. (1997) 'Towards a lifelong curriculum', in F. Coffield and B. Williamson (eds), *Repositioning Higher Education*. London: SRHE/Open University Press.

Dunkin, M. and Biddle, B. (1974) *The Study of Teaching*. New York: Holt, Rinehart & Winston.

Eisner, E. (1994) *The Educational Imagination: On the Design and Evaluation of School Programs*. New York: Macmillan.

Eliot, T.S. (1961) 'The hollow men', in *T.S. Eliot: Selected Poems*. London: Faber & Faber.

Entwistle, N. (1988) *Styles of Learning and Teaching*. London, David Fulton.

Entwistle, N. (1997) 'Contrasting perspectives on learning' in F. Marton, D. Hounsell and N. Entwistle (eds), *The Experience of Learning*. Edinburgh: Scottish Academic Press.

Entwistle, N. (1998) 'Conceptions of teaching for academic staff development: the role of research', *Conference Paper on Development Training for Academic Staff*. London: Goldsmith College, 26 March.

Entwistle, N. and Entwistle, A. (1992) 'Experience of understanding in revising for degree examinations', in *Learning and Instruction*, 2 (1): 1–22, Oxford: Pergamon Press.

Entwistle, N. and Tait, H. (1990) 'Approaches to learning, evaluations of teaching and preferences for contrasting academic environments', *Higher Education*, 19 (2): 169–94.

Entwistle, N., Thompson, S. and Tait, H. (1992) *Guidelines for Promoting Effective Learning in Higher Education*. Edinburgh: Centre for Research on Learning and Instruction, University of Edinburgh.

Erhmann, S. (1996) *Adult learning in a New Technological Era*. Paris: OECD.

Feldman, K.A. (1987) 'Research productivity and scholarly accomplishment of college teachers as related to their instructional effectiveness: a review and exploration', *Research in Higher Education*, 26 (3): 227–98.

Francis, H. (1997) 'The Research Process' in N. Graves, and V. Varma, (eds) *Working for a Doctorate: A Guide for the Humanities and Social Sciences*. London: Routledge.

Freire, P. (1972) *The Pedagogy of the Oppressed*. London: Penguin.

Gardiner, D. (1989) *The Anatomy of Supervision*. Milton Keynes: SRHE/Open University Press.

Gardner, H. (1993) *Frames of Mind: The Theory of Multiple Intelligences*. New York: Basic Books.

Gardner, H. (1999) *Intelligence Reframed: Multiple Intelligences for the 21st Century*. New York: Basic Books.

GMC (1993) *Tomorrow's Doctors*. London: General Medical Council.

Gibbons, M., Limoges, C., Nowotny, H., Scott, P. and Trow, M. (1994) *The New Production of Knowledge: The Dynamics of Science and Research in Contemporary Societies*. London: Sage.

Gibbs, G. (1981) *Teaching Students to Learn*. Milton Keynes: Open University Press.

Gibbs, G. (1995) 'Changing conceptions of teaching and learning through action research', in A. Brew (ed.), *New Directions in Staff Development*. Buckingham: SRHE/Open University Press.

Gibbs, G. and Jenkins, A. (eds) (1992) *Teaching Large Classes in Higher Education*. London: Kogan Page.

Gibbs, G., Habeshaw, S. and Habeshaw, T. (1986) *53 Interesting Ways to Assess your Students*. Bristol: Technical and Educational Services.

Gibbs, G., Habeshaw, S. and Habeshaw, T. (1989) *53 Interesting Ways to Appraise Your Teaching*. Bristol: Technical and Educational Services.

Goodlad, S. (1996) *Speaking Technically: A Handbook for Scientists, Engineers and Physicians on How to Improve Technical Presentations*. London: Imperial College Press.

Goodlad, S. and Hirsh, B. (1989) *Peer Tutoring*. London: Kogan Page.

Gough, H. and Woodworth, D. (1960) 'Stylistic variations among professional research scientists' *Journal of Psychology* Vol 49.

Graves, N. and Varma, V. (eds) (1997) *Working for a Doctorate: A Guide for the Humanities and Social Sciences*. Routledge, London.

Greenblat, C.S. (1998) *Designing your own Simulations*. London: Sage.

Gronlund, N.E. (1982) *Constructing Achievement Tests*. Englewood Cliffs, NJ: Prentice Hall.

Habeshaw, S., Habeshaw, T. and Gibbs, G. (1984) *53 Interesting Things to Do in Your Seminars and Tutorials*. Bristol: Technical and Educational Services.

Hale, E. (1964) *Report of the Committee on Teaching Methods*. London: University Grants Committee, HMSO.

Hamilton, D., Jenkins, D., King, C., MacDonald, B. and Parlett, M. (1977) *Beyond the Numbers Game: A Reader in Education Evaluation*. New York: Macmillan Education.

Hanson, A. (1993) 'A separate theory of adult learning', in P. Edwards, A. Hanson and P. Raggatt (eds), *Boundaries of Adult Learning*. London: Routledge/Open University Press.

Harden, R. and Cairncross, R. (1980) 'Assessment of practical skills: the objective structured practical examination', *Studies in Higher Education*, 5 (2): 187–96.

Harre, R. (1981) 'The positivist-empiricist approach and its alternative' in P. Reason and J. Rowan (eds), *Human Inquiry: A Source Book of New Paradigm Research*. Chichester: John Wiley.

Harry, K. (ed.) (1999) *Higher Education through Open and Distance Learning*. London: Routledge.

Harry, K. and Perraton, H. (1999) 'Open and distance learning for the new society', in K. Harry (ed.), *Higher Education through Open and Distance Learning*. London: Routledge.

Hartley, J. (1998) *Learning and Studying: A Research Perspective*. London: Routledge.

Harvey, D. (1998) 'University, Inc.', *The Atlantic Monthly*, 282 (4), October: 112–16. Boston.

HEQC (1996) *Graduate Standards Programme: Draft Report*. London: Higher Education Quality Council.

Heron, J. (1976) *Six Category Intervention Analysis*. Guildford: University of Surrey: Human Potential Research Project.

Heron, J. (1981) 'Philosophical basis for a new paradigm' in P. Reason and J. Rowan (eds), *Human Inquiry: A Source Book of New Paradigm Research*. Chichester: John Wiley.

Heron, J. (1981a) 'Assessment revisited' in D. Boud (ed.), *Developing Student Autonomy in Learning*. London: Kogan Page.

Heron, J. (1989) *The Facilitator's Handbook*. London: Kogan Page.

Hewton, E. (1982) *Rethinking Educational Change: A Case for Diplomacy*. Guildford: SRHE.

Heywood, J. (1989) *Assessment in Higher Education*. Chichester: John Wiley.

Higgins, J.S., Maitland, G., Perkins, J., Richardson, S. and Warren Piper, D. (1989) 'Identifying and solving problems in engineering design', *Studies in Higher Education*, 1 (2): 169–81.

Hill, B.J. (1975) 'The reliability of marking in BSc. examinations in engineering', *International Journal of Mechanical Engineering Education*, 3: 97–106.

Hodgson, V. (1997) 'Lectures and the experience of relevance' in F. Marton, D. Hounsell and N. Entwistle (eds), *The Experience of Learning*. Edinburgh: Scottish Academic Press.

Holquist, M. (1990) *Dialogism: Bakhtin and his World*. London and New York: Routledge.

Hounsell, D. (1997) 'Contrasting conceptions of essay writing' in F. Marton, D. Hounsell and N. Entwistle (eds), *The Experience of Learning*. Edinburgh: Scottish Academic Press.

Hounsell, D., McCulloch, M. and Scott, M. (1996) *The ASSHE Inventory: Changing Assessment Practices in Scottish Higher Education*. Edinburgh: The

Centre for Teaching, Learning and Assessment, University of Edinburgh.

Hounsell, D., Tait, H. and Day, K. (1997) *Feedback on Courses and Programmes of Study: A Handbook*. Edinburgh: Centre for Teaching, Learning and Assessment, University of Edinburgh.

ILT (1999a) *ILT Consultation: The National Framework for Higher Education Teaching*. February, York: Institute for Learning and Teaching.

ILT (1999b) *The National Framework for Higher Education Teaching*. York: Institute for Learning and Teaching.

Ingrams, R. (1997) 'If Richard Branson wants to be a future president of this country, he really must try to get his trains to run on time', *The Observer Review*, 9 November.

Jaques, D. (1991) *Learning in Groups*. London: Kogan Page.

Jaques, D. (2000) *Learning in Groups*. London: Kogan Page.

Jarvis, P. (1987) *Adult Learning in the Social Context*. London: Croom Helm.

Jarvis, P. (1992) *Paradoxes of Learning: On Becoming an Individual in Society*. London: Jossey-Bass.

Jarvis, P., Holford, J. and Griffin, C. (1998) *The Theory and Practice of Learning*. London: Kogan Page.

Johnston, S. (1997) 'Examining the examiners: an analysis of examiners' reports on doctoral theses', *Studies in Higher Education*, 22 (3): 333–47.

Jones, C., Mackintosh, M. and McPherson, A. (1973) *Questions of Uncertainty: Non Cognitive Predictors of Achievement*. Centre for Educational Sociology: University of Edinburgh.

Kember, D. (1997) 'A reconceptualisation of the research into university academics' conceptions of teaching', *Learning and Instruction*, 7 (3): 255–75.

Kemmis, S. and McTaggart, R. (1988) *The Action Research Planner*. Victoria: Deakin University Press.

Kennedy, D. (1997) *Academic Duty*. Cambridge MA: Harvard University Press.

Kerlinger, F. and Lee, H. (1999) *Foundations of Behavioural Research*. New York: Harcourt.

Knight, P. (ed.) (1995) *Assessment for Learning in Higher Education*. London: Kogan Page.

Knowles, M. (1978) *The Adult Learner: A Neglected Species*. Houston, TX: Gulf.

Knowles, M. (1984) *Andragogy in Action*. London: Jossey-Bass.

Kogan, M. (1989) *Evaluating Higher Education*. London, JKP.

Kolb, D. (1984) *Experiential Learning*. Englewood Cliffs, NJ: Prentice Hall.

Kolb, D., Osland, J. and Rubin, I. (1994) *Organizational Behavior: An Experiential Approach*. New York: Prentice Hall.

Kolb, D., Rubin, I. and McIntyre, J. (1984) *Organizational Psychology: An Experiential Approach*. Englewood Cliffs, NJ: Prentice Hall.

Kuhn, T. (1970) *The Structure of Scientific Revolutions*. London: University of Chicago Press.

Laurillard, D. (1993) *Rethinking University Teaching*. London: Routledge.

Lewin, K. (1951) *Field Theory in Social Sciences*. New York: Harper & Row.

Lenzner, R. and Johnson, S. (1997) 'Seeing things as they really are', *Forbes Magazine*, 10 March.

Light, G. (1995) 'The literature of the unpublished: student conceptions of creative writing in higher education'. PhD thesis, The Institute of Education, University of London.

Light, G. (1996) 'The limits of literature: creative writing in the university classroom', *Writers in Education*, 9, Summer: 13–18.

Light, G. (2000) 'Lifelong learning: challenging learning and teaching in higher education', in A. Hodgson (ed.), *Policies, Politics and the Future of Lifelong Learning*. London: Kogan Page.

Lippett, R. and White, R.K. (1961) 'An experimental study of leadership and group style', in E. Maccoby, T. Newcombe and E. Harley (eds), *Readings in Social Psychology*. London: Methuen.

Loomer, B. (1976) 'Two kinds of power', *Process Studies*, 6 (1): 5–32.

Luft, J. (1984) *Group Processes: An Introduction to Group Dynamics*. Palo Alto, CA: Mayfield.

Lyotard, J.-F. (1984) *The Postmodern Condition: A Report on Knowledge*. Minneapolis: University of Minnesota Press.

Malcolm, N. (1967) *Ludwig Wittgenstein: A Memoir*. London: Oxford University Press.

Marton, F. (1981) 'Phenomenography: describing conceptions of the world around us', *Instructional Science*, 10: 177–200.

Marton, F. (1988a) 'Describing and improving learning', in R. Schmeck (ed.), *Learning Strategies and Learning Styles*. New York and London: Plenum Press.

Marton, F. (1988b) 'Phenomenography: a research approach to investigating different understandings of reality', in R. Sherman and R. Webb (eds), *Qualitative Research in Education: Focus and Methods*. London: Falmer Press.

Marton, F., Beatty, E. and Dall' Alba, G. (1993) 'Conceptions of learning', *International Journal of Educational Research*, 19 (3): 277–300.

Marton, F., Hounsell, D. and Entwistle, N. (eds), (1997) *The Experience of Learning*. Edinburgh: Scottish Academic Press.

Marton, F. and Saljo, R. (1997) 'Approaches to learning', in F. Marton, D. Hounsell and N. Entwistle (eds), *The Experience of Learning*. Edinburgh: Scottish Academic Press.

Mason, R. (1994) *Using Communications Media in Open and Flexible Learning*. London: Kogan Page.

Mason, R. (1998) *Globalising Education: Trends and Applications*. London: Routledge.

Mason, R. (1999) 'The impact of telecommunications', in K. Harry (ed.), *Higher Education through Open and Distance Learning*. London: Routledge.

McKeachie, W., Pintrich, P., Lin, Y.-G. and Smith, D. (1986) *Teaching and Learning in the College Classroom*. Ann Arbor, MI: University of Michigan, Office of Educational Research and Improvement.

Mead, G.H. (1950) *Mind, Self and Society from the Standpoint of a Behaviourist*. Chicago: University of Chicago Press.

Mead, G.H. (1964) 'Social psychology as counterpart to physiological psychology', in A.J. Reck (ed.), *Selected Writings*. Chicago: University of Chicago Press.

Merleau-Ponty, M. (1962) *The Phenomenology of Perception*. London: Routledge & Kegan Paul.

Merriam, S.B. (ed.) (1993) *An Update on Adult Learning Theory: New Directions for Adult and Continuing Education*. San Francisco: Jossey-Bass.

Mezirow, J. (1983) 'A critical theory of adult learning and education', in M. Tight (ed.), *Adult Learning and Education*. London: Croom Helm.

Middlehurst, R. (1997) 'Enhancing quality', in F. Coffield and B. Williamson (eds), *Repositioning Higher Education*. London: SRHE/Open University Press.

Moran, L. and Myringer, B. (1999) 'Flexible learning and university change', in K. Harry (ed.), *Higher Education through Open and Distance Learning*. London: Routledge.

Moro, B. (1997) 'A pedagogy of the hypermedia', in A.-K. Korsvold and B. Ruschoff (eds), *New Technologies in Language Learning and Teaching*. Strasbourg: Council of Europe Publishing.

Mortimore, P. (ed.) (1999) *Understanding Pedagogy and its Impact on Learning*. London: Paul Chapman.

NCIHE (1997) *Higher Education in the Learning Society* (The Dearing Report). London: National Committee of Inquiry into Higher Education.

Newble, D. and Cannon, R. (1989) *A Handbook for Teachers in Universities and Colleges: A Guide to Improving Teaching Methods*. London: Kogan Page.

Noss, R. and Pachler, N. (1999) 'The challenge of new technologies: doing old things in a new way, or doing new things?', in P. Mortimore (ed.), *Understanding Pedagogy and its Impact on Learning*. London: Paul Chapman.

Ong, W. (1982) *Orality and Literacy*. London and New York: Methuen.

Oppenheim, A.N. (1992) *Questionnaire Design, Interviewing and Attitude Measurement*. London: Pinter.

Owen, J.M. and Rogers, P. (1999) *Program Evaluation: Forms and Approaches*. London: Sage.

Parlett, M. and Hamilton, D. (1977) 'Evaluation as illumination', in M. Parlett and G. Deardon (eds), *Introduction to Illuminative Evaluation: Studies in Higher Education*. Cardiff-by-Sea, CA: Pacific Soundings Press.

Pask, G. (1976) 'Styles and strategies of learning', *British Journal of Educational Psychology*, 46: 128–48.

Penrose, R. (1989) *The Emperor's New Mind*. London: Vintage.

Perkins, D. (1991) 'Technology meets constructivism: do they make a marriage?', *Educational Technology*. May: 18–23.

Perry, W. (1970) *Forms of Intellectual and Ethical Development in the College Years*. New York: Holt, Reinhart & Winston.

Perry, W. (1980) 'Cognitive and ethical growth: the making of meaning', in A. Chickering (ed.), *The Modern American College*. London: Jossey-Bass.

Peterson, M. (1997) 'Language teaching and networking', *System*, 25 (1): 29–37.

Phillips, D.C. (1995) 'The good, the bad, and the ugly: the many faces of constructivism', *Educational Researcher*, 24 (7): 5–12.

Phillips, D.C. (1995) 'An opinionated account of the constructivist landscape', in D.C. Phillips (ed.), *Constructivism in Education: Opinions and Second Opinions on Controversial Issues*. Chicago: University of Chicago Press.

Phillips, E. and Pugh, D. (2000) *How to Get a PhD: A Handbook for Students and their Supervisors*. Buckingham: Open University Press.

Piaget, J. (1950) *The Psychology of Intelligence*. London: Routledge & Kegan Paul.

Pieron, H. (1963) *Examens et Docimologie*. Paris: PUF.

Pincas, A. (1999) 'Problems and principles in the use of computer networks for course delivery', *Certificate in Online Education and Training*. Institute of Education, University of London.

Pinker, S. (1995) *The Language Instinct*. London: Penguin Books.

Pring, R.A. (1995) *Closing the Gap: Liberal Education and Vocational Preparation*. London: Hodder & Stoughton.

Press, E. and Washburn, J. (2000) 'The kept university', *The Atlantic Monthly*, 285 (3), March: 39–54.

Prosser, M. and Trigwell, K. (1999) *Understanding Learning and Teaching: The Experience in Higher Education*. London: SRHE/Open University Press.

QAA (1999) *Code of Practice for the Assurance of Academic Quality and Standards in Higher Education, Postgraduate Research Programmes*. Cheltenham: Quality Assurance Agency.

Ramsden, P. (1992) *Learning to Teach in Higher Education*. London: Routledge.

Ramsden, P. (1997) 'The context of learning in academic departments', in F. Marton, D. Hounsell and N. Entwistle (eds), *The Experience of Learning*. Edinburgh: Scottish Academic Press.

Ramsden, P. and Moses, I. (1992) 'Associations between research and teaching in Australian higher education', *Higher Education*, 23 (3): 273–95.

Readings, B. (1996) *The University in Ruins*. Cambridge, MA: Harvard University Press.

Robertson, D. (1997) 'Social justice in a learning market', in F. Coffield and B. Williamson (eds), *Repositioning Higher Education*. London: SRHE/Open University Press.

Rogers, C. (1969) *Freedom to Learn*. Columbus, OH: Merrill.

Rommetveit, R. (1974) *On Message Structure*. Chichester: John Wiley.

Rommetveit, R. and Blakar, R.M. (1979) *Studies of Language, Thought and Communication*. London: Academic Press.

Rorty, R. (1982) *Consequences of Pragmatism*. Minneapolis: University of Minnesota Press.

Rorty, R. (1989) *Contingency, Irony and Solidarity*. Cambridge: Cambridge University Press.

Rowan, J. (1976) *The Power of The Group*. London: Davis-Poynter.

Rowntree, D. (1985) *Developing Courses for Students*. London: Harper & Row.

Rowntree, D. (1987) *Assessing Students: How Shall We Know Them?* London: Harper & Row.

Rowntree, D. (1994) *Preparing Materials for Open, Distance and Flexible Learn-*

ing. London: Harper & Row.

Rudd, E. (1985) *A New Look at Postgraduate Failure*. Guildford: SRHE/NFER Nelson.

Rudd, E. (1986) 'The drop-outs and the dilatory on the road to the doctorate', *Higher Education in Europe*, 11 (4)): 31–6.

Salmon, P. (1992) *Achieving a PhD*. Stoke-on-Trent: Trentham.

Saussure, F. de (1966) *Course in General Linguistics*. New York: McGraw-Hill.

Schon, D. (1983) *The Reflective Practitioner*. New York: Basic Books.

Schon, D. (1987) *Educating The Reflective Practitioner*. London: Jossey-Bass.

Sloboda, J. and Newstead, S. (eds) (1995) *Guidelines for the Assessment of the PhD in Psychology and Related Disciplines*. London: BPS/UCOSDA.

Smith, P.B. (1980) *Group Processes and Personal Change*. London: Harper & Row.

Stenhouse, L. (1975) *An Introduction to Curriculum Research and Development*. Oxford: Heinemann.

Talbott, S. (1995) *The Future Does not Compute*. Sebastopol, CA: O'Reilly and Associates.

Tang, C. (1998) 'Effects of collaborative learning on the quality of assessments', in B. Dart and G. Boulton-Lewis (eds), *Teaching and Learning in Higher Education*. Camberwell: Australian Council for Educational Research.

Taylor, J. and Swannell, P. (1997) 'From outback to internet: crackling radio to virtual campus', in *Proceedings of InterAct, International Telecommunications Union*. Geneva: ITU (CD-ROM).

Teller, E., Teller, W. and Talley, W. (1991) *Conversations on the Dark Secrets of Physics*. London: Pitman.

Tessmer, M. (1993) *Planning and Conducting Formative Evaluations*. London: Kogan Page.

Toohey, S. (1999) *Designing Courses for Higher Education*. Buckingham: Open University Press (SRHE).

Trow, M. (1981) 'Comparative perspectives on access', in O. Fulton (ed.), *Access to Higher Education*. Leverhulme Studies 2. Guildford: SRHE.

Usher, R., Bryant, I. and Johnson, R. (1997) *Adult Education and The Postmodern Challenge: Learning Beyond the Limits*. London: Routledge.

UTMU (1976) *Improving Teaching in Higher Education*. London: UTMU Institute of Education.

Van Ments, M. (1983) *Effective Use of Role-Play*. London: Kogan Page.

Van Rossum, E.J. and Schenk, S.M. (1984) 'The relationship between learning conception, study strategy and learning outcome', *British Journal of Educational Psychology*, 54: 73–83.

Vygotsky, L.S. (1986) *Thought and Language*. Cambridge, MA: MIT Press.

Warren Piper, D. (1975) 'Organisational points to bear in mind when designing a course, some analytic models', in D. Bligh, G. Ebrahim, D. Jacques and D. Warren Piper (eds), *Teaching Students*. Exeter: Exeter University Teaching Services.

Warren Piper, D. (1976) 'Educational objectives', *Improving Teaching in Higher Education*. London: UTMU, Institute of Education.

Watkins, C. and Mortimore, P. (1999) 'Pedagogy: what do we know?' in P. Mortimore (ed.), *Understanding Pedagogy and its Impact on Learning*. London: Paul Chapman.

Watson, D. and Taylor, R. (1998): *Lifelong Learning and the University: A Post-Dearing Agenda*. London: Falmer Press.

Webster, D.S. (1985) 'Does research productivity enhance teaching?', *Educational Record*, 66: 60–63.

Williams, R. (1983) *Writing in Society*. London: Verso.

Winter, R. (1996) 'Some principles and procedures for the conduct of action research', in O. Zuber-Skerrit (ed.), *New Directions in Action Research*. London: Falmer Press.

Wittgenstein, L. (1968) *Philosophical Investigations*. Oxford: Basil Blackwell.

Young, M. (1998) *The Curriculum of the Future: From the New Sociology of Education to a Critical Theory of Learning*. London: Falmer Press.

Zuber-Skerrit, O. (1992a) *Professional Development in Higher Education: A Theoretical Framework for Action Research*. London: Kogan Page.

Zuber-Skerrit, O. (1992b) *Action Research in Higher Education: Examples and Reflections*. London: Kogan Page.

Zuber-Skerrit, O. (1996) *New Directions in Action Research*. London: Falmer Press.

Index

271